The Life of
TED HORN
AMERICAN RACING CHAMPION

By RUSS CATLIN
(1908-1983)

> **DEDICATION**
> *To the youth of America.*
> *Ted Horn's greatest love.*

Published by
FLOYD CLYMER
America's Largest Publisher of books pertaining to
Automobiles, Motorcycles and Automobile Racing
1268 South Alvarado Street
Los Angeles 6, California
Copyright 1949 by Floyd Clymer

This Edition Reprinted 2024 by:
www.VelocePress.com

Best of Luck Always,

Ted Horn

Announcement

By Floyd Clymer

This book on the life of Ted Horn we believe to be a most accurate and interesting biography of a truly great racing driver and one who was beloved by the thousands who knew him and by hundreds of thousands who saw him perform on the race tracks of the nation.

Ted Horn was not only one of the world's outstanding drivers and a great champion . . . he was a man who came up the hard way . . . he asked and gave no quarter. He was honest and sincere in his desire to build interest in automobile racing. He planned his campaigns and races carefully and he injected business methods into the sport of automobile racing. His path was never a bed of roses . . . and his grit and stick-to-itiveness made him a leader in his chosen profession. He was considerate and thoughtful of his competitors and I am sure that Ted Horn never knowingly made an enemy. He had a great sense of humor . . . he liked to smile and make others happy.

The author of this book, Russ Catlin, has generously waived his right to the author's royalty in order that the royalties might be paid to Ted Horn's widow and his three children. The story was written by Mr. Catlin after a great deal of research and contact with those close to Ted Horn. It is written in an interesting, breezy style that will surely appeal to the racing fans of the world.

Index

	Page
PREFACE	5
EYLARD THEODORE HORN	9
A START IS MADE	17
EARLY ASCOT DAYS	21
THE EASTERN CAMPAIGNS	69
THE CHAMPION	121
HORN AND HOLLAND	147
THE YEAR OF FATE	177
DU QUOIN	205
REMINISCENSES AND TRIBUTES	211
STATISTICAL DATA	217
CREDITS	222

Preface

Auto racing is a dangerous and hazardous profession. None know this more than do the participants. Injuries and fatalities are a part of the vocation, and from this phase has grown a lore of superstition and habit that only those within the Inner Sanctum of racing can explain.

Auto racing champions are crowned as are those in any sport—on the field of battle. Down through the years there have been many champions, and each in his own right deserved his laurels. In no other sport is the period of preparation so long, nor so exacting.

The story of Ted Horn is the story of a champion. One who served his apprenticeship dutifully, and in this course suffered the hardships, adopted the superstitions, fought the battle, and finally emerged at the top of his profession —the Champion.

But here the parallel ended. For, in Ted Horn racing produced a champion not only on the field of battle, but in that field every man of every profession strives to attain, respect of his fellow man.

On December sixth, 1948, Floyd Clymer wrote me a letter saying, "We have many requests for a book on the life of Ted Horn. I personally feel that this great man's life and deeds should become a matter of permanent record."

That was the first signal tribute to come my way regarding Ted Horn. In the months that followed, I was to receive literally hundreds.

My first contacts responded at once. From practically every corner of the nation came bits of information, tribute, and offers of cooperation. Racing itself seemed determined that the story of Ted Horn be fully and truthfully told. But, the strange part of it all was, not only was the requested information returned, but also some story, some illustration of the subject's kindness, generosity, modesty, and love for his fellow man. Only a person such as myself, serving as a

PREFACE

clearing house, could fully feel the universal impact of this great Champion's life on so many people.

The story of Ted Horn is primarily the history of major league racing from 1931 to 1948. In this telling I had most of racing's individual authorities to help in verifying the facts. At the end of the book a credit section lists those who helped in this effort. But, before you begin the reading, it is important that you know the sources from which the material was gleaned. If, as you read, some incident or some happening is foreign to your impressions, the telling is not entirely the imagination of the author. Conflicting statements were researched until the truth was apparent. Many times Ted himself solved the problem. Solved it in the many letters he wrote over many years, and in his meticulously kept scrapbooks.

As an illustration, Pete De Paolo, twice National Champion, Indianapolis victor and author, actually wrote the story of the 1935 Ford team in this book. Harry Hartz, also National Champion, and Ted's car owner at Indianapolis in 1936, 1937, and 1938 and who in Ted's own words gave him his start in the big time, handled the telling of those years. Ed Metzger, chief mechanic and successor to Cotton Henning, the incidents of Ted's races for the lovable Cotton.

Al Bloemker, Director of Publicity for the Indianapolis Speedway, compiled the records of those races, and Tom Smith of AAA, Ted's overall statistics under their sanction.

Cliff Bergere, senior driver, his valuable observations; Tom Frost, member of the Contest Board, and newspaper reporters everywhere, Ted's many feats on the dirt tracks of the country.

Ike Welch, Chief Observer at the Indianapolis Speedway and Paul Johnson, AAA Steward, and the officials in charge at the Du Quoin meet, the events of that fateful day, as well as other phases.

But the greatest authentic help came from Ted Horn himself. Ted was a prolific letter writer. His letters over the years are now treasured keepsakes of many people. Dozens were given me to aid in the research. Each was full of rac-

PREFACE

ing lore, personal thoughts and the familiar ending. "Best of luck always—Ted Horn."

The final stroke of fortune came in the form of scrapbooks. It is amazing that any person, let alone a race driver, would have kept such a chronological and meticulously arranged record of happenings over so many years. Yet this is what Ted Horn dutifully accomplished. It was as if the man himself knew the use for which they some day would be put. The Ted Horn racing story is fully told in these valuable clippings, pictures and notes. Oftentimes Ted objected to the author's version and when he did his own remarks, in a bold hand, were injected.

Charles Lytle, probably one of the greatest authorities of today on racing history and collections, pronounced the Ted Horn collection the most amazing and complete he had ever seen. It is to the capable suggestion of Lytle that I am indebted for the manner in which this material is presented.

If, in some part you feel a story is not fully told, or some phase has been lightly handled, remember it is such because in the scrapbooks Ted so indicated that phase was unimportant to him.

Auto racing is a great sport. But auto racing lost its greatest asset when Fate decided it was the last lap for Racing's great Champion. Champion on the field of battle, and Champion in the struggle of life. That was Ted Horn, the man.

RUSS CATLIN.

Parents of Ted Horn. The late Armandus Horn, his father, a talented musician, and Mrs. Mary Horn, his mother.

ARMANDUS HORN
1875 — 1935
Photo taken in 1918.

MRS. MARY HORN
Photo taken in 1948.

CHAPTER I

Eylard Theodore Horn

THE morning of February 27, 1910, Destiny's favored hand touched the Bethesda General Hospital in the predominantly German Settlement along the Ohio river known as Cincinnati.

Fate, too, was there and after Destiny had indicated her wishes, took charge.

Fate and Destiny were team mates of the Universe, and of Time. Once they had selected a log cabin in mid-Illinois and a great President, Abraham Lincoln, was born. Again they chose a small farmhouse in Ohio and Thomas Alva Edison started life. Today it was another baby boy, and Fate duly recorded the happening and Destiny's wishes— a great Champion had been born.

Armandus Henry Von Horn was happy. So too were members of the Cincinnati German Theatre, for it was to this prominent member of their musical group that the beautiful curly blonde, violet eyed child had been born. Herr Von Horn had been summoned from a rehearsal to the hospital to attend the event and when he returned beamed, "He will be an artist . . . those long fingers, strong shoulders, high forehead . . ."

Eylard Theodore Horn was the baptismal name of the baby and as he grew, became a precocious child. He never had any fear, even as a baby, and at thirty months his mother found him clinging to the front leg of a superannuated old horse. That the horse was old and gentle was unknown to Eylard Theodore.

When four years old, the family moved to Pittsburgh, the German theatre having disbanded due to the war. Papa Horn had long ago dropped the prefix Von in deference to his adopted country's customs. Here he entered business as a representative of a Cincinnati paper house, and Eylard started to school.

As the son of a well-to-do business man, Eylard was sent to a private school — Seton Hill — in Greensburg. On Sundays Papa and Mama Horn would drive the thirty miles to visit the youngster for by now a brother had arrived. The "Standard Eight" with the little pull up seats afforded room for many of the youngsters to go along for the invited "ride." One Sunday there were more youngsters than seats, so Papa and Mama Horn remained behind while the chauffeur performed the rite alone. From then on it became a custom for there to be more youngsters than seats. Years later, as Ted and Al were reminiscing, the reason came to light. Once out of sight of the parents, the youngsters would encourage the chauffeur to "let it out," and Elyard would imitate a siren. Startled pilots of Maxwells and Overlands would pull to the side, only to see a car full of grinning youngsters whiz past.

Eylard became "Ted" as time passed, and there never was any indication of mechanical tendencies. However, the boys — and now there were three — nearly set the house on fire with chemical sets. Ted leaned to poetry and art. This was natural as his ancestry was filled with artists and musicians. The artistry won with Ted, and all his letters and notes had little "doodads" printed on the margins. When punished he would react with silent contempt, and a poem.

One Easter Sunday, the boys were promised a ride. When the appointed hour came, there were no boys. One hour later, in they tromped. They had been in the woods, and their fine Sunday clothing was a shambles. Papa Horn, in spite of the mother's feelings, decided the punishment would be to remain behind while the elders took the ride. With a heavy heart, but a Spartan, Teutonic heritage, Papa Horn held to his decision, and the Reo then left three very disappointed little boys behind. On returning, the mother found pinned to her dressing table —

> *I am sad and weary*
> *My parents do not care;*
> *I have lots of clothes*
> *But they watch what I wear.*
>
> *Happiness is their life;*
> *Sadness is mine;*
> *But I wear through the strife*
> *And drag along with time.*

Ted Horn — age 9.

In after years the true story of the delay came to life. A forbidden BB gun was hidden in the woods.

In 1920, the Horns moved to California. Mr. Horn's health was failing and he thought an ocean trip, down the east coast through the canal and thence to Los Angeles, would restore that which was failing. He was so impressed with California, that he requested a transfer from his company, and the little family located in San Mateo.

At 14, Ted was restless. He began to raise rabbits, and was doing well when the family moved to San Francisco. Here family finances dwindled, due to Mr. Horn's continued illness, so the habitual hired help was discharged, and the boys given the assignments — Ted's duty being dishes. The job became boring, and to an end in his mind when one day his mother found a very business-like statement for wages amounting to $74.60. Furthermore, if the bill was not paid by a certain date, dishwashing would be discontinued. In addition, a five dollar deposit would be required for any further dish dunking, until a decision was made.

When Ted was fifteen a group of boys, George Fisher of Hollywood Whispers, and his brother Ted, Demitre Romanoff, a pianist, John Condon, now Colonel of the Presidio, and the Horns decided on a peach picking expedition to Mountain View. All the parents were pleased with the idea of a summer's employment for the boys. However, the Horns were a bit apprehensive when after a season of peach picking the boys returned with but twelve dollars.

Casually, Mother Horn had noticed a chassis and four wheels on a side street, and one day when an officer came to the door and inquired if the "Jalopy" belonged at this household, an answer came from the back room, "It's mine." That is where the peach money went.

Although Ted despised the dishwashing chore, he rapidly adapted himself to his new duties as cook. He became proficient with corn muffins and devil's food cake. The result being "the kind mother tries to make." However, his first batch of root beer erupted at midnight and that ended that.

The family now contemplated a move to Los Angeles. The parents were reluctant to deprive the boys of their hard-earned Jalopy, so consented to their driving it to the new home. There was much joy as they loaded it with every imaginable knick knack, so precious to the heart of an American boy. Had John Steinbeck seen them, it very well could have been his inspiration for the "Joads" of his great novel, "The Grapes of Wrath."

At 3:30 in the morning the little Horns arrived, tired, dirty but happy. The car stopped sideways in a narrow street, gasping its last, and while three little workmen slept the clock around, the milkman had to back down the hill, and the ice man back up the hill. The jalopy ended its career some weeks later, wrapped around a telegraph pole on Ventura Boulevard, where it had gone "to get tested."

At sixteen, Ted started his racing career. Previously he had expressed the desire to become a farmer, so off again to Mountain View. Immediately the family's finances took an upturn. The farming was being done mostly at Jalopy tracks. Then Father Horn secured Ted a nice, safe job on the Los Angeles Times—safe for any boy but Eylard Theodore. He was dissatisfied with the manner water cleaned the floor, so he used gasoline and set the plant on fire. His burns were superficial.

Ted started as a swimmer at the early age of nine. L to R: Ted's brother, Al, unidentified girl, and Ted. Taken at Ocean City, N. J.

Ted didn't always ride on four wheels. At 5 years of age, he is shown here with his pony.

This picture of Ted at the right was taken when he was 16 years old, with his arm around his brother, Al.

When 9 years old Ted was maneuvering a four-wheeled vehicle in the form of a coaster. According to his mother, he disliked the white starched collars he wore at the time.

Shown here is Ted in his first racing car, taken in Los Angeles when he was 16 years old. He drove his first few races without the knowledge of his parents.

— Photos from Mrs. Mary Horn's Collection

An artist's conception of Ted at work — age 14.
Above: Even as a youngster Ted (then known as Eylard) had a sense of humor, which he displayed throughout his lifetime. Shown here is an interesting invoice he presented to his mother for dishwashing — proof of his business acumen when he was 14 years old. —Mrs. Mary Horn Collection

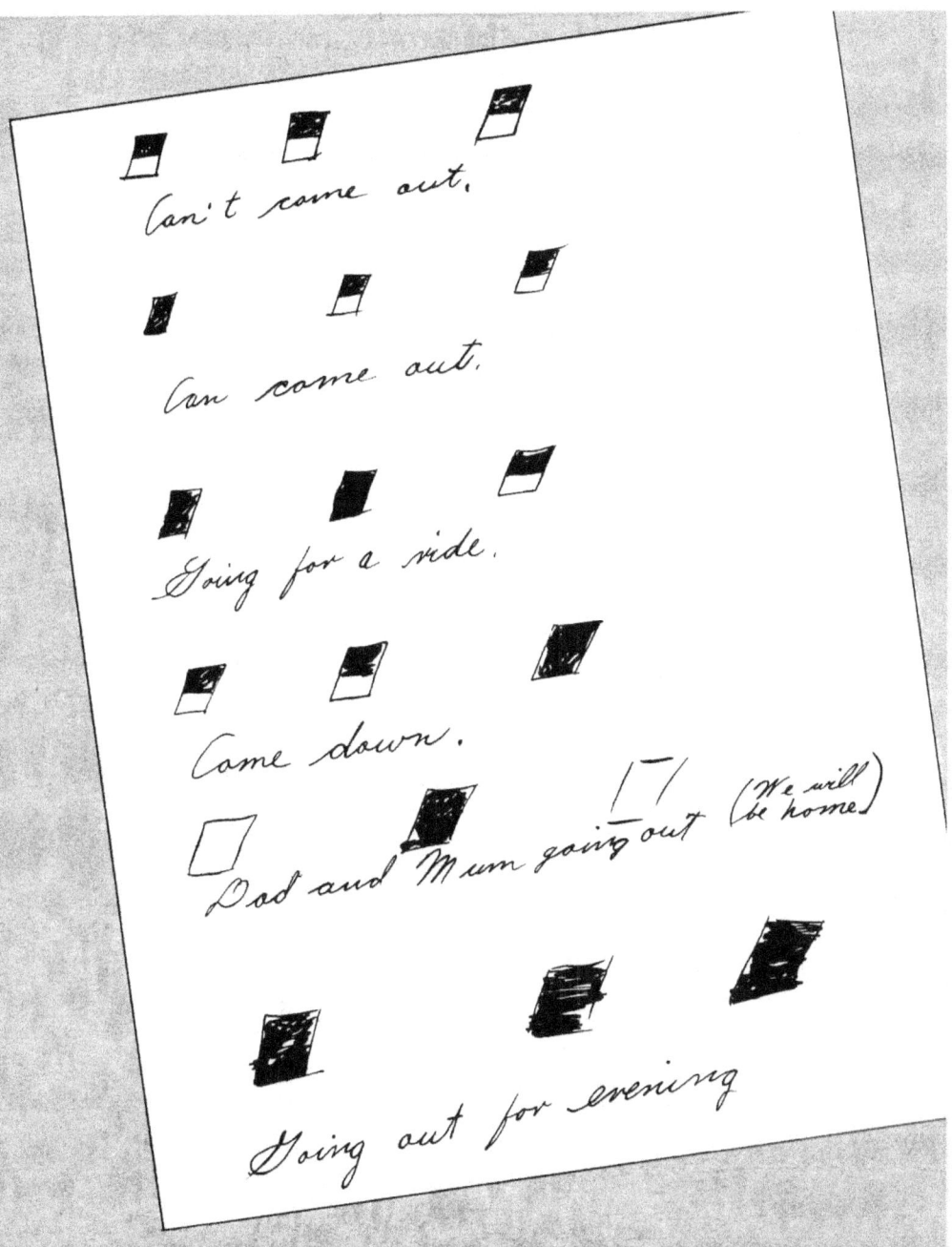

Here again is further proof of Ted's ability, even as a youngster, to plan "ways and means" of overcoming all obstacles. About the time he started going out with girls—when he was 15 years old—an attractive blonde lived around the corner from his home in Los Angeles. Ted devised this method of controlling the window shades so that he could keep his little girl friend advised as to his problems for the evening. His mother, Mrs. Mary Horn, found this in his early scrapbook. He kept a copy to be sure of his signals.

Ted Horn Racing Team
703 East 29th Street
Paterson, N. J.

DRIVERS:
TED HORN
BOB SALL
TOMMY HINNERSHITZ
REX RECORDS

The heading on Ted's stationery

Best of Luck,

Ted Horn

Throughout his career Ted had a flair for making little humorous sketches below his signature when he was writing to intimate friends.

CHAPTER II

A Start Is Made

FOR a week now, Officer 50 had been watching a black streak, too fast to catch, whiz down the level highway that stretches between Glendale and Los Angeles. Today it was going to be different. Officer 50 was parked at an intersection and here all traffic must stop.

So did the black streak and Officer 50 had his man. The man turned out to be a beardless and very frightened youth with a big smile that uncovered a row of white even teeth. Officer 50 opened his book of instructions and turning to page 23 chose a quote from form 17A. "Where's the fire? If you want to speed why don't you get on a race track?"—that was form 17A.

"Why, sir," stammered the youth—then with a grin and new found courage, "You see I work at a newspaper office and I'm late for work, and I really don't know of any race tracks."

If the youth thought the magic word "newspaper" would gain him probation, he was mistaken, but the grin did.

Officer 50 meditated. "Tell you what you do," Officer 50 returned, "You go to San Jose Sunday; there's a race track there and they usually have more cars than drivers. Get one of those cars, and when you get all the speed you have out of your system, come back to the station house and get your car. That's where it's going right now."

Ted appeared at San Jose on Sunday. That was 1926. Sure enough, according to Officer 50 he found an unoccupied race car. The only trouble was it was an almost stock Chevrolet and had been built by a blind man. It had never run, but this day it did—ran until the pistons fused with the cylinder walls and the entire motor was one solid molten mass. The race hadn't even started.

Going home that evening, Ted picked a ride atop a hay wagon. Lost in thoughts of his first experience on a race track, Ted failed to notice the approaching underpass, and neither did the driver. Hay, and one embryo race driver was neatly and quickly deposited by the side of the road.

The next week Ted picked a ride with a Goldberg film delivery truck. There was a race at Colton, and Ted had the promise of another car. Still wrapped in plans, Ted suddenly became aware that the truck had hit a ditch, the driver was gone, and the film was burning.

Kicking out the glass in the door, Ted made his exit, and headed for the race track.

Once again the car wouldn't run. But by now his face with the ever ready grin, was familiar. He picked a few conversations, and from them discovered he was "in."

One of his conversationalists was a car owner. "Listen kid," the owner countered, "Come down to Banning next Sunday and I'll give you a ride in my Rajo. It's a pretty good car, won the Pike's Peak once."

That was Noel Bullock, and Banning saw the Rajo and Ted Horn the following week. That is saw them until Ted and Ted Simpson locked wheels in a turn and the Rajo flew through the fence. There was no damage, but the following Monday Officer 50 had a quiet spoken lad's application for the return of one highway car.

That wasn't the end, however. Two years were to pass in which young Ted Horn tried stock car racing, outlaw barnstorming and finally an offer to appear at Ascot.

The offer was hardly one of star billing. A car owner, impressed with the youth's heavy foot on the dusty tank tracks, had simply offered him the chance to take a trial run on the famed banks of that immortal race track of the west, where such greats as Francis Quinn, Walt May, Carl Ryder, Stubby Stubblefield, Swede Smith, Shorty Cantlon, Ernie Triplett, Mel Kenealy, Babe Stapp, Bill Cummings, Arvol Brunmier, Kelly Petillo, Al Gordon, Les Spangler, Lou Moore, Wilbur Shaw, Chet Gardner, Billy Winn, Joe Russo, Cliff Bergere, Floyd Roberts and even Ralph DePalma were appearing, and were making history in motor racing.

It was an auspicious beginning. Tightly strapped in the cockpit, Ted turned his first three laps slowly to allow the oil to warm. Then, down went his foot. Through almost shut eyes he noted he was through the turn and the car was picking up speed on the backstretch. This was the life. Head into the wind, and a motor that was screaming, the pair sailed into the second turn. Suddenly there was a crash—100 feet of guard rail disappeared, and so did the race car.

That night Papa Horn and Ted had one of those talks. A bargain was made. As is always the case, especially in well regulated families, the bargain was consummated before the conference had started, and was to the effect Eylard was to drive no more race cars. Eylard's spoils from this meeting was the permission to return to his job as a photo engraver without admonitions of becoming a virtuoso in drawing a horse's tail over cat gut, or to blow his lungs out into a twisted piece of metal called a horn.

Most of the bargain was kept. Until 1934, Ted remained as a photo engraver, and no horn, save that which sport's writers were to blow about him, was ever tooted by Eylard Theodore Horn.

> Shiek:
> I want the (car) tonight
> (Tuesday)
>
> Ted
>
> You   Me

When Ted was 16 he wrote this humorous note to his brother, Al.

CHAPTER III

Early Ascot Days

LEGION Ascot Speedway was a five-eighth's, banked, dirt racing oval, with 60 percent of its length taken up in turns. Leased and operated by the Glendale Legion Post 127, it ran weekly events year 'round. Competition, first of the local variety, soon attracted all of the great performers in speedway competition, and in due time became the most popular, and heaviest populated speedway in racing history.

Ascot was the first to present night racing on a regular schedule. It featured color, uniformed attendants, a band, and a program of point competition that set the standard for embryo speedways to follow for years to come.

Movie stars mixed elbows with the hoi poloi, and figures prominent in the social, business and sports world served in honorary capacities. They sought the honor.

Ascot carried AAA sanction, which was under the direction of Art Pillsbury, who built many of the board tracks which mushroomed into prominence during the twenties. Many of the present-day driving stars got their start at Ascot, and all of the drivers making racing a year 'round vocation, competed. Bill Cummings used Ascot racing to train for the Indianapolis grinds, and "500" winners Wilbur Shaw, Lou Meyer, Ralph DePalma, Mauri Rose, Floyd Davis, Floyd Roberts and Kelly Petillo were regular competitors. Ascot produced such nonpareils as Ernie Triplett, Al Gordon and Stubby Stubblefield. Its overall history is unmatched in speedway competition.

It was into this maelstrom of activity that Ted Horn emerged the Sunday afternoon of March 8th, 1931. Preparing plates for the Roto sections of the newspapers, Ted's knife had many times traced the features of Ascot drivers and events taking place there. "Once a driver, always a driver," is the axiom of the track, and Ted was no exception to the rule. His visits to the pits became regular, and once his mind was made up to return to the sport, he used his selling ability to secure a car, even to the point of fabricating a racing history. All eyes were on Triplett, the blonde terror, who was making a run-away of the point standings even this early in the season, and no car owner save a very few even hoped to catch the blonde bombshell.

On the strength of his showing three years previous, Ted managed to get his former Rajo to drive. He bought the car, but failed to get the ever-necessary AAA driving permit. Two programs later Ted had the valuable piece of paper, but the Rajo was sick. Finding the L & C Special without a pilot, the young car owner talked himself into a time trial.

Once again Ted journeyed onto the hallowed oiled surface. Two laps later the L & C was seen to disappear over the south brim into darkness, hit a tree, then turn over.

The crushed foot and badly burned back kept Ted in the hospital many weeks. Two starts at Ascot and two crashes, plus the burning film truck and the upset hay wagon, one would think the young driver would have had enough.

Yet, late that October, Ted and the Rajo appeared at the Oakland mile track, taking a bang-up last in each event.

The next week the embryo was back at Ascot, and on the first of November completed his first successful time trial—33.84 the clock said, the slowest trial of the program by almost a full second. The next week it was 35.20 and the following program 34.80.

Going nowhere in a hurry could be the proper term. Yet, in one department Ted was scoring. Everyone liked the gangly good-natured kid with the ever ready grin, and the determination to become a race driver. One night a portly white-clad figure called at the Horn pit. Chet Gardner, second only to the unbeatable Triplett in Ascot points in the now closing days of the 1931 season, and a respected veteran of eastern, western, and Indianapolis campaigns, halted for a social visit. Nodding to the youth in the black cloth helmet, the pair sauntered away. Gardner spoke:

"Ted, your trouble is getting out of the turns. Get up off of the pole, let your nose down and when you feel it is going to spin, straighten your wheels. Then you'll find you are out of the turn. The faster your speed on the stretch, the higher you go on the turn. Soon you'll find the groove and then you will get to race."

That favor and that word of advice turned the trick. In the years to come, Ted paid back the veteran's advice many times. Always, as the immortal Gardner had done, to some aspiring newcomer with demonstrated ability.

That night Ted turned the oval in 31.13, almost three full seconds faster than his previous time and on the scorer's chart accepted the signal honor of being faster than both Floyd Roberts and Floyd Davis. That he drifted to fifth place in his heat did not bother Ted—he had made the program.

December 21st of 1931 closed the season at Ascot. Ted's 31.30 placed him well ahead of such drivers as Bob Austin, Tommy Cosman and Hugh Schuck, and his last in the ten lap preliminary to the 100 lap feature, earned his first AAA points—three-fourths of one point.

Bryan Saulpaugh won the long feature almost a lap in front of Bill Cummings. Babe Stapp was third, followed by Wilbur Shaw, Gardner and Gus Schraeder. Triplett won the Pacific Southwest title over Gardner by almost 300 points, with Stubblefield a close third. In 83rd place was Ted Horn—none were lower.

1932 became the year when racing reached its zenith in popularity at Ascot. Ernie Triplett won the opening 100 lap feature on January 10th, with Shaw a close second and Gardner, Brunmier, Petillo, Martino and Tomei following in that order. Before the season was to close, auto racing, through Ascot, became the most popular sport on the west coast! 8,000 average attendance jumped to 12,000.

By mid-April, Wilbur Shaw had wrested the point lead from Triplett. Dual wheels on his Gilmore Miller had given Wilbur much publicity, as well as the added traction to front Blonde Ernie. Movie stars were falling all over themselves to get into the Ascot limelight. "The Crowd Roars," one of the best of the movie racing thrillers, was made starring Jimmy Cagney and Joan Blondell. Race drivers took prominent roles and the action scenes were shot at Ascot.

Stubblefield, Shaw, Arnold, Frame, and Hepburn held leading parts, and on April 27th, the James Cagney trophy was presented at the 40-lap feature. In attendance that night, as Arvol Brunmier sped to an impressive victory, was Edward G. Robinson, Doug Fairbanks Jr., Jimmy Dunn, Constance Bennett, Andy Devine, Buster Keaton, Jack Oakie and Clark Gable. The next day advance publicity on "The Crowd Roars" hit the American public. It ran to the best of Hollywood tradition—

—It's a matter of Life and Death—

THE CROWD ROARS

James Cagney   Joan Blondell

With Ann Dvorak, Eric Linden . . . Directed by Howard Hawks

". . . Speed demons with goggled eyes glued on glory . . . grinning at death . . . laughing at love . . . Breaking necks to break records . . . Never-Never-NEVER has the screen shown such nerve-racking action—lifted right off the track of the world's greatest speedway—It's the thrill epic of all time . . . the talk of every town that's seen it . . . Forty men risked death to film it . . . miss it at your own risk."

Ted Horn won the three lap wheel-changing race that night. An added attraction in place of intermission.

The first program in May, Ted electrified no one but himself, and probably his car owner, Leo Champion, when he turned the oval in 29.55. Brunmier had the pole with a 25.91, and with the bulk of the stars leaving for Indianapolis, Ted managed a close third in the last heat to make the feature. Gardner won the 40-lap affair, and the black helmeted neophyte in the white Fronty Ford ran last. But he was now a feature driver at Ascot, albeit a synthetic one.

Fred Frame won the Indianapolis race, and in the same day Ted turned in a neat 28.46, to be third fastest at Ascot. It mattered little that less than 20 cars took a time trial, Ted again made the feature by a third in the second heat. Carl Ryder and Clyde Bloomgreen finished in front. The feature found the Fronty sour, and after a few laps, Ted pulled into the pits. Martino won the big race with Gardner second.

These two showings won Ted a new car. Bill Rasor and his number 21 signed the lanky youth, and the pair were due to climb much of the racing ladder together. The fact was hardly pit gossip, the news of the day being the coming marriage of Arvol Brunmier, popular winning Ascot pilot. The terms of Arvol's marriage included his retirement from the sport. Betting was even money it wouldn't last a month.

On June 22nd occurred one of those things so common on a race track. Triplett had the feature won with a lap to go, when a slight skid let another youngster, Les Spangler, squeeze through the inside to victory. Earl Cooper, immortal of the roaring road from the Oldfield days, crushed a straw hat in his excitement. Gilda Grey awarded the happy victor with a big kiss and the crowd went wild. So did Spangler, and there was no stopping the chunky pilot from there on. Spangler took every helmet dash in sight and the kisses that went with it, until late in August when Fifi Dorsay was the scheduled osculator. Blonde Ernie Triplett scored that one with his wife attempting nonchalance as the Dorsay caress shook the foundations of the stands.

So hectic were the proceedings those days that the management had to take space in the program to draw attention to the antics of the "Busy Bees"—the little known drivers with the slower cars, who were providing the bulk of the racing program. Named as drivers to watch were Bob and Art Scovel, Bob Austin, George Connor, Ted Horn, Frank Suess, Art Boyce and Pinky Richardson.

The first race in August was to be a 100-lap affair. Spangler grabbed the lead only to be passed by Mel McKee. On the 38th lap McKee blew a tire and Shaw took over, to be chased the remaining distance by Triplett. Prentiss won the 15-lap B feature, with an accident on the ninth lap causing some consternation. Horn's car skidded and he was thrown to the track. The car rolled over his prostrate body, but a quick checkup at the hospital tent uncovered only a few scratches. Leon Duray appeared this night and finished 8th, after driving the entire distance without goggles. They had been smashed at the outset by a flying rock.

The night of September 14th was one Ted would never forget. He won his 5-lap B heat, and in the 15-lap B final had third spot safe when the leaders Cosman and Tomei locked wheels. Ted went on to win and make it a gala night in his career. Kelly Petillo took the 60-lap feature after two thrown wheels and ten "gilhoolies" spiced the program. The 9,000 patrons talked of this evening for many moons.

Ted repeated this performance a month later at San Jose. Taking his heat and the 15-lap B. Spangler bested Petillo in the feature. Shaw and Duray had left for Italy and the Monza road race, and Spangler had passed the little Indianapolis pilot in points, to crowd the champ Triplett as the season neared a close.

At the season's final, Triplett's lead was cut to the point he had to finish fifth or better in the 200-lap feature. Chet Gardner held pole position in the long grind and took an early lead. Shaw who had returned unexpectedly from Italy, took over when Gardner crashed, only to see his lead vanish to Bill Cummings.

Wild Bill was plagued with tire troubles. Twice a blown shoe wrested the lead from him; meanwhile Triplett had closed on Shaw. Near the finish Shaw's motor seized and Triplett flashed over the line a winner. Stapp was second and Cummings third, Ryder fourth, Stubblefield fifth, Kenealy sixth and Tomei seventh. Triplett for the second straight year was the Pacific Southwest Champion.

Without official records showing it, three events occurred in 1932 that were important to Ted. The first was the double win of September 14th, establishing him as a front runner. The second, pairing up with Bill Rasor, and the third, a comparatively minor 5-lap event the night of September 7th. Ted was leading the affair with one lap remaining, when a white streak flashed past him on the outside to grab the lead and the checker flag. The pilot, driving his first AAA race, was such an unknown that the papers recorded the event in 28 words, including the mis-spelling of the winner's name. It ran thus:

"Rex Mayes, a Colton youngster, drove his first AAA race

and showed a lot of promise in winning a 5-lap event." That was the understatement of 1932. The names of Ted and Rex were to be linked in a speedway rivalry that was to last 16 years.

The final point standings for 1932, released from AAA headquarters were:

    1—Ernie Triplett   6—Bob Carey
    2—Lester Spangler   7—Babe Stapp
    3—Wilbur Shaw   8—Kelly Petillo
    4—Chester Gardner   9—Sam Palmer
    5—Bill Cummings   10—Arvol Brunmier

In 20th position was Ted Horn. 84.8 points.

The 1933 California racing season opened on New Year's day at Ascot. The new season was to bring many changes, chief of which was the establishing of both class A and B divisions. Car specifications was the dividing line, and programs were scheduled to fit the entries. Points were to be awarded in each classification and so recognized by AAA.

The racing was getting faster. Where once the record stood at 28 seconds, it now was nearing the 25 second mark. At a time when the country was plunged into a terrible financial depression, Legion Ascot played to full houses. More and more celebrities were fastening their names to that of the speed sport. It was a promising new year.

Ernie Triplett started the season on New Year's in the same manner in which he had commenced his title winning 1932 effort, by winning the 50-lap feature with Shaw hot on his heels. An East versus West match race, pitting Carey and Cummings of the East against Shaw and Triplett of the West drew much attention, with Shaw emerging the victor.

Al Theisen copped the second feature and Triplett came right back to nab the third. Carey, now National Champion as a result of his many eastern victories, returned to Ascot on February 26th amid much fanfare, and won the feature. Then Triplett took over again.

Meanwhile, the B's were having a race all of their own. Swede Smith, a Pacific Northwest veteran, sailed into the point lead with Vest, Tomei and Cosman pressing him.

Horn was far down the list with a balky motor failing to respond to treatment.

Engaging in pit gossip before a March race, Ted became imbued with his first taste of superstition. Kelly Petillo was fastening a baby shoe to his dashboard and that started the conversation. One tale after another was told of the effect of hoodoos to race drivers. One that stuck in Ted's mind was the telling of the immortal Jimmy Murphy's last ride at Syracuse in 1924. A woman and child had been photographed sitting in his race car just previous to the event that was to take his life. Ted made a mental note right then that such would never happen to him.

On April 16th, tragedy struck Ascot. Bob Carey, National Champion went over the wall to his death in his qualifying attempt. The affair sobered the populace. Triplett was again running away with the championship. Gardner was second and Stapp third. The last day of April, Rex Mays shocked the entire west coast by taking a class A car for a trial spin, turning turtle and crashing the fence, only to come back and pass Gardner to win the feature race—his first feature Ascot victory. The event took the headlines away from the breadlines, and the gate groaned under the impact of new auto racing boosters.

Meanwhile two new names were added to the prominent B lists. Herb Balmer and Art Boyce, an ambulance driver. Both were forging towards Smith, while Horn continued near the tail of the list.

As per habit, the month of May saw the bulk of the stars leave for Indianapolis, and the B's took over the program. Elliott Roosevelt visited the races and pronounced them as being the most thrilling sporting event he had ever witnessed. Al Gordon won two features in a row and young Roosevelt presented a cup. Both Gordon and Mays moved up on the absent Triplett.

On Sunday preceding Decoration Day, Silvergate Speedway at San Diego carded the Ascot stars. It was to be a gala affair, featuring the B's, but again tragedy struck. Harry Gentry, taking his time run, dived through the south

TED SCORES CLEAN SWEEP AT SAN DIEGO

turn fence and bounced 73 feet through the air before hitting an embankment. His injuries proved fatal.

Horn scored in the Helmet Dash over George Connor. He repeated in the first heat with Frenchy La Horgue third, then smashed the track's 50-lap record in taking the feature, again besting Connor. Swede Smith was third.

On the 27th lap of the main event, Tex Peterson and Ray Durling hooked wheels and turned over. Pinky Richardson's car stalled and was hit by that of Ed Walker. All in all it was a wild afternoon, but Ted had scored the first clean sweep of his career.

Returning to Ascot, Mays took his third feature as the month ended.

The first event in June found the headliners still in the east for championship events. Still hot from his San Diego clean sweep, Ted made the feature with a third in his heat. Carl Ryder, veteran of many seasons, led from start to finish of the 50-lap feature, with Smith close until the latter stages of the race. Ted running with the confidence of a veteran, following his victories, engaged Smith in a spirited duel, and edged the B point leader for second spot. Frank Suess was fourth after throwing a wheel and finishing his last lap on three.

Ted was elated. In two races he had earned himself more money than he would earn in six months at his job. His mind was made up to now seriously pursue a racing career. Previously it had just been an outlet to his enthusiasm. From this point on, it was to be a serious business.

One week later Ted knew his car was ready. He scored a 27.27 in his time trial, in one of those evenings that everyone was on edge. You could practically feel the excitement that was coming. All the big names had returned from the east, and tales of Lou Meyer's Indianapolis victory filled the pits. The only sad note was Les Spangler's tragic death during that great classic.

Ted won his heat with Frank Suess half a lap behind. Ted didn't use full throttle for his victory, being content to coast to victory. Earlier in the program, Mays had crashed while engaged in a match race with Gordon. Therefore, the anticipated Gordon-Mays-Triplett duel in the feature became just a two-way affair, with Triplett chasing Gordon all the way.

Ted started the 15-lap B final in third spot. Directly behind him came Suess, with Frenchy La Horgue alongside Suess. Roaring into the south turn on the first lap, Ted's car started to spin. Suess struck the tilted car, and in turn both were hit by La Horgue. Suess and the Frenchman went over the wall, while Ted's machine remained on the track, badly damaged.

Suess never regained consciousness. A quiet spoken, likable chap, Ted felt his loss immensely. Suess had started his career long before Ted, but his only claim to fame was that of an "also ran." La Horgue recovered.

Rex Mays was running wild at Ascot. A registered driver less than a year, he was to take 11 of the next 18 feature events, with Triplett, Gordon and Petillo the only drivers able to head him. By mid-July, he had moved into second spot in the standings, passing Gardner, while Gordon was fourth. Triplett's huge lead was now narrowing perceptibly, and the season had not yet reached the half-way mark.

July was to chalk up another tragedy in Ascot history. The races were now carded for Wednesday nights and on February 19th Mays and Triplett were dueling for points. Ernie had broken Rex's string of victories and had two of his own. This night he grabbed an early lead, while Rex was boxed in traffic. Only Gordon was free to give the Bombshell chase, but on the 30th lap, Triplett's transmission gave out. Mays cleared himself of traffic and set out after Gordon. Eight laps later and the "Colton youngster" had another victory. Such were the typical phenomenal performances of Rex Mays.

In the B final, Ted had a long lead, while trailing in last place was Harold Proven. Suddenly Proven's car shot to the top of the bank, hit the guard rail and burst into flames. Horrified, 10,000 spectators watched as Proven was tossed to the ground and his car consumed by fire. He was dead on arrival at the hospital.

The Proven accident provoked comment in the newspapers. Racing fatalities of the young season were listed, and it was apparent there were people who would like to see the end to the Ascot tragedies. None were more sincere in this than racing personnel themselves, yet, true to the belief of the track, such an avalanche of bad accidents were one of those things to be expected. Always they will come in bunches. In spite of safety precautions some mythical power sees to it that the death cycle is repeated. Always it ceases just as suddenly as it starts.

Death did take a holiday, although the racing got faster and presumably more dangerous. Two weeks after the Proven accident, Ernie Triplett crashed while riding hub to hub with Gordon. At first it was feared the champion's name would join that of Carey, Gentry, Suess and Proven. Luckily his injuries proved superficial, but confining.

Gordon and Mays were trading victories, and closing in on Triplett. In mid-August, Gordon had passed Gardner in third spot, and was close on Mays' heels. Triplett was still out of action, but rapidly approaching the point where his return was imminent.

Among the B's, Swede Smith was emulating Triplett's 1931 and 1932 campaigns. His lead was a long one, but Horn continued to climb. As Gordon and Mays traded firsts, so did Ted and Art Boyce. The fans, following a hub-to-hub 15-lap race between Boyce and Horn, which was won by the ambulance driver, clamored for a series of match races between the two. The management agreed, and in addition, also carded the same between Mays and Gordon.

Gordon was the victor in his match, and Boyce bested Ted. It was a friendly rivalry which the matches far from decided.

September 13th was another typical Ascot program. Roy Russing, a new driver, in attempting to miss stalled Frank Wearne, went over the fence. He was unhurt. Swede Smith stalled in the B final, and Pinky Richardson went end over end three times in the mixup that followed. The feature had hardly started when Gordon lost control, side-swiped the fence, then caused Mays to do likewise. At the same instant,

Mel Kenealy lost a wheel, and it was a merry mixup all over the track. That Fate was in attendance was evident. There were no injuries and Petillo went on to win, breaking the Gordon-Mays-Triplett grasp on those laurels. Balmer was second and Mays third.

Boyce again bested Horn in the 15-lap affair.

Opening October, San Diego carded another race for the B's. This time it was returned Franchy La Horgue who was to take Horn's measure. He sailed to victory in three events, while Ted was hard pressed to hold second spot from Herb Balmer. In one way Ted had to eat Crow. Five months earlier he had cleaned house at the same track. Today, against practically the same field, he was just an "also ran."

October 29th proved another Ascot tragedy, as well as three spectacular accidents. The main event was one of 100 laps, and on the 76th lap, George Connor locked wheels with Carl Ryder riding in third spot. Ryder freed himself to continue, but Connor took a "loop" and headed for the fence. The car turned over and brushed crazily along the guard rail, finally falling back onto the track, pinning Connor beneath. While horrified spectators watched the car burst into flames, Connor could be seen slowly climbing out unhurt. Mays won the event with a sick motor, after both Gordon and Triplett had been forced out. Petillo was second and Gardner third.

During the time trials, Ted had "lost it" on the turn and crashed. Later, writing of the event, Ted had this to say, "My car swung too wide, spun and leaped the bank twenty feet high. For a moment it looked bad for me and especially so when the car hit and began rolling. It took three complete loops on the ground before it stopped. Although this was enough to put anyone in the hospital, I strangely didn't feel so bad excepting that my sides hurt. Nevertheless I righted my car, found it in good condition, went back to the track and later won the race. Afterward I found I had broken two ribs."

In the race Ted won, tragedy struck. Babe Stanyer, 25-year-old Alhambra driver, riding far back in the field, blew a tire. Like a bird the car sped towards the guard rail, then out into space. The mass of shattered metal came to rest thirty feet from the track, and Stanyer died in the wreck.

To this program of ill fortune, the public press devoted much space. Where before opposition to the racing had been a whisper, now it became a shout. Yet, when November rolled around, and Al Gordon smashed all existing records up to 100 laps, in an accident-free program, public sentiment was still with the racers.

Gordon was not to be beaten the rest of the season, and his victory on November 5th shot him into the point lead ahead of Mays and Triplett. Meanwhile Ted had matched Gordon's victories in the B field, and now was second to Smith, but too far away to hope to catch the veteran. The A's however was a different story. A change in one position in any of the three remaining events, could eliminate Al, Rex or Ernie.

The December 17th race settled things. Triplett grabbed a long lead to be followed by Gordon, then Mays. A win for Gordon at this point would cinch the crown for him. A victory for Ernie would leave the decision for the last race, December 31st. Mays could cinch the crown only by taking both races.

Near the close of the race, Triplett pulled in with a flat. As he sat in his car he watched Gordon roar into the lead. Suddenly he noticed the tread coming loose on Al's right rear tire. Pulling onto the track, the champ wildly waved to the front running Gordon and pointed out his danger. Gordon slowed at once and coasted to the victory that clinched the crown for him.

This was sportsmanship to the highest degree. If Triplett had not warned Gordon of his impending danger, Al's high speed would have certainly resulted in his crashing. Thus Triplett stood to hold his crown. His act cost him the title, but won many friends on the track. One of these was Ted Horn.

The final standings for 1933 were as follows:

CLASS A

1—Al Gordon
2—Rex Mays
3—Ernie Triplett
4—Kelly Petillo
5—Chet Gardner
6—Mel Kenealy
7—Herb Balmer
8—Carl Ryder
9—Wilbur Shaw
10—Babe Stapp

CLASS B

1—Swede Smith
2—Ted Horn
3—Lou Tomei
4—Art Boyce
5—Al Reinke
6—Herb Balmer
7—Woody Woodford
8—Bob Austin
9—Frenchie La Horgue
10—Tommy Cosman

Ted Horn was awarded the trophy for the best appearing driver and crew for the season.

What was to be an ill-fated 1934 season opened late. Janaury 28th was the date, and on hand to award the traditional kiss was Sally Rand. Specifications had been drastically changed on cars, thus the late opening was arranged to give car owners a chance to make the necessary changes.

Harry Hartz, 1926 National Champion, had this to say of the new rules. "It is one of the best moves made in racing in the past decade. It is truly a new era. It is going to make all cars more evenly matched, and discourage 'parades.' I look for nothing but a better brand of racing."

Art Pillsbury was quoted, "We are going to see some new stars in the local picture. No longer will the Gordons, Tripletts and Mays dominate the picture. Look for such drivers as Herb Balmer, Harris Insinger and others to be right up in the running. Racing fans do not want speed with a lack of competition. They want competition. That is why this change was made."

Gordon won the feature again and also the next. This time he equalled the late Jimmy Sharp's long standing record of nine straight feature wins.

Gordon received his title and trophy in front of the stands. The first to grasp his hand in congratulation was Ernie Triplett. The immortal Ernie was quoted, "One can't be on the top all the time and I'm glad to see Al win the crown. Good luck Al, and here's hoping you keep up the good work." He then announced that the coming Mines Field race would be his last. He was retiring from the sport in which he had dominated for so long.

The Gilmore Mines Field was the first in a series of three road races designed to bring back stock road racing. It was to be over a 2-mile course of 125 laps, and attracted the biggest names of the day in racing. Ted joined the Ford team and practiced diligently on the course. Years previous he had scored nominal success with the stocks, and now felt that with his track experience he could make a favorable showing.

The hue and cry against auto racing had subsided somewhat, with but an occasional bleat from a non-racing editor. One of these went as follows: "The comeback of road racing scheduled over a 2-mile course within the boundaries of the municipal airport at Mines Field Sunday, is away to a bloody start with the death of Kenny Willens yesterday in a practice spin."

The Mines Feld race was a success. More than sixty thousand spectators were held breathless for more than four hours, as the strictly stock cars slithered and slashed over the rough and dusty course.

In the late stages, Stubblefield who was leading, stopped for gas. Gordon then grabbed the lead and finished a half mile in front of the luckless Stubblefield. His average speed including two pit stops was slightly over 60 mph. Lou Meyer was third. Pete De Paolo fourth, and Rex Mays fifth. Ted had started in 18th place. At the 100-lap mark was 13th, but at the finish sixth. Tomei, Connor, Reinke and Nelson followed.

Later a recheck of the tape placed Stubblefield as the winner, Gordon second, De Paolo third and Meyer fourth. In spite of the checking mixup, the race was declared a success for all but the morbid. The only serious accident was Chet Gardner's flip, with his riding mechanic suffering a broken pelvis.

Ascot then announced a programmed road race for March 21st to be known as the Targo Florio, after that famous event in Italy. Again stock cars would be used and following this event Ascot would revert to a half mile track in the interest of safety.

El Centro carded a Sunday event for race cars. The success of the Mines Field event, plus the fact Ernie Triplett had announced his entry in a comeback effort, resulted in another huge throng for the races. For some reason the track was in bad shape. Rains of the previous week, plus a last minute watering failed to settle the dust. After a few laps of the feature, it was impossible to follow the events, save on the straightaway.

On the seventh lap a car stalled in the center of the north turn. It was stopped directly in the middle of the "groove." Each of the following racers had to leave the groove at this spot, to miss the car. On the 21st lap, one car failed to clear the stalled machine. It was Swede Smith, two months earlier crowned Pacific Southwest Class B champion. His brush with the stalled car sent his own into a slow side-over-side roll.

Immediately Hap Hafferly, pit hand, rushed onto the track to aid Smith. He was directly in front of the oncoming leader Triplett. Blonde Ernie swerved to miss the mechanic, but dust hid his vision. The Triplett machine struck the luckless man, then continued into the fence, bounced high in the air and caromed off that of Gordon's now in the midst of the dust whirlwind.

Officials stopped the race at once, Hafferly was dead and Triplett dying. Smith lived only a few hours. Triple tragedy of the starkest nature, and soon to become the case celebré in auto racing annals.

The anti-racing press now had the incident they wanted. Black banner headlines screamed defiance at the sorrowing race followers. Morbid pictures appeared and sob sisters had a field day. The public was stunned and extras sold as fast as printed.

Prominent people were quoted. Spokesmen for racing, trying to explain, were misquoted until the whole affair took on the aspects of a Roman holiday during Caesar's heydey.

Feature articles screamed the following headlines:- "Widow-In-Waiting-Faints-As-Mate's-Car-Goes-Into-Spin" ... "She sees mate fight for life in flaming car" ... "Auto Racing Faces Storm of Protests" ... "AAA Chiefs Will Make Racing Safer" ... "Auto Racing Brutal Says Barney Oldfield" ... "More Assemblymen Join War Against Auto Racing" ... Horror pictures appeared under such banners as, "Just to provide a thrill," and "Is it worth the price?"

Midst all this furor, racing buried its dead. The funeral home was jammed with people from every walk of life, as the final rites were said for the three men. So huge was the crowd that very few took notice of an incident taking place on the front lawn. Press photographers were having a field day snapping celebrities. That is, all but one. He was seen to get into a car parked at the curb, in company with several men.

The next day, the triple tragedy was all but forgotten with sensational news of another nature. Blazoned across the front page of a morning paper, was a story of kidnapping and beating at the Triplett rites. The story that ran was as follows: "Resorting to gangster tactics and desecrating the sacred soil of the cemetery during the burial of Ernie Triplett, courageous driver, whose life was sacrificed at El Centro last Sunday, a dozen drivers and race track hangers-on viciously beat Bennus, a World War veteran. The kidnapping followed. Both the reporter and the photographer were manhandled and forced into separate cars. After being threatened and menaced, the two men were taken to the Examiner editorial offices, where the kidnappers openly admitted they had seized the newspapermen and declared it was a direct result of the Examiner's vigorous campaign against legalized murder on the race tracks of Southern California.

It was a sensation.

The "Stop Auto Racing" headlines gave way to those of another sensational nature. "Racers Face Kidnap Charges" . . . "Fitts Quizzing Racers" . . . "Fitts hurls threats of raid on Ascot track". . . . "Fitts issues Ultimatum to Racing Drivers" . . . "Seven Racers answer Edict."

It was truly racing's darkest days. Sorrowed and grieving at the loss of the brilliant members of their fraternity, now hounded by sensational charges that threatened their very existence.

Even the neutral and sympathetic press couldn't tell the racers' side. There was little defense. To be sure AAA officials were on hand, obtaining testimony into the triple tragedy, and seeking a cure for the hazards of the game. Their plea that the advancement of the automobile was credited to the racing sport fell on deaf ears. Even the fact that previous to the Triplett rites, racing had asked the press, not in deference to them, but for the sake of good taste and common decency, to refrain from more horror pictures. That the kidnappers were actually a committee requesting no pictures from the assembled photographers, and that all were willing to cooperate save those who were kidnapped. Also that the kidnapping was merely the forceful removal from the scene of the objectors, and that any rough stuff was perpetrated first by the newsmen. The fact that the party ended in the newspaper offices was overlooked.

District Attorney Buron Fitts had a hot potato on his hands. On one side was the press, loudly calling for the racers' scalps, while on the other hand in response to his surrender plea came seven open faced individuals, willing to tell their story and asking no mercy. The seven that appeared were Babe Stapp, Jack Siveritz, Tony Gullotta, Al Reinke, Earl Brentlinger, Ed Steever and Ted Horn.

Ted's only comment on the tragedy was, "Ernie shouldn't have come back. He shouldn't have told anyone he was quitting. That jinxed him. When I quit, I'll do it after a race, and I won't come back."

The Targo Florio was nearing. Ascot officials had charted a trying course of one and a half miles. It utilized part of the track, then wound for a mile over a hilly course that included a 28 and a 25 degree hill. Herb Balmer died testing his car but strangely the press paid little notice.

Ted again was a member of the Ford team, and again he practiced diligently for the coming event. Al Gordon and Lou Meyer were installed as early favorites, with Rex Mays coming in for much backing.

Early race day crowds jammed the course. Well laid out parking lots were soon overrun with spectators. Many brought their lunches and more than one homemade grandstand was noted, built on top of automobiles. April 15th was the day selected, and many of the drivers charted an exodus to the east and Indianapolis following this event.

Ted too was making plans. Into his life had come a robust, soft spoken man, with opportunity concealed in his billfold. It was Ralph (Pappy) Hankinson, eastern promoter and the man responsible for auto racing's popularity at the big eastern fairs. He sung the praises of the western drivers and openly offered many contracts. One of these was to Ted Horn.

Ted was undecided. To be sure the offer was flattering, but Ted was not one to let flattery turn his head. He really had not amounted to too much in the racing game. Second in the B division was really his outstanding accomplishment, but to place that against the unkown competition of the east was doubtful in Ted's manner of thinking. But of one thing he was decided. He would be at Indianapolis, not as a driver, but to see the great event. Then, he told Hankinson, he would give him an answer.

The young driver wanted to make the change. He was determined to make his mark on the west coast, but the kidnapping affair, plus his lack of ability to get class A mounts, made him want to change. It was a question time had to answer.

There were 22,000 paid admissions to the Targo. How many more came in free, over the hills, and through the thin lines of guarding Legionnaires will never be known. It was a tremendous throng.

Ted grabbed much space in the papers by qualifying third fastest. Yet, in a race of this nature, like that at Indianapolis, a front starting position counted little advantage save for lap money in the early stages of the event.

As the starter dropped the green flag, Horn shot to the front. Car after car came after him, but not until the 18th of the more than one hundred laps, was a car able to get in front of him. Ted's mount skipped a beat on the 25 degree hill, and Mel Kenealy edged in front. Lap after lap the pair rounded the curves, climbed the hills, and sped down the straightaways. Mays challenged, then Gordon and finally Bergere, but none could get past the pair.

On the 65th lap Ted again went to the front when Kenealy broke a spindle. Very few of the cars were going out with mishaps, and it truly became a race of driving skill.

Starting in 18th position, Lou Meyer, Indianapolis winner and National Champion picked up car after car. On the 75th lap he challenged Horn. Curve after curve they rounded as a team, but always the white V8 of Horn's slightly in front. All was forgotten in the race, save these two masters. One the veteran and the other the youngster.

Twenty laps of this and a slight skid by Ted let the master through. But, here the act changed. Ted tore after Lou like a madman, and in the next lap, when Lou suffered a slight slide, the youngster was again in the lead. With only two laps to go, Horn's car slowed slightly. Meyer took him on the inside and at the finish had a lead of 250 yards. Gordon was third, Bergere fourth, Danny De Paolo fifth, Stubblefield sixth, Mays seventh. Woodford eighth, Gardner ninth, and Lou's brother, Eddie Meyer, tenth.

There was demonstrated joy in the Horn pit, and a swelling of pride in Ted's heart. He knew in his own mind that he had made the grade. Even though he had finished second, it was to one of the greatest drivers ever to don a glove and but for a loose brake rod in the final stages of the race, Ted would have had his first major victory. It was this result and no other incident that decided Ted to go east. He had bested many of the greatest names in racing that day and held his own with the National Champion.

Lou Meyer when asked for a statement had this to say: "That fellow Horn certainly gave me a battle and my mitt is out to him. He drove a marvelous race and it was a break for me that his brake rod loosened. Otherwise I might not have been able to beat him."

That night Ted sought his friend Bill Rasor. He told him of his decision, and Bill agreed the choice was a wise one. "I'll take your car Bill," Ted said. "Babe Stapp wants me to drive a few races with his at Winchester, Langhorne and such, but after that I think I will campaign at some of the little spots Hankinson told me about. I'll make my headquarters in Paterson, as there is some sort of a gasoline alley established there, and we will see how good I really am."

Ted stopped at Indianapolis and watched the great race that Bill Cummings won. Earlier he had been offered a car to drive. A Mick Special, which had been entered by Jimmy Kemp and then sold to a local Hupmobile dealer, J. J. Mick, lacked a driver, and when Ted arrived at the track someone told the car owner of his availability.

However the car failed to respond to treatment, and Ted felt satisfied to sit this one out. He neither had the desire to drive this track before he had seen it, nor rebound from his Targo reputation to a poor showing with inferior equipment. Ted had a goal now and a set purpose. It was to be proved that once he had made up his mind as to the right course nothing short of a court order could stop him.

As was the habit following Indianapolis, the western drivers scattered to the four winds, with the wind blowing directly east. Some went straight to the Atlantic seaboard, while other appeared at many of the mid-west tracks. Al Gordon headed east, while Rex Mays and Ted traveled to Winchester in Indiana.

Ted had both Bill Rasor's McDowell and Babe Stapp's No. 10 along. At Winchester he drove the Stapp beauty to a spot in the feature starting lineup. Shortly after the start, a rock hit the cloth-headed driver and he had to retire from the event in which Mays sailed to victory. It took three stitches to close the wound.

The next week a leaky radiator put him out of the event at Dayton and then the entire contingent converged at Langhorne—the Ascot of the east. Ted got away fast and was running third in his heat when a broken piston ended that effort. Gordon won the feature.

Three starts in the east and three failures. Parting company with the Stapp car, Ted joined forces with Gordon and headed for his first look at the eastern circuit. That was to be at Hohokus, a popular half mile track located just outside the municipality of Paterson, New Jersey.

Hohokus was promoted by Jack Kochman, then just starting a promotional career that was to last a lifetime. The Hohokus bull ring was popular with the eastern drivers, and although attendance was not to be compared with such tracks as Langhorne, still it enjoyed the patronage of both the home talent and barnstorming pilots. It was hardly a soft touch for a west coast B driver who was making a habit of blowing up or finishing second.

June 17th was the date set for Ted's first appearance at Hohokus. As planned, he located a garage in Paterson and spent his first week on the east coast readying the Rasor McDowell. Each evening Ted would journey out to the track and walk its entire length. He studied every pebble, every rut and now and then would stoop to feel the texture. By so doing Ted formed an opinion where the soft spots were liable to develop on the track, once the racing started. He mapped the course in his mind, and thus set a precedent he was to follow for a decade. In fact, fourteen years later, at Du Quoin, Illinois, one hour before that fateful race, Ted could be seen taking a mile long stroll around the race track.

Sunday dawned bright and clear. True to tradition, Hohokus had attracted a galaxy of stars including Johnny Han-

Ted in his early racing days, taken at Ascot (Los Angeles) 1932. — *Kozub Photo*

Woodbridge, New Jersey. Taken July 1, 1934 during his first year of racing on the East Coast. Car is Bill Rasor's McDowell.
Kozub Photo

Ted alongside Paul Fromm's Rocker Arm Special, Hohokus, N. J., 1935.
Kozub Photo

Goshen, New York, 1936. Ted in 100-mile championship.

CHAMPION
100-MILE-AN-HOUR CLUB

Know all men by these presents that Ted Horn *has qualified for membership in the Champion 100-Mile-an-Hour Club having averaged* 108.170 *miles per hour for 500 miles without relief in the Memorial Day Race at the Indianapolis Speedway on* May 30th 19 36.

IN WITNESS WHEREOF ARE HEREWITH AFFIXED THE SEAL OF THE CHAMPION 100-MILE-AN-HOUR CLUB AND THE SIGNATURES OF ITS BOARD OF GOVERNORS

BOARD OF GOVERNORS

non, Ben Shaw, Billy Winn and Lloyd Vieux. Car after car took a time trial, and when it came the black No. 1's turn, the spectators did not realize a potential winner had posted the second fastest time of the day, so effortless was his performance.

Ben Shaw had the pole for the first heat with Ted alongside. Ted beat Ben to the corner and won the heat handily. The performance was repeated in the feature, of 30 laps. The black car increased its lead to almost a full lap at the finish, and when the dust had settled the spectators, who had remained on their feet during the entire running, heard a new track record announced. The smiling young Californian with the trace of a moustache had taken everything in sight. He was a sensation.

When the shouting and celebrating had died, Ted had time to reflect. Two things had contributed to his victory. The week long personal preparation of his car, and the minute study of the Hohokus track. Without either Ted very easily could have had another close-up finish, or a sick motor in the pits.

Thus, the next week at Woodbridge, Ted repeated these preparations. The result was another clean sweep of events, with Malcolm Fox taking Shaw's place as the runner-up. Ted was the only driver, and the black No. 1 the only car to break 29 seconds. It was a new track mark of 28.6.

At Flemington the streak was to end. Writing of the event later, Ted indicated he might have been able to keep the victory string alive, but his pre-track stroll revealed a condition not to his liking. Ted wrote, "That's the dilliest track I ever saw. It's got four corners and four straightaways and only half a mile around. Maybe you don't have fun. Another thing, they still have the blue laws, and you don't start a motor up on Sunday until 1 o'clock. That means you get no practice whatsoever when you go to a new track. That probably explains why Gordon and myself did not do so good. I think I've found out how to drive the track now that I've had one race on it, but that didn't do me any good the first time."

Billy Winn won Flemington, with Bobby Sall second, Johnny Hannon third and Ted fourth.

July fourth the entire field returned to their favorite track, Hohokus. The buildup for the race was good and the largest crowd of the season was on hand. Ted opened festivities by setting the fastest lap in the trials, 29.8. The crowd was given its choice for a match race, and chose Ted and Walt Brown. Ted led from start to finish. The first heat was another "Brown chase Horn," but in the feature, Harry Angeloni, in a matching McDowell, pushed Ted to a new track mark of 15:25:00 for the fifteen miles. Brown was third. Harris Insinger, coming Philadelphia ace, soured in this event.

During the program a telegram arrived from ever-popular Bobby Sall. He announced he would be at Hohokus the following week and would meet anyone in a match race that the management was to choose. The public indicated Horn.

Altamount had a race carded for Saturday. For some reason, Ted's AAA registration became confused, and the track officials refused to let him run. However, Ted seconded his pal Gordon, and later wrote that "Al for the first time tried to fly like a bird without wings." The west coast champ parted the fence and collected a few painful bruises. Bobby Sall was on hand, and the pair engaged in some good natured ribbing over the coming match race.

Returning to Paterson, Ted had his first taste of sloppy reporting. So huge was his following at this time, that an enterprising reporter had picked up a chance remark, and weaved a story of the coming match race now becoming a three way affair, with Al Gordon as the third party. The account also had Ted, the California champion, and taking credit for a victory over Bill Cummings, then leading the National Championship as a result of his Indianapolis victory.

It didn't take Ted long to act. He appeared at the newspaper office at once, and the Sports Editor wrote the following account of the meeting.

"A trim, blonde youth with very blue eyes walked into the office yesterday and introduced himself as Ted Horn, who is recognized pretty much as an auto racer with a win over Bill Cummings to his credit this year.

"Except for a grease-stained shirt and hands soiled by labor inside the bowels of his machine, Horn looked like a book salesman. Racing drivers always deceive me. Instead of the gruff, hairy persons you visualize when you see them roaring around the track, they always turn out to be mild, gentle, and soft spoken individuals. It seems to be an unwritten law, too, that racing pilots must either wear glasses or sport a mustache. Horn wears a mustache, which is set off effectively by even, white teeth.

"R. E. Mattade, the Clifton motor vehicle agent, had Horn in tow, acting as his manager. He probably authored the typewritten letter Horn offered for inspection, but Ted verbally sanctioned its contents so they must be accepted as official.

"With commendable honesty, Horn waived all claims to the Pacific Coast championship of the AAA, and steps back for Al Gordon, who is officially recognized as the title holder.

" 'At no time since I have been in the East,' reads Horn's letter, 'have I represented myself as champion of the Pacific Coast. Al Gordon is the champion. The car I will drive at Hohokus Sunday is the machine which the late Swede Smith rode to fame last year. He was class B champion and I finished second to him.

" 'It has been reported by the papers that I consented to a match race against Al Gordon and Bob Sall. Only last Tuesday when the Hohokus promoter approached me in regard to the matter, I informed him that I would be unwilling to make the race a three man affair.

" 'The track is only forty feet wide, too narrow for a race of this kind. I know how I would ride in that race, and havign competed against Sall and Gordon, I know how they would ride. It would be suicide on the turns.

" 'I suggested that the original match race between Sall and myself go on, with the understanding that the winner will meet Gordon the same day. I'll give my best Sunday and if I am defeated I will not alibi.'

"Horn refused to take seriously his victory over Cummings at Woodbridge a month ago. He pointed out that the

Indianapolis star did not have his car geared for the small dirt track, and was not anxious to risk his neck for a comparatively few dollars anyway.

"'Cummings gets a flat sum simply for just appearing at a race,' explained Horn. 'He could pick up a few more dollars by winning, but why should he run the gamble of getting hurt? He is being paid for oil, gas and cigarette testimonials and can continue to get guarantees for personal appearances. If he got hurt while trying for a few extra dollars, all that would be lost.'"

That Ted was naive about the incident could be charged, but as the Sports Editor so ably pointed out, the man was honest and sincere.

The article served as a boomerang for advance publicity. July 22nd marked an exodus of the entire state of New Jersey to the Hohokus track. Not only were the participants of the match races on hand, but so too were Ben Shaw, Eddie Staneck, Chuck Tabor, Walt Brown, Walt Keiper and Johhny Hannon.

Ted beat Sall by 30 yards and set a new track record for the three miles. He then duplicated the feat over Gordon, and lowered the record set some ten minutes earlier. But in the first heat a piston let go and Ted was out for the day. Angeloni won the feature with Gordon and Sall following him to the checker.

An incident occurred just previous to the start of the heat in which Ted was to blow the piston. Returning to his car, parked in the pits and cooling off, a small youngster had climbed into the cockpit. Ted at once made friends with the tyke and invited the mother to bring the youngster to his pit anytime.

Following the racing, Ted noticed the pair approaching, but appeared to be busy elsewhere. Questioned later on his reaction to the fan's interest, Ted muttered, "Did you ever hear of Jimmy Murphy? I only got a busted piston today."

Closing July, Ted joined the troup going to Harrington, Delaware. Again it was a new track and Ted was cautious. The finish of the feature, saw six cars in a blanket finish. Ted, Winn, Gordon and Drexler were involved and first place money went to Winn, with Ted taking third. All were happy over the near perfect finish, and Gordon was heard to say, "Now some guys will tell you that was arranged, but honestly if I had tried I couldn't have made it look any better." Ted wondered, did such things actually happen? He had never experienced it but did not want to show his inexperience before such veterans as Gordon and Winn. He wondered. In 1946 he was to refer to this race in a remark made concerning "putting on a show."

August found Ted hitting the circuit. At Hamburg, he was second with another new track mark; Rhinebeck, third; blew up at Langhorne, and again returned to Hohokus to score a pair of victories and run second to Winn. As the first of September rolled around Ted decided to return to the Coast. A race was scheduled in Chicago and he decided this to be his swan song to a very successful and exciting visit in the east.

Making the trek back was Bobby Sall, the eastern sensation. Ted and Bob had formed a strong friendship. Rivals on the track, but the best of friends once the racing was over. Al Gordon too liked the bespectacled easterner, and told the pair of his plans to open a night club once he returned to the Coast.

Ted wrote a letter. It was to a friend of influence on the Coast. Its entire contents consisted of a buildup of Bobby Sall. His own victories over the Jerseyite he belittled, as matters of accident. His sole purpose was to pave the way for acceptance of the visitor.

At Chicago Ted was to meet Frank Brisko, Johnny Sawyer, Wally Zale, Pete Romcevich, Emil Andres, Myron Fohr, Shorty Sorenson, and Harry Lewis. Once again his billing was as the Pacifiic Coast Champion, but there was little time for Ted to rectify the error. This bothered him no end.

Rex Mays was leading things back home with Floyd Roberts his closest competitor. Bill Cummings continued to lead the National chase, although Cantlon scored at Syracuse, Winn at Milwaukee and later Atlanta. Doc Mac-

Kenzie followed Ted's eastern circuit and broke many of his records.

At Chicago, Ted worked himself up to third spot, and seemed to have the speed to gain the front of the pack, when suddenly he slowed and pulled into the pits. "What's wrong?" a pit hand asked. "Don't know," Ted replied, "Just had a feeling I should come in."

The pair went over the car before loading it on the trailer. Everything seemed to be in perfect shape, but as they pushed it towards the tow platform, the right wheel collapsed. The spokes had worked loose and but for some sudden warning in Ted's mind, that would have happened during the race. The first of the often referred-to "Ted Horn hunches."

The return back to the Coast was uneventful. Ted made himself and his car owner some money. Not anything to match the success that appeared. He had raced and won mostly at small tracks, where the purses were not too large, but he had beaten the cream of the east, and more than held his own against the western drivers engaging in those events.

Mays was blazing an unbeatable trail at Ascot, but the new half mile track was unpopular and rumor had it the return would soon be made to the five-eighth's. The Coast papers, especially those devoted to racing events, made much of Ted's return. His first scheduled appearance was for the night of October 24th, and Ted's unfamiliarity with the new half mile strip worked to his disadvantage.

During the running of the feature, a tangle on the turn, and Ted joined Harris Insinger in running out on the five eighth's track and out of the event. Previously, Ted had won his heat handily. Floyd Roberts took the 100-lap feature, with Mays a close second.

Bob Sall viewed the proceedings, and the following week took a time trial, but not fast enough to make the feature. On the 18th of November, a race was scheduled at Phoenix, and both Ted and Bob entered.

Well up in the heat in which they both were placed, the pair locked wheels in an innocent "gilhooley," to ruin their chances for a front spot in the feature. The following heat was a ding-dong affair, with the easterner winning and Ted a close second.

The 40-lap feature had Insinger in front, until taken by Roberts. Ted and Sall waged a merry battle for sixth place, and at the finish it was Mays, who as usual came from nowhere, the winner. Roberts was second, Gardner third, Red Clark fourth, Insinger fifth, Sall sixth, and Ted seventh.

Ted was happy. He had a little money in his pocket— at least an eastern reputation. He had made a good showing at Phoenix, as had his protege, Sall, and he was going hunting. But his joy was to know no bounds at the piece of news that reached him. Harry Miller wanted Ted to drop into his office for a chat.

When and if Racing's Hall of Fame is to be established, the name of Harry Miller will have to be included. Never successful as a financial giant, this west coast builder of motors scaled the heights of immortality with his "Miller Specials." They were as near to the perfect racing motor as could be assembled. An invitation to see Harry Miller was tantamount to a command performance. It could only mean one thing to a race driver—opportunity.

Ted lost little time contacting the genius. Greetings over, Miller launched into the business at hand.

Preston Tucker, a man Ted knew by sight, was a promoter. Not of the race track, but of great ideas. Through the years he had been attracted to the Indianapolis race and finally to Harry Miller. Tucker had an idea, and after months of careful spade work had been rewarded with success.

The Ford Motor Company had set up a racing division of engineers. So phenomenal had been the success of the Ford in the California road races, that Tucker's idea of a Ford team for Indianapolis fell on willing ears. Henry Ford himself had used the race track in the early days of the development of his car, and once, on the sands of Daytona Beach, Henry Ford had set the world's one mile straightaway record.

Tucker went direct to the head man himself. Out of their

conference emerged the idea. Tucker was to sell the Ford dealers throughout the country the plan. They were to back the team. Ford himself would furnish the technicians if Harry Miller could be secured as head engineer.

That was the picture of the moment. Turning to a drafting board, Miller indicated a blue print. "That," he said, "Is the plan I have drawn for a front drive Ford V8 race car. This first year the team will be comprised of ten such units, and the Ford factory is ready to start the first right now."

To all of this, Ted sat spellbound. Finally finding his voice he asked, "Where do I fit in these plans?"

Looking the young driver straight in the eye. Miller answered, "Ted, you're ready for Indianapolis. The Ford people like what you did in the Targo, and in the east this summer you proved your capabilities. Now, in picking this team I am not depending on my own judgment. Naturally, very few people know about it at this time, but there is every chance that Pete De Paolo will captain the team. Cliff Bergere too will be a member, and it is our opinion, as well as Harry Hartz' that you should have one of these opportunities. Now, what do you say? Any more questions?"

Ted counted a very fast ten — by fives — before answering with his acceptance, then added, "And if there are any more spots open, there is a driver I met in the east this year that can run rings around me — Bobby Sall." "We know about Sall," Miller answered, "He will get one of the cars."

There was no person on the West Coast happier at the moment than Ted Horn. He went hunting and he fished. He little cared for the happenings at Ascot. The track was being rebuilt back into a five eighths racing strip, and the accidents of the past year ceased. The sun was shining again, the birds were singing and Ted Horn was a full-fledged major league race driver. Nine long and fruitless years of apprenticeship, since that day back in Glendale and Officer 50.

But, Ted wasn't the only person with hopes for the embryo race team. As Miller had predicted, Pete De Paolo accepted the captaincy, although his return to the speedway was in direct violation of his announced retirement following a near fatal crash in Spain.

Pete left for the Ford factory in Detroit. It was obvious to him that his presence on the team was vital. As twice National Champion, plus the fact the power of his name as a capable team manager, would do much to allay the fears of the investors. Then too, glancing over the list of proposed drivers, with the exception of Bergere, it looked as if much teaching would have to be done. Most of the drivers would be first-time starters at Indianapolis.

Arriving at the Ford factory, Pete developed other worries. In spite of best intentions, it was perfectly obvious to him that progress was far from the point that ten race cars would be ready by Decoration day. Two might be ready, was his opinion.

But, Tucker was Tucker, and Ford was Ford, and an engineer was always an engineer, be it a baby carriage or a naval dreadnaught, and a delay seemed imminent.

Ted made a few half-hearted appearances at Ascot. The season ended in a blaze of glory for Rex Mays, as he copped the West Coast title, and in spite of a very brief appearance in the mid-west around Decoration Day, was second to Al Theisen in mid-western standings. Johnny Hannon took down eastern AAA honors, and although Ted finished in 14th place in the East Coast ratings, Hannon had never bested him.

Ted also had a few points in the Mid-west, and in spite of only a few appearances, was placed in tenth position in the all important Pacific Southwest Championship.

Cars were now coming to him. The news of his Ford team alliance had spread, and one offer Ted accepted was the Gilmore Miller that Mays had driven to his championship at Ascot, to campaign on the half mile tracks back east. Ted planned to return to the east following a 100-mile event at Oakland late in April. He might engage in one or two mid-western affairs before Indianapolis, but the big 500 mile event was his goal. He talked of little else, and planned nothing definite until that event was history.

Ted turned author. In "Coast Auto Racing" appeared a

poem credited to his pen. It was entitled, "God Save the Connecting Rods," and might have reflected his overall attitude.

Oh God save the connecting rods,
  Those precious little things
That keep the motor all intact
  While she sings and sings and sings.
Four little jumping irons,
  Always on the hop—
Oh God save the connecting rods;
  May they never stop.
Oh God save the connecting rods
  And make them last forever,
Hopping merrily up and down;
  Never let them sever
And bust our racing engine up
  By looking out the side.
Oh God save the connecting rods
  On this Sunday's ride.
Oh God save the connecting rods
  If just for one more race.
Leave them turning on the crank
  At this headlong pace.
If they finish just this time
  In their strenuous task—CRASH—
Oh God save the connecting rods
  Was just too much to ask.

Ted Horn

Ted went to see the two-man National Championship race at Mines Field. Here his coming adversaries at Indianapolis staged the last of the big point races in California. It drew not only the western name drivers, but those from the east such as MacKenzie, Haustein, Snowberger and Barringer.

It was a miserable race and day. Driver after driver tired and had to seek relief, and long before the 200 miles were completed the race was called due to a fog condition. Kelly Petillo was the winner, Shaw second and Hepburn third, although Roberts was giving relief at the checker. Then followed MacKenzie, Gardner, Gordon, Cantlon, Cummings, Miller, Haustein, Brisko, Meyer, Sall and Stubblefield.

Al Gordon's Club Rendesvous was enjoying success. Back

of the bar was a new bartender, Bob Sall. Everywhere the air was filled with laughter and the racing entourage, with their troubles and tragedies behind them, felt new and bigger things were ahead. The proposed Ford team came in for much of the conversation, and the general opinion seemed to be that its success was a foregone conclusion. Race drivers' aversion to factory engineers was brushed aside in this instance. Wasn't Harry Miller the head man, and wasn't little Pete De Paolo in Detroit right now? It looked like the perfect setup from a race man's angle, and Ted was in full agreement.

Sall left for the east, and was the subject of much conversation at the Rendesvous when a letter arrived telling of Sall's confinement in a Dallas Texas hospital. Driving into a filling station late at night, Bobby had opened his door, then stepped out into space. He had tried to walk on air directly above an open grease pit, and a few broken ribs was the result. "Probably thought he was full of that hot air we fed him," Gordon remarked.

Mays, Petillo, Insinger and Roberts were all in a dog fight for the point lead at Ascot. Ted was little interested. He made the feature each night, but coffee money was all he was after. His chance was coming, and he was determined to make the best of it.

Practice opened at Indianapolis and Tucker scheduled a preview of his new race team. Over a hundred Ford dealers were invited and both De Paolo and Bergere were on hand to do the demonstrating. Miller was in Detroit and through his efforts two partially completed race cars arrived at the Indianapolis track. In looks they were a thing of beauty. Low slung and embodying all the elements of streamlining —in looks alone one would know Harry Miller had scored again.

Writing of what then transpired, De Paolo had this to say, "After my first glance at the jobs I knew my part of the deal was off—not good. Pointing to the steering box located alongside the cylinder block, where constant heat would prevail, I informed Miller that it would be almost impossible to keep lubrication in the unit, in addition to the fact that the steering gear unit resembled the size of a gear driven oil pump."

"He pleaded to have me drive at least a few laps for the benefit of the Ford dealers present that day. I did, only to learn the gear box tightened up going out of the south-east turn almost causing me to wind up over on the golf course —then and there I resigned as Captain of the Ford V8 racing team."

Bergere followed suit. He immediately signed with another car owner while De Paolo took over the management of Kelly Petillo.

The Ford factory started pouring out race cars on a production line basis. The plan was to do the basic building at Detroit, then let Miller finish the job at Indianapolis. A dozen hungry young race drivers stood around awaiting the completion of their cars. Meanwhile, Ted took in a 50 mile race at Milwaukee. MacKenzie walked off with the major honors, as Ted scored fourth place in the feature.

Johnny Hannon died at Indianapolis in a trial spin. Crowned eastern dirt track champion a short five months earlier, he was a popular driver.

Ted's No. 43 was ready. Now the race was for time as the field was rapidly filling. Mays was the pole, with Gordon and Roberts in the front row. An all-Ascot lineup. Then came Lou Meyer, Bill Cummings and Tony Gulotta. Hepburn, Frame and Gardner. Happy-go-lucky Stubby Stubblefield's car dove over the retaining wall and ended his brilliant career. Two fatalities and only eight spots remaining in the starting field.

Then Ted faced the starter for his time run. The first of the V8's to hit the line. The hood was unpainted. The flag fell, Ted raised his arm and the ten lap race against time was on.

Straightaway speed was blinding, but the curves were disappointingly slow. Yet, his average was very near the 115 mark. Six laps, seven, eight, then he began to slow down. Lap nine and the white flag. Around the north turn the unpainted car sped and the checker fell.

High up in the Pagoda, Chet Ricker, made a quick calculation. "One-one-three-point-two-one-three." Ted was *in* and the first of the Fords had qualified.

Johnny Seymour was next, and 112.696 placed him alongside Ted. Only three hours left to qualify and six of the Fords on hand were unfinished.

The last day of qualifying at Indianapolis is always a hectic session. Time runs out with many cars unqualified—just putting the hood on. 1935 was no exception, and the Ford team was the worse sufferer. George Bailey and Bobby Sall got in, but the rest had to wait for another year to race on these bricks.

Ted was worried. He had trouble in those turns. Not to the extent he wanted to tell it, but each of the four corners was a new experience to him on that time run. Ted liked a front-drive car—he liked the license it gave him to stand on it until well into the turn. Near the end of his run he had slowed ever so little. Not wanting to crowd his luck, and paying homage to that hunch he had.

Race day Ted rose and dressed early. He dismissed his fears and took a solemn vow unto himself. Today was the day. When the race was over, everyone would know he was an established driver. This was the real big time. This was one race he would win. Maybe not today, but if not today, someday. Regardless, today one Ford was going to do some important running.

Ted and his riding mechanic, Bo Huckman, shoved their car to the starting line. They were in the ninth row between Clay Weatherly and Seymour. Ted glanced first at Johnny, then Clay. Neither spoke, but all nodded the same greeting, "Good Luck."

The first row moved out, then the second and the third. The Fords started then gained momentum on the backstretch. Ted watched Weatherly and kept even with him. They made the turn in front of the stands and the speed increased. They were over the line and away . . . Now Ted watched directly in front. Weatherly was pulling away on the inside. Ted nearly reached him at the turn, then fell back as they pulled on the backstretch. The field was stringing out, but no one had passed Ted . . . Now they were in the front stretch again and running easily.

Mays was out in front with Rose right after him. Now Rose had the lead. Still Ted was holding his own—no one had passed him. The stands took on a solid look, and not the blur he had noticed at first, and the yellow flag was out—that meant slow down—here on the north turn was the reason, a big hole in the concrete wall and a race car was upside down, hanging on the wall. It was Gordon, and he was standing alongside the wreck. Didn't look hurt —good old Al—but that was a nasty hole he made.

The "hole" marked the spot Clay Heatherly had gone through five laps earlier. His luck had run out just fifteen minutes after that "Good Luck" wave, and in the same car Johnny Hannon had ridden into eternity.

The green was on again, and Ted opened up. One car passed him, then another, Mays and Meyer. Cars were stopped along the pit wall—one was Sall and he was walking towards the garage. Ted wanted to open up, but at every turn his car seemed to tighten. Now it wasn't his imagination—it was a fact. Yet on the straightaways it went like a bullet. Bo kept punching him in the leg—cars coming up—Stapp, Petillo, Gulotta, Shaw, Cummings, Cantlon. Ted looked at the pits again; there was George Bailey's Ford and George wasn't to be seen.

Now Ted was gripping the wheel with both hands to get around the corners. It wasn't his imagination that was working, the steering was going bad. He slowed, but only on the turns did it tighten. He tried a burst of speed on the backstretch and grinned as Petillo couldn't get away from him, but on the turn again it tightened—this time he almost didn't get it back. Seymour was in the pit now and watching him. Next time around, Ted looked at Johnny and got a sad shake of the head. Ted looked at Bo and got no response. Obviously the passenger was enjoying his ride and perfectly oblivious of the trouble.

Then Ted felt a bit sick at his stomach—months and months of planning and here he was without a chance. Fate was certainly against him, or was it?—that last time on the north turn he felt he had lost it for a minute—he didn't think he could get the wheel around. He looked at Bo again and he knew Fate was with him. Fate was holding off disaster because he had an obviously dangerous car in his hands, and he was risking not only his own life but that of others, in his desire to win this race. Win?—that is a laugh—he didn't have a chance now.

Ted signaled his pit he was coming in. The last lap he slowed to a crawl on the inside. He was glad he had made the decision because on the last turn into the stretch he had to use both hands and brace his feet against the floor boards to get the wheel around. He pulled to a stop and pointed to his front end. A jack went under it and a husky pit man tried to turn the wheels by hand—they wouldn't budge—frozen solid.

Another dream shattered. Nothing to do now but dress and wait for the results. Shaw was in the lead but had a pit stop to make. Petillo was second and De Paolo was pacing his countryman from the pits.

Ted dressed in the garage. A mechanic ran in with the news—Petillo has it. Shaw's a half lap behind—say, what happened to you?

Ted wanted to get away. This party was for those who earned it. He certainly didn't belong here. Now, his chance was gone. Nothing but junkers to drive in this race—well, I won't take them. I'm a dirt man and I'm going to stick to it.

A slender man with a noticeable limp walked into the garage. "Ted, I've been looking for you. That was a great race you drove. I mean it. Those cars weren't ready, and how you lasted as long as you did I'll never know. None of them could handle you on the stretch. How would you like to drive my car next year,"

Ted looked up. It was Harry Hartz. Immortal of the board tracks and National Champion in 1926.

The grin came out—gone was the look of disappointment. The two men shook hands. No words were spoken. None were required. Ted had a lump in his throat.

"Ted," Harry finally said, "I'm going to rebuild my car completely. It'll be a brand new job next year and if we have luck we ought to have a chance. Good luck this summer and I'll see you when you get back to the Coast."

That race marked the last time, and only time Ted didn't get the checkered flag, denoting the finish of a race at Indianapolis.

The Indianapolis drivers were planning a summer of National Championship events. Lacking a championship car, and not wanting to accept the second grade equipment he could get, Ted decided to return to Paterson and Hohokus.

June 9th an event was carded at Chicago, and Ted planned to give this event a try before heading east, but so did many of the other 500 drivers. Petillo, Snyder, Willman, Andres were a few on hand as another tremendous crowd awaited the start of festivities.

Ted was ninth in time trials, third in his heat behind Maynard Clark and Floyd Davis, but won the next event, beating Jimmy Snyder and Fritz Tegtmeir.

The main event went to Emil Andres, with Ted well back in seventh spot. The dust was so bad that Ted had little liking for taking chances, so settled on the small paying spot, to race another day. Tony Willman was second.

All plans to return to Paterson were halted when Ted got word in Chicago that his father had died in California. So Ted packed up and headed west once again.

Arriving on the Coast Ted found that the news of his signing with Hartz had preceded him. Everywhere he went he found a decided public interest in his welfare. Paul Fromm offered Ted his very rapid Lion Head Winfield Rocker Arm No. 4, and Ted made plans to enter the July 4th events at Hohokus.

A year ago Ted had won a trophy for having the neatest appearing pit crew and car at Ascot. At the time he was driving the Atlas Chrome Special, and as he reflected on the event, he was able to reason some very sound logic. He noted that the drivers who were really big time, and who seemingly enjoyed the most success, not only on the track but socially and financially, were those whose devotion to appearance was outstanding. Shaw, Gardner, De Paolo, Bergere, and back east MacKenzie. Doc's beard gave

Ted a laugh. Still, it was color, and color paid off in many ways. The Fromm No. 4 was a beautiful car, and Ted took the $500 he had won at Indianapolis and bought himself a new Ford coupe. Before taking delivery however, Ted left these instructions. Have the car painted snow white, and on the door sill, letter this signature and the wording "AAA DRIVER."

Thus, it was little wonder that the outfit speeding eastward near the end of June, attracted a second glance.

Ted wasn't prepared for the reception he was to get in the east. His first race at Hohokus found him eating dust to Ben Shaw. Furthermore, the Fromm, so hot on the Coast, couldn't break 30 seconds at Hohokus. At Woodbridge the next week, Ted withdrew when he couldn't locate the right gear. Back to Hohokus again, and another second. This time to Chuck Tabor, after MacKenzie had taken a long lead, only to spin out. At Woodbridge a motor support gave way and the following week Ted had to be content with a third in the consolation at Hohokus.

Then, for four races in a row, Ted had to watch the tail of MacKenzie's car as the bearded ace went on a rampage. At Langhorne the rains came, and so did the bill for his new car.

Ted didn't mention it, but he was hungry. Some drivers were known as hungry drivers, but to Ted, he was actually lacking in funds to eat properly. This had happened before, but long ago. Back when he was hitch hiking to those first races, it seemed as if he was always hungry. One time he and his friend George Burch had thumbed to a track where Ted had the promise of a car, but they were so dirty and hungry looking the guard wouldn't let them into the track. A hole in the fence on the backstretch had been their method of entry, and the two dollars Ted made driving went for food for their stomachs.

Now, Ted reflected, he wasn't any better off. Three thousand miles from home, in debt, and hungry. Still, on that car door was emblazoned the words, "Race Driver." Almost ten years as a race driver and he was still hungry.

Another thing that bothered him—he was having a rough

time in the competition. Where before, even the uneducated-in-racing Press had remarked of Ted's clean driving and racing ethics, of late Ted had noticed a tendency of writers to gang up on him. Nothing to put your finger on, but here and there the holes just wouldn't open up. Still, as MacKenzie, or Sall, or Shaw came up, the holes miraculously would be there.

Then he knew. He had a big reputation—in fact off his 1934 showing he was number one man, and always it was to be thus—the number one man had the field against him.

Ted wrote a letter. Maybe his disillusionment of the moment was reflected in it, but it was to someone back home in California who had written for advice on becoming a race driver. Ted wrote:

>Now we're going to take for granted that you want to drive a race car, you're half crazy (or better yet, all crazy). Well, the first thing to do is to find a guy as crazy as yourself (you may think this hard to do but it's easy, look at all the drivers and car owners there are). He'll be the guy that owns a race car. The fact that he owns a race car is a good sign that he's cracked, or anyway half cracked.
>
>You tell him how good you are (it makes no difference if you are or not, he'll find out soon enough anyway). Tell him how many times you won on different tracks, even if you haven't been there. Anyway talk yourself into a ride. (Sometimes bringing the car owner a jug of wine helps.)
>
>O.K. here we go, you get in after almost having to use a shoe horn. Well, at last you're in. You'll probably find that on a race car the clutch is in the most difficult place to get at. If it isn't, the guy who built the job didn't do a good one. They really take great pride in building goofy clutch pedals. Get the yannigan who owns it to show you where all the gadgets are; you'll never find them yourself. The only things they all agree on is, the throttle is always worked with the right foot, except maybe the steering wheel.
>
>You'll find air pumps on the right or left side, hand brakes, switches, shutoff buttons (if any) on the right or

left side. Spark advances (if any) either on the right or left —in fact you know exactly where not to find them, in the starter's hip pocket.

They put a rope around the front axle and hand you the end to hold. That's so if you can get the motor started, you just leave go and you can go about your business driving the fool contraption (if it will run).

Take about three or four slow laps to warm up the oil and say your prayers, and if you're mad at your Guardian Angel, make up, but fast, HERE WE GO. Grasp the wheel firmly, set your head into the wind, and grit your teeth (like all the posters that advertise auto races). Press down with your right foot (which should be on the accelerator).

You're having lots of fun till you come down the straight-away and don't shut off till way past where you should have, and the throttle "she no back off." Well, all you have to do is kick it out of gear by disengaging the clutch. (Don't worry about the motor flying apart, you only have one neck and how easy it breaks and stays broke.) Well, well, the bolts that held the clutch pedal on have fallen off and the pedal is sliding around somewhere down in the oil pan. Well, steer for the infield and pull back hard on the brake. The brake lever is outside the fence on the right, or left side. Aw hell, find it, it probably won't work anyway . . . ain't you having fun?

If you are still on the race track you will be looking back where you came from and be nonchalant as the excited car owner comes running up. Tell him you knew just where it was going all the time. (Even if you know you are a darn liar. He may suspect it, but he can't prove it.)

Anyway, your first practice is over, and you'll show up race day all primed and ready to make lots of money (OH YEAH!), to go home all sore and weary, your arms weary, your sides and legs all skinned up. (You'll have to eat off the mantelpiece till the next race.) You'll have to pay a dentist $100 to put back the teeth you had knocked out by a rock while following some goof like yourself in the race, and you made a dollar and a half. And, you're not satisfied? Neither is anyone else but you'll be back, and that's all I can tell you.

Have a good time,
Ted Horn.

A race was coming up at Lewistown. Ted had the Fromm torn down but he needed some money. A car was available to borrow, so Ted journeyed to the Pennsylvania track, vowing that today he would not step out of the way for anybody. In the elimination heat he found himself in the No. 2 spot, alongside a newcomer to AAA driving ranks.

On the first turn, the new driver skidded and came to the top of the bank where Ted was vainly attempting to jump into the lead. Ordinarily, Ted would have backed off, but today his mood was different. He stepped on it, but the strange machine, lacking the pickup of the Fromm, only dug in. The cars met, and both sailed through the fence.

A piece of railing pierced Ted's shoulder, and his shoulder and collar bone were broken, plus a general shaking up. At the hospital the Doctor shook his head and notified the luckless, hungry man lying on the operating table, "That's all the driving you're going to do this year."

Late that fall Ted returned to the coast. While in the Lewistown hospital he had a lot of time to do some thinking and planning. One of his visitors had been the kindly, mild mannered man who had first induced Ted to come east— Pappy Hankinson. As yet Ted hadn't joined the fair circuits, but Pappy, wise in the ways of the track, had let the youngster feel his way. He knew the young driver would be in need of funds and also some encouragement. On his third visit, and after he had found his deductions to be correct, Pappy made an offer. "Ted, get your own car. I'm willing to advance you the money, and I know you will build a good one, so that next season you can pay me back after Indianapolis and you run a few races for me. I'll make your guarantee enough that the car will be yours if you don't win a dollar all season, and if you do have some luck, the outfit will be free in a hurry."

Ted accepted the offer, and the broken bones started their mending.

While in the hospital, Ted got a package. It bore a Los Angeles postmark, and contained an Ascot program of the events that night. Ted scanned the contents quickly, and tears came to his eyes. Scribbled and scratched on every page were messages of cheer and get well, from every driver and car owner present. It made a big lump come in Ted's throat, and a swelling in his heart. "What a swell bunch that is," Ted said, "They sure remember a guy." But, on the Coast it wasn't just "a guy." It was a quiet, smiling friend of theirs, who never would take unfair advantage of anyone on the track, and who never spoke a word of ill will be it friend or foe.

A hand drawn character with a long beard and frock making a speech was labeled, "That's me—Rex Mays." Another, "Hello Ted, hoping you'll be back soon—Al Putnam," "Best of luck—Carl Ryder," "Nuts to you—Al Gordon," "Stay away from midgets—Doc Allen." "Lots of luck and a speedy recovery—Floyd Roberts," "Don't stay there long—Red Garnant," "If there's a blonde reserve me a room—Bob Biggs," Hal Cole, Ralph Gregg, "You were thinking of Margie—Bill Rasor," "Ted, do not be so damn polite next time—Chris Vest," "Hurry home, Ted, and we'll pour some beer on your Elm tree—Ed Kalin," and then, "Go get 'em, Ted—Lou Tomei," "With all of my best wishes, and luck—Bob Swanson."

Ted's jaw muscles tightened, and he uttered never a word as he read the next inscription, "Dear Ted, let's try to be OLD race drivers—Harris Insinger." The morning's Philadelphia Enquirer had contained a one sentence news item: "Harris Insinger, Philadelphia race driver, was killed yesterday in a race at Los Angeles."

Ted in his Vanderbilt Cup car at Roosevelt Raceway, 1936. — *Lytle Photo.*

Famous early day racing car driver and designer, Art Chevrolet, and Ted Horn. Taken at Roosevelt Raceway, 1937. — *Lytle Photo.*

Horn in Hartz Special chasing Goldie Gardner, England's entry (No. 48) at Roosevelt Raceway, October 12, 1936.
— *Kozub Photo.*

This photo taken at Williams Grove, Penn., shows a youngster waiting with program in his hand to be autographed by Horn.

Always fond of children, Ted is shown here giving one of his toy Maserati cars to Eddie Pettillo of Atlanta. Eddie is the youngster in the story suffering from pneumonia and befriended by Ted.
—Floyd Jillson Photo

Character study of Ted taken shortly before his death. The immaculate appearance of the Champion was always a credit to automobile racing.

— Nalon Photo

CHAPTER IV

The Eastern Campaigns

TED appeared at Hohokus once before returning to the coast. An innocent affair in which Ted ran sixth to Floyd Roberts, and just ahead of Bill Schindler. He found his shoulder was stiff, and that he had to do most of his driving with his left hand. Roberts told him to carry a rubber ball in his right hand, and keep squeezing it until strength returned. Ted tried the ball trick, but discarded the attempt when he found his trouble was in movement, not strength. He was always to favor this arm and shoulder.

Back home Ted found the racing in a state of dormancy. Another shutdown of Ascot for alterations and the Legion showed every sign of never reopening. Bill White, car owner and enthusiast, secured terms to take over the track, and for the first time Ascot was to be under private promotion.

Mays, Petillo and Gordon were waging a merry battle for the championship. Rex had arrived to the point where there was no disputing his leadership, his only trouble being cars which could not withstand his heavy foot. At the season's end, Mays had his second successive Pacific Southwest championship tucked away, with National Champion Petillo second and Gordon third. Following this trio came Wearne, Pixley, Cole, Connor, McGurk, Vest and Gardner. In spite of meager appearances, Ted was listed in 20th position.

Ted also got an eastern rating of 23rd place, and midwestern of 39th, from his one race in Chicago. MacKenzie ran off with the Eastern title, and Babe Stapp the Mid-Western.

Ted found a motor and a chassis. It was a Miller with a long and successful history. Shorty Cantlon had once driven it to a new world's straightaway record in its class at Muroc Dry Lake, and at one time Mel Kenealy had scored feature Ascot victories with it. Ted busied himself preparing for the coming campaign, visited Hartz and watched the completion of his Indianapolis job and hung around the Club Rendesvous.

Most of the talk centered on Bill White's chances of operating Ascot, the coming two-man race there, and the 1936 Indianapolis Classic.

Hartz's car took on the appearance of being a big job. With the reduction of gasoline allowance for the long race, most car owners were looking for means of cutting weight. Hartz reasoned, and Ted agreed, that the secret lay in correct carburetion, and a planned, even race. "Of course," Harry offered, "Weather conditions race day will have a lot to do with it. We will meet that when we face it, but if we don't sacrifice weight, you will have a safe car and one with the power to put you right where you want it."

Ted was satisfied. Here was a man who knew what he was talking about. In five races, from 1922 on, Hartz had finished second three times and fourth twice. It was the most consistent record ever made at Indianapolis, and as a car owner he had already placed two cars in the winner's circle, Arnold and Frame.

January 26th, Al Gordon took his last ride at Ascot. In the two-man race, his big car went over the wall, killing both himself and Spider Matlock, colorful riding mechanic and race starter. It was the beginning of the end for Ascot.

Early in March, El Centro, in the Imperial Valley programmed a race. Ted had the Miller ready and was anxious to give it a baptism. Every driver of note was on hand, and more than 5,000 people watched as Roberts set a new mile record in the one lap time trial, of 38.68. Roberts headed the first heat with Mays in the ultra rapid Sparks-Weirich job hot on his heels.

Pixley took the second with McGurk following, and Hal Cole was victor in the third. Gardner after leading, had to be content with second to the Tacoma Ace, and Ted was third.

Ted started the feature in ninth spot. Mays grabbed the lead with Cantlon on his tail. Roberts, Gardner and Pixley made up the next echelon, and Ted gained on the lot.

ASCOT BURNS

By the 25th mile it became dusty, and a few of the cars were sliding out. Gardner quit entirely, and so did Cole. Ted advanced to third spot behind Cantlon.

With ten laps remaining, Ted came into the pits. His grin was unmistakable, and he waved his pit crew off. "Done for today," Ted said, and he wouldn't explain his grin.

Back home in the confines of his garage, Ted grinned again, "Baby," he said, "You got it. Had you a little rich today and I don't blame you for heating near the end, but don't worry, I'll never make you work when you aren't feeling right. We gotta long summer ahead, and there will always be another race."

Ted had held his first communion with his first "Baby." Later, his "Little Gems" were to join his "Babies," but always his race cars were to be a part of his family. They were to be groomed, petted and cared for. They were to earn the living. Like a good horseman cares for his horse, Ted was always to see that his car was cared for before himself. Stooping over the cockpit, Ted fastened a little metal object on the dash. The first of many he was to place in his own race cars. A Saint Christopher Medal.

ASCOT DESTROYED — READ ALL ABOUT IT — ASCOT DESTROYED! Ted got up and dressed. The newsboy's shrill voice had awakened him. Reaching a phone, Ted called first one, then another. Finally, Harry Lewis answered at his garage. "Yeah, Ted, it's true," Harry reported, "Don't know what caused it, but it's my guess those bums sleeping underneath the stands did it. Getting pretty old anyway, and they say the stands went in twenty minutes. Well, that's the way things are in this game. How's things look in the east this summer?"

Ted walked past his garage, stopped, and went in, "Baby," he said, "There's a guy named Fate following us. He just burned down Ascot last night. Guess he figured you and I would be foolish enough to hang around here this summer instead of going east, so he took it on himself to make our minds up for us."

The latter part of April, Ted was ready for the trek east.

Hartz and Riley Brett had left a day earlier with the big front drive job, and Ted followed by 24 hours, in his Ford, and hauling Baby. He didn't remember much of the trip, and he drove slowly. He was remembering his disappointment of the previous year, and how badly all his hopes and plans had been ruined in those first few laps. Outside of the usual best wishes, not much talk had been going on in racing circles, concerning the Hartz car. That is, none that Ted heard. Most were concerned with the gasoline reduction to 37½ gallons for the race. Shaw's new streamlined car was installed as the early favorite, with only the first year jinx held against it, but the "Catfish" type of body streamlining had caught the public's fancy.

Roberts and Lou Moore were thought to have a good chance with their Burd Piston Ring jobs—in fact you could get favorable comment on many — but of Ted, it was, "Too big."

Ted was surprised to see Hartz wearing a helmet the first day he arrived at the track. Harry didn't leave him wonder long. "Get in," he indicated, "We're going for a ride."

The rides lasted for a week. "The job is ready, Ted," Harry said. "We can take it the first day, but I want to show you some tricks I picked up here a few years back."

Slowly at first, then at an even keel, the pair rode. There were few speed trials, until Ted took the wheel. The old master had done his job well. Ted took to the front drive like a duck to water. "Let 'er out in the backyard," Hartz said, "when you're ready, but keep it down in front. No need to advertise what we have."

They ran mileage tests. Not so good. "Too hot today," Harry said. "Yeah," Ted came back. "But what will we do if it's hot race day?" "Lean it up and sacrifice speed," was the answer.

On the 15th the time runs opened for the pole, and qualification. Ted fully expected to shoot for the one slot. His mind was made up for it, but arriving at the Hartz garage, was surprised to find it locked. "Too hot," Harry said. "Tomorrow's another day."

LOU MEYER QUALIFIES

Ted watched as car after car took its ten laps. Bergere, Tomei, Connor, Stapp, then Mays with a pole winning 119.644. Ardinger, Chet Miller and MacKenzie. Ted met Doc on the apron and congratulated him. "The beard comes off," laughed the eastern champ, "Just as soon as I win this one."

The next day it was cooler, with a slight threat of rain. Hartz had a big smile, just a shade under Ted's in width, as they met. "Der tag," said Ted. "Eh," smiled Harry. "The day—don't you understand perfectly good Dutch?" "Well, we're going after it today, regardless of what you're trying to sell," Hartz admonished.

Ted "took it" on the first time around. This time there was no tightening on the turns. Half throttle out of the turn, and Harry standing on top of the concrete abutment at the starting line gave him the double handclasp overhead.

Lap two and a big 117 was on the blackboard Brett was holding. Lap three, four, five — eight, nine and the white flag—now the checker. Ted slowed and cut the motor as he glided to a stop at the finish line. Hartz was just looking, and happy—nervously so. Brett, wearing a greased stained "Champion" Spark Plug cap, swarmed over the hood, and a committee advanced to measure the remaining gasoline.

One-one-six-point-five-six-four, came down from the beret-topped Chet Ricker, high atop the Pagoda. "Gotta pint extra, Horn," announced an official. "Get your picture taken, then take your brake test."

Shaw got in, and Cantlon, Roberts, Barringer, Winnai, Cummings and Jimmy Snyder. Only the first two had better time than Ted, and one of Ted's laps was 119.

Lou Meyer was having trouble. He blew a complete motor and had to get a new one by air from the coast. Then the valves wouldn't seat, a piston broke. He tried a qualifying run and had to pull in to completely overhaul the motor. The last day, with only an hour remaining, he had the motor together again. No time to experiment, he shot for the trial at once. 114.171 was sufficient, but he had a funny look on his face as he pulled into the garage lane. "Blew it again," he said, "Guess we aren't supposed to ride this one."

Ed Wintergust, long-time titled "Mayor of Gasoline Alley" looked up. "Bad luck turns into good luck, Lou."

Race day was clear and warm. Ted was in the fourth row — again the sandwich spot between Cantlon and Winnai. This time he didn't look around, but adjusted his helmet as Hartz leaned over the cowl and said, "She's all yours Ted. Just keep out of traffic the first part of the race and drive at a speed you feel is safe. We didn't lean it any, so you have the speed you want, and we'll just have to hope it doesn't close in and get muggy. Good luck."

The big 22 gathered momentum. Seth Klein was leaning far out of his martinet tower—the green was out—the race was on.

Mays shot in front like a cannon ball, Stapp, then Chet Miller as the first lap was completed. Ted passed Tomei, then Bergere, Cantlon was directly in front. Lap two and MacKenzie was drifting back toward Ted, still no one had passed him. Lap three and Ted glanced at his pit— someone was motioning with a backward sweep of the hands—slow down—the 22 slowed.

Wilbur Wolfe, the riding mechanic, was punching Ted's side—someone coming up—Winn, Roberts, Ardinger. Lap 10 and more rib punches—Gardner. Cummings was out of it and so was Frame—running easy now. Litz went by, but Mays was in the pits. The big board says 21 leading—that's Stapp. Seymour is out of it and ten more laps are gone— the big board still has 21 in the first slot, then 3 and 6. That's Shaw and Gardner and Jimmy Snyder is in the pits. Ted glances at his pit and gets a "safe" hand signal. The big board is changing, number 3 now leading—that shovel nosed car of Shaw's, Ted thought. Winn now third—two quick punches in the ribs and Hepburn and Meyer went by. Hey, that 8 of Lou's is supposed to blow. Gardner and Litz both in the pits: so we are holding our position. Ardinger is out and traffic is thinner. Ted lets it out a little and the big brute picks up speed—going past cars now. Hepburn's in the pits and Meyer isn't in sight—Harry is holding up the board and it says "Pos 9"—that means we're ninth. Tomei is out and so is McGurk—there's a car ahead and we're going to take it—MacKenzie. Ted grinned and rubbed his chin as he passed the easterner, then another Wolfe punch in the ribs—that's starting to hurt, who is it this time, Meyer?—say, how many times does he want this race, anyway. Hang on, Wilbur, we're heading up front. Roberts, then Winn, Connor, Miller and Meyer—he's slowing on the inside. The pit now signals "Pos 4"—that means we're fourth—Geez, forgot all about the gas. The big board is changing again, 3 still leading—that's Shaw, now 21 second, that's Stapp—and 22 third—HOLY COW, THAT'S US! Winn is out and Harry is waving us in. Ted signals one finger, then starts to slow, around the turn and on the inside. The crew is waiting—the car stops.

Seventy-five seconds later and Ted is back on the track with a new front tire, full gas tank and radiator. While in the pits, no words were spoken, but Hartz held up two fingers—did that mean 200 miles or seconds? Stapp is pushing his car towards the garages and the big board says 8 leading with 22 second. Meyer, then Horn. No more signals from the pit and everyone looks as if it would be a long afternoon. O.K. this is it—no one is going to get past us and we're sticking right to this groove. Harry had said that when the black line appeared on the track to ride high, and fast—we're riding.

The big board says 7 is third and that's Cantlon—that is one car that isn't getting past—22 is singing like a humming bird. The pit signals O.K.—it's a long afternoon.

The big board is changing—22 now leading—and that's us—hope they're not wrong. Ted glances at his pit and the board is out, "Come in." Gee, that gas thing again. Ted signaled two more laps, and let the big Miller out a little more, then slowed, the long glide and a stop.

Three new tires, water and more gas. This time Hartz spoke, "That's the last of the gas Ted. Do you think you can make it?" About 50 laps more! Ted just grinned, but he was worried. Meyer went by and Ted swung into traffic.

Ted completed five laps before he would allow himself to look at the big board. It showed him second to Meyer.

That was good, now what to do? Watch the pits for signals—there it is, and it's a safe signal with upturned hands at Harry's knees. That means hold my speed and play it safe. Now it's up to that guy Fate. Will the gas hold?

Everyone is on their feet as Klein waves a white flag and holds a cardboard out with number 22 on it—one more lap. Ted relaxes as he swings into the stretch—the checker, and he salutes Seth with a wave, but keeps on going—one lap, then two—then the glide into the pits, and there is Hartz, now grinning and holding up two fingers.

Ted and Harry closeted themselves in the garage. Hartz spoke, "Ted, you drove a marvelous race. Now a lot of things are going to happen. You aren't any longer just a barnstorming race driver; you are in the big time, and should go after that National Championship. It pays off. If you want, we will get the Miller ready for Roosevelt. I'm not too sure of our chances there, but regardless, it's yours if you want it, and next year too. What say?"

Again the two men shook hands. Ted was visibly happy, but for a moment he sobered, "Anything happen today?" "A perfect race, Ted. Al Miller did the Charleston on the stretch and got dumped, but he isn't hurt too badly. By the way, you broke the old record, did you know that?"

Ted was almost two miles per hour faster than Petillo's winning time of the year previous. In addition, he had qualified for the Champion Spark Plug 100-Mile-an-Hour Club, the most exclusive organization in the United States. Limited to just those men who had driven the Indianapolis race at an average speed of better than 100 MPH, and without relief.

The next night at the Victory banquet, Ted experienced a new sensation. As the checks were doled out, he found himself holding paper totaling more than $15,000. Then there were a couple of testimonials to sign, Pyroil and a shaving advertisement that necessitated him stripping to his undershirt, squirting some lather on his face and getting his picture taken.

The winning checks, Ted endorsed over to Hartz; then accepted a personal check for his percentage of the winnings. The Pyroil and shaving money he pocketed, but the race winnings went into a cashier's check and in the mail to Pappy Hankinson. Wires were arriving too, with guarantees for personal appearances, but Ted looked over the National Championship schedule, and decided on that program for the season.

Broke again, but he owned Baby, and a summer of guarantees ahead. Now for the campaign.

On the 6th, Ted appeared at Roby. Baby was hot and Ted sailed into third place in the early stages of the feature race, when a stone broke his goggles and he had to retire. Mays won the event. Two nights later Ted appeared at a midget race in St. Louis and got $100 for the effort—the first of the appearance deals.

Then came successive 100 mile Championship races at Goshen and Langhorne. At the kite shaped New York track, Baby acted tired until the consolation, and Ted won it over Tabor, Tomei, Walt Brown and Joe Thorne. Mays again was the victor. At Langhorne, Floyd Davis romped and so did Baby's connecting rods. On the 18th lap, Ted and Baby were moving up when it happened.

Ted surveyed the damage. There was only one thing to do—get Baby to a doctor, and those specialists were in California.

Baby and Ted got back from the Coast in time to take in the 100-miler at Springfield, Illinois. Baby romped in the second heat, right behind Chet Gardner, and the pair were in the feature. But here the long ride from the Coast took its toll. Baby sprung a leak in the radiator, and every five laps Ted had to stop for water. Shaw won the event, setting a new 100 mile record that eclipsed that set by Frank Lockhart nine years previous, at Cleveland.

The next day tragedy struck at Milwaukee, when bearded Doc MacKenzie rode his last lap. Doc had just married and, consenting to his wife's plea, shaved the now famous beard before winning the Indianapolis race.

Ted's only comment was "Doc shouldn't have shaved. That jinxed him." From that day on, Ted Horn never shaved the day of a race.

At Roby, near Chicago, Ted was leading a poorly started heat, when Ray Pixley was killed. George Connor and Jimmy Snyder also crashed in the same mixup. Winn took the feature event, with Gardner second and Bill Cummings third. Ted retired following the Pixley crash.

On the 20th, the pair returned to Roby. Ted had the third fastest time, behind Mays and Cummings, and was matched with the pair in a special event. Ted took the lead at the first turn with Rex at his elbow. Cummings seemed content to watch the pair from a trailing spot. Time after time Rex came at Baby, but at the checker Ted and Baby had a half length advantage.

Ted made the feature through a fourth in his heat behind Gardner, Mays, and Cummings. Gardner copped the lead in the long race, followed by Mays, then Connor and Ted. Midway, Chet spun and Rex took over. At the same time, Ted passed Connor, but the length of the stretch separated the pair and Mays had another feature with Ted in the familiar second spot.

A week later the pair returned home to New Jersey. Here Ted was happy. It meant the dusty bull rings, where the purses were lower and the competition just as stiff, but these were folks. Stopping long enough for a fresh change of clothes, the pair headed south, Richmond. Ted and Baby had a field day. 10,000 fans screamed themselves hoarse as the Black Beauty cleaned house, taking the time trials and a new record, the heat and the feature of 40 laps. Hurrying back to Jersey, the pair repeated at Union, setting a new record for 30 laps and finishing in front of Sall, Ronny Householder and Staneck.

Watertown, N. Y. was the next stop and another romp. In this event, Bill Schindler parted the fence, and Baby had a slight scare when her right rear tire blew on the 37th lap. Ted fought the wheel and gave a masterful exhibition of staying right side up as Vern Orenduff passed him for the checker.

On the fourth the pair went to Goshen and watched Mays win another 100 miler. Ted and Baby sat this one out after taking a qualifying run. "Just tired," Ted said, "Baby's

Ted at Uniontown, Pennsylvania, August 11, 1940. Above: Tony Willman, at left, putting on helmet.

— Lytle Photos.

been pretty busy lately." But alone, turned to the car and in a half whisper repeated, "Just a hunch Baby."

Roosevelt Raceway is probably one track that should never have been built, and the renewal of the Vanderbilt Cup, a race that never should have been run in 1936.

The country was in the midst of a depression, yet this track, built at great cost, and embodying all the features of European road racing, less hills, with that of the American speedway saucer, was designed to sell the foreign race plan to the public, as well as settle the question of supremacy between the two groups.

The course was four miles long, made up of 15 straightaways and 20 curves, right and left. The longest straight stretch was 5/8 of a mile, and the shortest, 125 feet. Pre-race publicity was beamed to the elite, who could afford the exorbitant entrance fee, and the little man was forgotten. The Cup race, which attracted such European stalwarts as Jean Wimille, Phil Etancelin, Sommer and Raph of France; Pat Fairfield, Brian Lewis and E. K. Rayson of England, and Count Brive, Giuseppe Farina and Tazio Nuvolari — the man with the date with the Devil — from Italy, was scheduled for 400 miles over this pretzel shaped course.

When the first cars started to practice, it became apparent that an average speed of 60 MPH would be the best the contestants could do. Quick calculation revealed the fact that 400 miles would require almost seven hours of watching, obviously too much, so the race was cut to 300 miles.

American pilots, busily engaged in championship, fair ground, and other dates, accepted Roosevelt as just another race. Most took one look at the winding course, then at the specially constructed European road cars, and snorted, "Well, a lot of dough went in here and we'll put on a race of some kind, but don't blame us if it stinks," was the average racer's thoughts.

They cared little for the so-called American versus European car and driver ballyho. European racing was government subsidized, with the taxpayers footing the bill for the costly race cars, while theirs was of Yankee ingenuity and more often than not, financed by the time payment loan.

The race that ensued resembled nothing more than a Sunday afternoon's traffic surge in Central Park. Nuvolari led from the start to the finish, and the bull-like rushes on each straightaway did little to whet the appetite of the spectator. Such remarks as, "Nuts, crazy man's dream, going everywhere and getting nowhere. Roosevelt 16 ring circus," were heard as the more than 50,000 spectators filed out.

Midway through the race, American drivers, trailing far behind, threw caution to the winds, and emulating that great of former years, Frank Lockhart, fishtailed their cars through the curves. Mauri Rose was sixth, to be the first American to finish, but earlier, Billy Winn had made Nuvolari think his friend the Devil had already called, so reckless was his performance.

Ted and the big Miller lasted only a few laps. A suspicious noise developed in the motor, and the pair withdrew, to race another day.

Two weeks later Ted drove Baby for the last time in 1936. At Union, N. J., the rear end went out in a heat, and Ted loaded for the long trip back to California.

In eleven years, he had a stiff shoulder, aversion to women and children in his race car, shaving the morning of a race, to announcing a retirement and a fervid belief in hunches. He wanted nothing more than to do some hunting and fishing, work on Baby, and rest.

The first of May, 1937, rolled around all too soon for Ted. He had enjoyed the winter in California, and had taken one long hunting and camping trip to Wyoming, fished, and made plans. The gasoline restrictions at Indianapolis had been lifted. There was an oil limit, but the big Hartz-Miller was not an oil hog, and Ted knew, in his own heart, that this could be his year.

Indianapolis held no awe for him. True, it was faster than any race he had to drive, but in the end equipment and strategy plus luck was what that race required for winning. He felt he had them all, save the latter, and in that there was no method mortal man could use to control.

NEW PAINT JOB FOR BABY

Baby was ready for the eastern campaign. Ted had changed her coat to white, with a maroon tail and a splash of maroon running over her hood. Somewhere, he had developed a dislike for the color black. Of the fatalities of past years, Ted gave little thought. They had ceased, and as he reflected, he formed some very strong convictions. Each and every one he could recall was caused by either the failure of some piece of equipment, or sloppy thinking on the individual's part. Probably, as he listed his gone friends, the thought came to him of how many had ridden black cars. Anyway, Baby's color was changed.

Ted and Baby made their first start at Phoenix early in April. The race-hungry clique on the Coast took a "busman's holiday" to a new ⅝'s mile track in Arizona, and Ted went with his friend Walt Woestman, whose car was entered to be driven by "Wild Man" McGurk. Ted turned out to be the wildman, however, and spun out on a turn, raising such a cloud of dust that the spectators were sure they had witnessed a most horrible accident.

When the dust had settled, there sat Baby and Ted, right side up and grinning. Spinouts were to be numbered for Ted, from this point on. McGurk sent Woestman into hiding when he scored a bang up second in his heat, and Ted did likewise. In the 25-lap feature, both Ted and Mays lapped the field, but the Pacific Coast champ had a 200 yard advantage, and Ted again had started a season looking at the tail of Rex May's race car.

At Indianapolis, predictions were rife of a new record from one lap to the finish. Everyone was happy over lifting of the fuel restrictions. Ted and Harry were no exception.

Baby had her picture taken. On the bricks she was never to race, the Pyroil people had requested her picture, with the owner at the wheel. This pleased Ted no end, as he knew his attention to the little things was paying off. Baby was brightly painted, not gaudy, but clean, attractive and pretty.

Five days before the race, Ted attended the Champion 100 Mile banquet. This was his induction to this famous group, and he kept a respectful silence as immortals of the great race spoke and engaged in good fellowship. That Ted was destined to become one of the most illustrious in this gathering never entered his head. Ted enjoyed the turkey dinner, the spirited affair, and his humble position.

Qualifying opened and the Hartz-Miller was not ready. Attempting to take advantage of the new rules, Harry had installed a supercharger, lengthened the wheel base from 101 to 104 inches and increased the tire size.

The impeller shaft broke on the supercharger, and Hartz removed the blower, and replaced the carburetors and manifold. Ted started a time run with three days remaining to qualify, and after the first lap, broke a valve.

The midnight oil burned in the Hartz garage. The motor was torn completely down and reassembled. Brett and Hartz were concerned; yet other inhabitants of gasoline alley loaned their tools, advice and time, to help the pair. "Didn't Lou Meyer run the same course last year?" thought Ted. He sought jovial Ed Wintergust for consolation.

Finally, on the last day, the car was ready. Replacing Bo Huckman of the previous year was Harry Dean, a smiling, happy-go-lucky type of riding mechanic and Ted liked him. In fact Ted liked anybody who could smile.

This time the qualifying run was completed without trouble. The 118.220 average was 2 MPH faster than the year previous, and still Ted didn't let the big motor have its full say.

Some phenomenal performances had been turned in in the qualifying. No less than eight cars and drivers; Tomei, McQuinn, Swanson, Petillo, Connor, Cummings, Shaw and Jimmy Snyder, had all averaged over 120 MPH. Snyder especially had the rail birds on fire. He was driving one of the new Sparks-Thorne six cylinder jobs, and it had screamed to a 125.287 average speed in the trial. Earlier it had been unofficially clocked at better than 130 MPH. It looked like a fast, dangerous and tough race.

Race day dawned hot, sticky, and with a threat of rain. The largest crowd in the history of the event was on hand as Ted settled into his seat, again the sandwich spot, but this time in the last row. Starting ceremonies were lost to his view, he was so far back and this time he had little instructions from Hartz. "Drive your own race Ted, and watch us, we'll keep you informed as to your position and speed."

It was awfully hot as the field started. Clouds had moved away and the sun was beating down. Ted swung into position on the backstretch, and moved up close on the car in front. As they reached the stretch, the pack picked up speed, and Ted passed his first car just as they swung over the starting line.

Ardinger broke in front. The field was off on what was to be the most thrilling 500 mile race in history. Foreign to last year, Ted didn't keep out of traffic and conserve his speed. He was far back in the field and had a lot of driving to do before he reached a contending position. A blue streak surged from seventh place, to wrest the lead from Ardinger, before the sixth lap had been completed. It was Snyder, and the Sparks-Thorne entry was running wild. Shaw was trailing Ardinger, in his Porpoise nosed speedster, and Lou Meyer close behind Shaw. Hepburn, in Meyer's winning car of 1936, was next. and then came Swanson, Cummings, Bergere, Connor and Gulotta, as the first 50 miles were reeled off.

Ted was driving hard. The only car to pass him was Snyder, but Jimmy had the field lapped, all but the first five cars. Now the big board was changing, No. 6 was leading, 54 second and 2 third. That meant Shaw, Ardinger and Meyer were in front. Ted glanced along the pit wall, and there sat No. 5—Snyder, out with a broken transmission.

100 miles reeled by, and Ted was oblivious of his blackboard. It signaled "POS 8." Heat was coming back in Ted's face in waves. The motor was running smoothly, but heat off the bricks was being picked up underneath the car and eddied into the cockpit. It was becoming a hard race to drive. Shaw went past, then Cummings and Petillo. Ted let it out some more, and his board read "POS 6." The next time it read "150 mi."

Ted glanced at the big board, and it read 6, 16, 25.

That was Shaw, Cummings and Petillo. Gardner and Hepburn were also ahead.

At 200 miles cars were stopping at the pits. One was Shaw, and this meant Ted had made up a lap. Cummings was in too, but Hepburn sped past on the outside. Now the pit signaled "Come in," and Ted slowed.

The pit stop was less than a minute. A new tire, gas, and water, and Ted was off with tires screeching. Hepburn was now leading and Shaw right behind him. No more cars passed Ted, and his board read "250." That meant the race was half over. Ted glanced at the big board on the next lap, and there was his number AT LAST, he was now third.

Shaw was right behind and Hepburn right ahead as the trio pulled into the back stretch. Shaw went wide on the outside, and before the north turn was reached had taken both Ted and Ralph. Shaw was leading again.

The pair stayed in sight, and Ted kept his position. Lots of cars now in the pits. The heat was taking its toll. Both men and machines were giving way to the humidity. Bergere, Cummings, Gardner and Petillo had all gone in for relief. A riding mechanic had to be bodily lifted from the cockpit, overcome by the heat. Now Hepburn was slowing, and he too asked for relief. Before Ted had time to complete another lap, Swanson was wheeling No. 8 after Shaw. Hepburn was taken to the hospital tent and given aid. Then he climbed to the roof of the structure and watched the race. Veteran that he was, he knew it would be a close finish, barring accidents.

Accidents? There hadn't been any. The pace was fully five miles an hour faster than last year, yet, save for the heat, not a single accident had happened to cause the caution flag to come out.

Now Shaw was heading for the pit row. The big Hartz car screamed as Ted made use of his advantage. The big board read 8, 3, 6. That meant Ted was second to Swanson and Shaw third. Hartz was signaling "Come in" and Ted slowed.

Shaw went by, and Ted was off. The stop took almost two minutes, and Ted was now determined to last to the finish.

THIRD BY ELEVEN SECONDS

The heat was almost unbearable. It seemed to get hotter as he sat in the pit, but this WAS a race. Ted had nothing to fear from any car or driver, and he was happy. Happy because of the close competition. He loved it.

Swanson was coming in, and Hepburn was relieving him. Ted's board had been signalling "—1 lap." That meant he was a lap behind. Shaw was not in sight, and neither was Hepburn. Wait . . . There was the 8 spot just rounding the curve at the end of the straightaway. Three-quarters of a mile ahead, now where was Shaw?

Ted kept Hepburn in sight. Next time past the Pagoda he glanced at the board, and this time there were no figures underneath his number. That meant he was on the same lap as the leader. Ted glanced at his pit, but there was no signal. The heat didn't bother him now. He looked at Dean, and back came a smile and three held fingers into the breeze.

Now Ted was oblivious to the stands. Everyone was on their feet. So were all the mechanics and stooges along the pit wall. Activity had ceased, and all were standing, watching the drama unfolding.

Hepburn was now coming back towards Ted. Shaw was in sight as they hit the stretch, and like three fixed buttons on a string, the cars made the circuit of the huge track.

There was excitement at the finish line. Klein was giving him the white flag . . . ALREADY? . . . One lap to go? It must be . . . If he wanted Ted in for a rule infraction the color would be black . . . Ted shot a glance at Dean, then pushed the accelerator to the floor. The motor responded and they picked up speed down the back stretch around the turn onto the short straightaway, then the next turn . . . Shaw was at the end of the pit row and Hepburn just crossing the finish line . . . 11 seconds later and Klein waved the checker for the third time . . . the race was over.

Ted slowed on the next lap and gave his pit a wave. They were motioning him to the garage, and the next lap Ted unbuttoned his helmet. The sweat was pouring off his forehead, and he swung leisurely into the garage lane. Hartz was there waiting for him, and his face was drawn and pale.

Neither man spoke, Harry had driven this race too many times to try conversation before the motor noise had left the driver's head.

Finally Ted grinned. "Swell race, eh Harry?" and Hartz spoke what was in his mind.

"That was my fault Ted. You had the car, the speed, and the will, and I didn't give you the go signal until too late."

"Forget it," came from Ted, and the ever-ready smile, "Next year is another year for us, and anyway, with all the trouble we had, we were lucky to finish."

"It's a deal," Harry returned, now smiling, "See you at Roosevelt in July."

The next day Ted picked up some more checks. There was the usual wires, and offers, one which read, "Langhorne 19th, signed Hankinson." A man from Hudson was there too, and Ted smiled as their conversation ended.

Among the well-wishers was a huge man. Primo Carnera, heavyweight champion, and his buddy, Enzio Fiermonte. Ted laughed at their enthusiasm, and together with Fiermonte, bought a ticket on the French lottery. They shared the cost.

The next day Ted and Baby arrived in Chicago. At the Fairgrounds they got a second in their heat, and had a car length advantage in the feature when Baby got hot. Hal Cole took the event.

At Langhorne, Ted met Hankinson. Together they mapped a schedule for the summer, and Pappy, true to his flair for showmanship, took advantage of the conference by calling in photographers. Ted met Sall again, and he joined the "signing" party. Baby was acting up, and Ted loafed to a poor finish in the 50 mile feature won by Mauri Rose. Then back to Chicago, and a fifth to Jimmy Snyder. Ted talked to Jimmy about the Indianapolis race. He was interested in that six cylinder motor of Spark's that Jimmy had pushed to a new record in the time trial. Snyder agreed it was the best thing he had driven to date.

The Roosevelt Raceway had been changed. Nine of the curves had been taken out, some now banked, and the straightaways lengthened. The overall length of the course was 3-1/3 miles. The 300 mile race was scheduled for July 4th, and this time drew a heavy entry from Europe.

Italy, Germany, England and Norway were sending teams. The German entry of Auto Unions, with Rosemeyer, Delius, Stuck and others drew much attention. Not only to their weird looking cars, but their method of operating—just as if they were the well oiled part of a machine. The Hitlerian swastika was very much in evidence and the team kept pretty much to themselves.

Ted was interested in their tires. "Ersatz," they called them, they were synthetic. As a car sped down the course, little chunks would fly off and would burn like a piece of punk for minutes afterwards.

The track improvements produced a much better race. Many of the American drivers had secured foreign mounts, and this time the entries from across the pond got a battle. Rosemeyer and Seaman, the Englishman, hooked into a duel for first place, with Billy Winn in striking distance. Seaman would pull away from Winn on the stretches, but Billy barreled the turns ahead of the Limey.

Fiermonte had bought and qualified a car. This he turned over to Wilbur Shaw, and the field roared to an 80 MPH average.

Rosemeyer won, with Seaman second. Winn was in tears as his driveshaft broke. He was in striking distance when it happened. Mays was third, and as usual, "came out of the clouds." Nuvolari withdrew almost at the start, as did Rudi Caracciola. Ted again had motor trouble, and felt the car was just not suited to the 990 turns it would have had to make.

Chicago, Springfield, Milwaukee, Syracuse, Hamburg—all followed in succeeding weeks for Ted and Baby. Ted was riding the Hankinson circuit and finishing second or worse to Mays, Winn, Rose, Wearne and Sall. Still the guarantee was good, endorsements continued to come, and there still was that man from Hudson, back at Indianapolis.

Ted liked the fellowship of the Hankinson circuit. The

THE EASTERN CAMPAIGNS

jumps were scheduled close together, and the racing clean. There had been no accidents and esprit de corps prevailed. He and Bobby Sall were hitting it off in fine shape. The pair were the nearest thing to team-mates on the circuit.

Another thing that pleased Ted was that Hankinson's races were mostly at county fairs. These were the affairs that each community looked forward to all year long and served as a treat for the youngsters.

Ted liked the children and they liked him. Their carefree attitude pleased him, and where the oldsters stood in awe at times, children were more apt to treat him as an equal. An observing person would have noticed that Ted gave just a little more attention to those with patches on their overalls, or worn gingham dresses.

Near the end of September the troupe moved on Nashville, Tennessee. Ted bought a new Ford tow car just before the Nashville race, and wanted to get it painted. Some drivers had an aversion to the color green, but Ted hauled Baby to the fairgrounds with the new truck still carrying its original green paint.

Vern Orenduff, Duke Nalon, Howdy Cox, Tony Willman, Chet Gardner, Monk and Morris Tadlock were a few of the drivers on hand as Ted arrived. Scuttlebutt and ribbing was going on in the pits, and one stooge was belaboring another for his belief in the bad luck peanuts brought at a race track.

"Look," he said, "I'll show you how screwy you are," and he proceeded to break peanut shells over the hoods of the first five cars in line.

It had rained for almost a week in Nashville. The track was heavy and sticky. Probably that was the reason it hadn't been treated race day, for dust. By the time the feature rolled around, huge clouds of the yellow stuff raised each time a car made the circuit of the oval.

Nalon, just then in the early stages of a brilliant career, had the pole for the feature race of 25 laps. Near the 20th circuit of the track, his lead was almost a lap. Only Cox remained to be passed, but he couldn't see him. The dust

SUPERSTITIONS 91

was so thick the drivers were watching the trees to give them the outlines of the track.

Suddenly there was a piercing scream. People with their radios tuned to the race heard the announcer's voice rise. Cars were hurtling end over end. Dust hid the vision, but people were running to the head of the stretch. The announcer screamed to keep off the track, but still they ran. One car emerged out of the cloud, braking and fishtailing from side to side in an effort to get stopped.

There were sounds of wood breaking, metal meeting metal, screams—then all was quiet and the dust settled.

Five cars were in a smoking and battered pile. Cox was lying on the track beside his demolished race car. Nalon and Orenduff were slumped in theirs. Gardner was being helped out of his car in the infield, where he had driven it to miss the body lying on the track. One car was overturned, pinning the unconscious driver underneath. That was Baby, a twisted broken thing.

Ambulances were summoned for all but one. The white clad interne took one look at Howdy Cox and said, "Take the injured first."

Gardner was released as soon as his cuts were bandaged. Nalon was seriously hurt and Ted listed as critical. Nalon reconstructed the accident for the reporters; "I knew Cox was ahead of me, but I couldn't see him. Suddenly there he was, sideways in the turn and that's all I remember." Orenduff told the same story and Ted, when he regained consciousness, remembered little. But to himself he said, "Those peanuts. Gardner. Cox, Orenduff, Nalon and Baby—those were the five cars."

There were months in the Nashville hospital. The truck was repainted from its ill-omen green to a deep maroon. Ted wrote a few letters and did some mental calculating. He had heard of Red Cambell's last ride at Winchester. Ted remembered Red well. He had chided him when a youngster wanted to take Red's picture, and Red had refused. "Not before a race, Ted," Red had admonished, "bad luck."

That day at Winchester the last race was late starting. Red had waved to a photographer who had pleaded for a picture and had been promised, "Right after the last race." "Go ahead," he shouted, "It'll be too dark when this thing is over." Red had died on the first turn, sixty seconds after the picture was taken.

Ted's money was going. Baby must be completely rebuilt. Ted wanted to do it anyway, this winter. Baby was good enough for the fair circuit and the half mile tracks, but he needed a bigger car for the mile and championship events. He figured what it would cost him. He had enough—but just enough. That Hudson man would take care of the eating this winter and with the rest of his money Ted would build a championship car.

Back in California, Ted found the market on race car parts a "seller's market." Parts were scarce and so were chassis. This was a disappointment but nevertheless he arranged to rebuild Baby for the coming season. Gone were his dreams of a championship car; Baby would have to do the job.

Then he headed east, and for the Hudson factory.

Babe Stapp was there, and so were Ira Vail and Chet Miller. Hudson had a new car ready for the market—the 112—and these four famous race drivers were asked to take a car each and in a few weeks put it to every known test they could devise in 15,000 miles of highway travel. Ted's route was laid out through Minnesota, Idaho, Wyoming, the Dakotas, Oregon and Washington—just what he needed to strengthen his body and test his reflexes.

The Hudson trip was a success. In Wyoming, Ted missed the road and ran into a snowbank. In Idaho, he hit a ditch and had to be hauled out when he tried dodging a herd of sheep which suddenly decided to cross the road.

At Fargo, N. D., Ted gave an interview. "The highway is more dangerous than the track" was the lead line. Ted told how Baby had cost him $7,000, and now was a junk heap in a Los Angeles garage. "Two minutes on a Nashville track did that," Ted countered, "but a racer can live to be just as old in this business as any other. I like racing, but it's just a job now. I'll probably stick to racing because I'm too lazy to work."

That was Ted. Modest, belittling his own prowess, and giving credit to those of his own profession.

Ted did a good job for Hudson. His testimonials smacked of sincerity, and he never failed to display his modesty while representing his chosen profession. Like the reporter back in Paterson, two years before, Ted Horn impressed these far western news chroniclers with the same high regard for the speedway and its habitues.

Baby was ready in March—so was Ted. Again El Centro was the scene and again a huge throng attended. Mays set the early pole mark with a 38.89. Others shot at it and missed—then came Ted and Baby's turn.

Although Ted had driven El Centro many times in the past twelve years, today he walked the full mile again, stooping to test its surface here and there. So, as he and Baby gathered speed for the start, Ted knew right where he wanted his car to run.

The flag dropped and they were off. High into the first turn, then down across and onto the backstretch. The pair negotiated that strip as if they were a meteor, and high again on the far turn — out into the straightaway and straight as a bullet for the finish line.

As Baby slowed on the backstretch, Ted heard the announcement, "38.14." "Phew," he thought, "Stroking a little that time."

George Connor was waiting at the finish line when Ted and Baby pulled in. Angular George put out his hand and Ted took it. 'What's up?" asked Ted. "Don't you know?" came back George, "That lap was the fastest mile ever traveled on an American track under AAA sanction, and it breaks my world's record by one-hundredth." "Phew," whistled Ted, "Just phew!"

Eleven years later that track mark was still standing.

Ted won the feature that day, Wearne was second and Jimmy Wilburn third. Mays, Jimmy Beeder, Jimmy Snyder and Lou Durant trailed. Mel Hansen won the consolation.

The next week the pair headed east and stopped long enough in Phoenix to engage Mays on even terms until the feature, and even then leading the race until Rex took advantage of a skid to nose in front. From there to the finish, Baby and Rex traveled as a team, with the record holder now a close second.

Ted didn't stop at Indianapolis, but headed for the opening of the Hankinson circuit at Reading. Here, Baby unlimbered a few more spurts and the pair romped in front of Gardner and Nalon. Reading took Ted to its heart and he was an hour signing programs, following his victory.

At Hohokus his old nemesis met up with him, and Baby was content to finish second to Sall. Baby now had a tire sponsor and before leaving for the "big brickyard," Ted had Baby's new name inscribed on her cowling. From now on she was to be known as "The Riverside Special."

Ted gave another interview and this time revealed he hadn't made enough money the previous season to pay his income taxes—this in spite of the fact that he held second place in the national standings, and would carry that number in the Indianapolis event. The Nashville accident and the rebuilding of Baby had put him right back in the hungry class.

Back at Indianapolis Hartz and Brett were busy. In two races, Ted and the big Miller had trailed the winner by a total of a little over 60 seconds. This time they wanted that first place, and if eliminating one pit stop would do it, the race was as good as won. With no limit on gasoline, or gas tank capacity, the pair were installing a huge tank to hold the Gilmore product, and reasoned that only one refilling would be required.

Ted went to the 100 mile banquet again. He couldn't help noticing on the program that only eight men had qualified for this club more than once, and he was one of them.

On race day, Ted sat alone at the starting line. Gone was the riding mechanic, to return no more to Indianapolis—the car was now a single seater. For the first time Ted didn't have the sandwich spot, but held seventh position; pole in the third row. His qualifying run had been effortless—

121.327, the fastest he had ever qualified, and still eleven others had made the trial run faster. Householder, Roberts, Snowberger, Snyder, Mays, Gulotta, Cummings, Brisko, Miller, Tomei and Wearne. Householder and Snyder had the Sparks six cylinder jobs, and they were awfully fast—Ted's choice, after his own mount.

Once again there were no specific instructions from Hartz. "She's all yours, Ted," was all he would say, and the manner in which he said it gave Ted confidence. Roberts was on the pole with Snowberger and Mays alongside. Then came Gulotta, Chet Miller and Stapp. With Ted in the next row were Shaw and Rose. They waved as the field got under way.

Roberts brought the field to a fast start at the line, then dropped back when Mays shot to the front. Ted felt a bit uneasy as they roared into the first turn. Not that he was afraid, but those 27 cars coming in back of him—all anxious to get up front, as he had been the year previous, was his concern.

Going up the backstretch, the car seemed a bit sluggish. Ted pulled ever so slightly on the wheel, and the response didn't satisfy him. The car didn't handle this way in the time run. Ted wondered if it was the front tires, then his mind went back to that 1935 race and his disappointment with his first car.

The thought spurred him on. He hadn't noticed, but cars were passing him. No Huckman or Dean to punch him in the ribs now. He was on his own. The motor was sweet. Ted listened. Just like a kitten, he thought.

The board said 8, 6, 16—Mays, Snyder, Householder—those Sparks jobs second and third. Ted's board said "Pos 9" and he let it out. He was a bit sorry he did. It brought back that uneasy feeling, and it didn't feel just right. Now the board was changed—6, 8, 16, it read. That meant Snyder had passed Mays and Ted smiled to himself. He knew from experience, going way back to that innocent heat race at Ascot years ago that when you got past Rex, you really had it.

Ted's pit signaled "Pos 6," and he let it out some more.

This time he knew something was wrong as the tail felt as if it were coming around to meet him. It left him a little cold, and he slowed perceptibly. Without glancing at his pit he held up a clenched fist with one finger—coming in for trouble, that meant.

Hartz was standing in front of the pit as Ted came to a full stop. This time there would be conversation, and he told him the trouble. Harry shook his head and placed his mouth close to Ted's ear, shouting, "It's that big gas tank Ted; when it empties more it'll handle better."

Then with a pat on the back, Ted was off.

Turning to Brett, Hartz said, "He'll have to make another stop now, and at the pace this one is being run, he'll be lucky to get in the first ten. Too bad we didn't think of the difference in weight a full tank would make."

Snyder was out again, and Roberts leading, Petillo second and Shaw third. Ted was out of the first ten, but running fast. Once the caution came out but Ted didn't see the cause, and soon the speed was resumed.

Snyder passed him and Ted waved. His pit hadn't given him a position for an hour, but he knew he was climbing. Then came "250," and on the next lap "GAS?" Ted looked at the gauge and it read a quarter full. The car was handling now and Ted was picking up other cars. He shook his head negatively.

Thirty minutes later he gave the pit the "coming in" signal. They were ready, and as the big tank was filled, Ted vaulted the wall and got a drink. This time he was prepared for the pulling when he went into the turn. His speed didn't slacken. Now came a position signal—"POS 8". That sent his right foot down some more. The big board said 23, 3, 1—Roberts, Miller, Shaw. Ted drove steadily and another sign came at him, "POS 5."

Ted knew it was late in the race. The sun was in his face as he went down the back stretch. That meant it was past noon, way past. He felt a little tired. When Seth Klein gave him the white flag he was glad. He took the checker without smiling, and without too hearty a wave. He didn't even look up when Hartz told him they had taken fourth and

Floyd Roberts had averaged a sparkling 117 MPH to win.

The next night at the victory banquet, Ted was his old self, smiling and greeting friends. One of these was a kindly faced little man, with a quiet voice and a way with motors. Cotton Henning had already had two winners, De Paolo and Bill Cummings, and there had been a lot of talk Cotton was coming up with a new car soon. Not just a new car, but one that would put everything at this speedway to shame.

Ted liked Cotton. Liked his modesty, his smile and the quiet manner in which he conducted his affairs. His workshop took Ted's eye too. If ever there was an establishment that observed the rule of "A place for everything, and everything in its place," it was Cotton Henning's garage.

Cotton spoke, "Ted, you are one of the best front-drive chauffeurs in the business. I'm going to Europe this winter for a new car for Bill, and I'm in the market for a front drive man to take over the Miller. Just wondered if you and Harry had plans for next year. I'd like you to drive for me if you haven't."

Ted felt a warm glow come over him. He didn't answer for a minute, then spoke slowly, "Thanks Cotton, I'll talk to Harry. But, Harry gave me my chance, and taught me all I know about this track, and I'll have to see what his plans are first."

Hartz seemed glad. "Take it Ted," he answered, "I don't feel like devoting full time to the speedway anymore, and you certainly deserve the best. In Cotton, you have it."

And thus the Horn-Henning team was formed, to become one that was to write speedway history to last into eternity.

Ted headed for Milwaukee and the Hankinson races at the fair. Once again Baby was hot, and set a new one lap record for the mile, 38.7. "Grandpappy" Gardner won the feature, with Snyder second, Winn third, Ted fourth and following Baby with a soft tire, Mauri Rose and Duke Nalon.

Then at Chicago, Ted, Snyder, Wearne and Roberts traded the lead in the 50-lap battle that had never had an equal. Snyder got the nod, but the entire quartette was applauded for twenty minutes.

On the 19th, Nalon scored his first victory on a mile track, when he led the almost duplicate field at Indianapolis home in a 25 mile event. Ted ran fifth ahead of Roberts.

At Atlanta, the Hankinson stars put on a thrilling show both the 3rd and 4th of July. Willman won the first day and Billy Winn the next. Ted ran third and fourth, but ahead of Gardner, Nalon and Fire Chief Waller. Back at Hohokus, disaster struck when a race car ran wild and plowed into a crowd at the pits, which wouldn't move back after repeated warnings. Two spectators were seriously injured, one dead and a total of seventeen treated for injuries. The catastrophe was to close the famous old track for good.

Back to Chicago on the 10th, and a fifth behind Nalon, Mays, Willman and Wearne. Ted and Baby closed July at Langhorne second to Nalon.

August opened at Springfield, and it was to be the last race for colorful and popular Billy Winn. On the fourth lap of the feature, Winn's tire went flat and the car rolled, throwing his body clear. Willman won and Ted was second. In three successive days at Milwaukee, Ted gave the fans all they wanted to talk about when he won the feature the first day, led the second until a soft tire caused him to slow behind Mays and Gardner, and run second to Gardner the final day.

September opened with Ted at Altoona and running sixth behind Rose in the feature. Ted had a feeling that day —another of those hunches, so took it easy. The next morning's papers told him why he had that feeling. Goodnatured Grandpappy Gardner, had sacrificed his life to keep from hitting a child that had run onto the track at Flemington. Ted said, "They never happen singly. Always in bunches, Winn and Gardner."

At Syracuse Ted ran fifth behind Snyder, then jumped to Richmond where he was well liked, and to a track Ted liked. Again he walked the circuit, and when his time trial was over, a new world's half mile mark was set. 25.5 . . . Now Baby had them both. At Trenton the pair ran third to Nalon, and Ted called it a season.

It had been a successful year. Two new world marks, a

fourth at Indianapolis, two major fair victories, and enough closeups to send him back to California hunting a championship car. Ted left Baby in New Jersey after dismantling her, and this time made the trip without the familiar tow car.

Back in Los Angeles, Ted went calling. Now he was a buyer with the cash in his pocket, and he knew what he wanted. Finally, a chance remark led him to his purchase. The Haskell-Miller was for sale and Ted bought it. The original had quite an Ascot history. Built in 1932 and changed many times afterwards, it now was to become the Championship car for Ted.

Seeking his friend Harry Lewis, and taking his purchase to the McDowell shops, Ted laid his plans. Lewis was to build the body and Ted and McDowell would do the rest. Thus, that winter, the new car was built.

Walt Woestman was in a dither. He had a race car, a contract and no driver. "Burn Em Up O'Conner" was demanding race cars and drivers and Walt had half of the full solution. Then Ted and Walt met on an L.A. street, had a beer, a long one with Ted doing the listening and Walt the drinking. At the end a very formal handshake took place and the Woestman 54 had a driver; Ted Horn was now a movie actor.

"Burn Em Up O'Conner" was a movie that featured a race track theme, written by a sponge diver in Alaska. It wasn't Ted's first movie. Previously he had worked a Pete Smith two reeler with Cliff Bergere, and Cliff did the fancy spinning, crashing and directing. "Burn Em Up O'Conner" offered pleasant relaxation, and at the finish Ted gave Walt back his car all in one piece. Woestman had another beer.

As Ted returned east in 1939, he realized he was in business. Two race cars, a contract with a leading racing stable, another with a racing circuit, one excellent sponsor and another to sign. Ted stopped in Rockford, Illinois, and met F.M. White, president of Burd Piston Ring Company and liked what he met. The man smiled. That interested Ted more than the contract, but for the business at hand

Ted was serious. White asked that in return for their sponsorship, Ted drop them a letter occasionally informing them of the performance of their rings, and in case of an impressive victory, they would appreciate a wire to the effect.

He wasn't ready for the deluge of letters that followed. If ever a company needed a research laboratory, Ted Horn was it. For his end of the contract, Ted performed fully. In one of Ted's letters he mentioned that, but for such companies as Burd, racing would be hard put. Purses hardly met expenses, but sponsorships kept big timers like Ted solvent. Ted was attempting to keep racing's part of the bargain. There was no question of his fullfilment.

At Indianapolis, Ted joined the Cotton Henning "Boyle Team." Mike Boyle, wealthy Chicago labor leader, sponsored and financed the clean cut outfit. In some ways it reminded Ted of the Auto Unions, back at the now-defunct Roosevelt. Bill Cummings, slated for the new Maserati, would never feel its power. In February, a skidding car on the highway had slammed into the one driven by Bill, and his life had ended in the accident.

Wilbur Shaw had the mount, and Chet Miller drove the Offy of the team.

Ted qualified handily, with 127.723. Only Shaw, Snyder and Swanson were faster. The race was destined to become a "team" victory, and another thrilling event. Snyder went out in front at once, followed by Meyer and Shaw. Ted found he could handle any of them, but Shaw and Snyder. Near the half way mark, the spectacular accident occurred that took the life of Floyd Roberts and injured Bob Swanson. Chet Miller was also involved.

Ted's car heated at high speed. He made four pit stops and was never higher than fifth. Near the finish, Shaw and Meyer hooked into an Alphonse-Gaston duel that had the specators gasping from the sheer excitement. Three laps from the finish, Lou's car started a deadly slide, hit the inner rail and tore out a huge section. Meyer was uninjured, but that crash ended a long and brilliant career. Meyer retired. Snyder got the checker second, Bergere third, Ted fourth.

The famed team of Ted Horn and Cotton Henning, taken at Indianapolis in 1939. This was the first year that Ted drove for Henning.

Coming into the pits, Indianapolis, 1941.

Ted leaving the pits for a practice run. Cotton Henning at right.

Indianapolis, 1946. L to R: Johnny Moore, Clair Zook, Otto Wolfer, Ted Horn, Ed Metzger.
— Lytle Photos

Happy Freddy Carpenter taken after he had beaten Horn in a heat in 1948 at Reading, Penn. Immediately after this shot was taken, Ted proposed the match race described in story. — Frank Smith Photo.

Probably the last picture taken of Fred Peters, famous race car owner. This photo taken on a fishing trip in Florida shortly before the death of Peters. L. to R.: Unidentified guide, Peters, Mrs. Peters, Ted Horn. — Michael May Photo.

TWO STRAIGHT WINS AT MILWAUKEE

June 4th found the Indianapolis stars at Milwaukee. Ted drove the new car to second place in the feature, and Jimmy Snyder took down third in Baby. The next week they had fourth fastest in qualifying, but withdrew due to dust. Ted wrote Burd:

> Have just re-ringed my old engine in the car I was using last year and am sending you the slip that was in the box of new rings.
>
> The rings I took out had about 600 miles of running They were in the race at Milwaukee right after Indianapolis when Jimmy Snyder drove to third in the feature. I took second with my new car besides winning the heat race and the match race for five fastest cars.
>
> I intend to be at Milwaukee July 2nd with both my cars. Rex broke my qualifying record there this last race and I intend to try and get it back and also bring to Milwaukee the world's record for that type of track, which I hold at El Centro, Calif.
>
> Best of luck always,
Ted Horn.

But 4th was the best Ted could do at Milwaukee in qualifying. He won the feature. Two weeks later he won his heat at Williams Grove but had motor failure in the main event.

> Have just torn down the motor in my new car and found all the ring lands broken, but the rings were not ... I am rebuilding my old car for the Championship races. The motor is getting a new crank and set of rods, besides new mains, rebore, new pistons, new valves and guides, so it ought to be in the best of shape.
>
> Take it easy and I'll be seeing you, Best of luck,
Ted Horn.

Baby responded. Two straight features at Milwaukee, August 20 and 24th; a new five mile record and a feature at Hamburg. In the championship event at Syracuse, Ted and Baby were running fifth when they picked up a nail, then a fourth at Flemington, and a second at Hughsville. Ted wrote:

> Sorry I have no more wins to report at the present time, but hope to have a couple more this season yet. Broke the track record at Hughsville last Saturday. Former record 27.3 by Frank Bailey. My record 25.8. In winning at Hamburg set new record of 26.02 for that track. There are no other

races scheduled but half milers. Fact is, it's a lot harder to win on the halves than it is on the miles . . . This year I am the high point man, or champion, or whatever you want to call it for the Mid-West district, so will carry No. 1 on the little Dandy next year.

I'll be seeing you, Best of Luck
Ted Horn.

A third at Allentown and motor failure again at Williams Grove. The explanation:

Well, we had a little trouble over at Williams Grove yesterday. Broke all the ring lands out of one piston and all the little pieces got under the valves and bent every one of them beyond saving, so I have to completely rejuvenate the Little Dandy.

Then followed two straight feature wins at Richmond and Danbury, Conn., before a failure at Trenton. At Raleigh, he led the feature until hit and spun out. Ted explained:

Have been keeping quite busy lately as I have been having a lot of piston trouble. Lost one at Trenton and washed out a block beyond repair and also one rod and all the valves . . . Won everything at Danbury with a couple new records. Set a new qualifying record at Raleigh and was leading the main with four laps to go, when Buddy Rusch who was trying to get by all the time and couldn't, ran into me going into a corner and spun me out . . . Am racing at Charlotte on the 28th and I think this will be the last race this year. Hope to send you a victory telegram.

Best of luck always,
Ted Horn.

But at Charlotte the track was dusty and Ted and Baby, or Little Dandy as he now called her, refused to run after winning the heat. This closed the season and Ted, never one to leave a job half finished, painstakingly compiled his complete record for the year. It showed:

Competed in 18 race meets; had fastest qualifying time 6 times; won 12 out of 18 heat races; won 6 main events; won 4 out of 5 match races; had motor failure 3 times; withdrew account of dusty track twice; set 8 new records at Hughsville, Raleigh and Danbury.

He then wrote:-

> Dear Mr. White: Have just compiled the data enclosed in this letter and thought that maybe you would like to have it. I didn't have it at the time you asked for the photographs or I would have sent it along. I trust that you got a picture to use. I am sure sorry that I didn't have any and that my car was not in shape to get one taken, but I am rebuilding it, and as soon as finished, I will have some made immediately. Hope that I have as good a record for 1940 for you which means that I am entirely satisfied with the performance of Burd rings in my motor for 1939, and that I am looking forward to the privilege of using them again in 1940 . . .
> Best of luck always.   Ted Horn.

That winter Ted went to Florida. He had something on his mind and needed advice. At Vollusia, and after a day-long conference, Ted had the advice he sought, and it was his trusted friend, Pappy Hankinson who gave it.

Ted then wrote his friend Harry Lewis back in Los Angeles, and went in training. From this point on, Ted's training schedule was never slighted. Road work, regular hours, swimming and rowing. Of it all, Ted considered rowing the most important. It served to strengthen his arm muscles. His grip was not a valuable part of the training. Ted's comments were: "You drive race cars with one hand anyway, and your grip is light. The guy who hangs on with both hands belongs on the highway where it is really dangerous."

Ted met Lewis back in Paterson. He bought the little wooden garage he had been renting. Then he secured additional property, and the Ted Horn Engineering and Ted Horn Enterprises were started. Lathes, drills and other machinery went into it.

Ted's problem consisted of lots of money, a big cut for Uncle Sam in the form of income taxes, and the belief in his theory that all his money should go back into equipment, parlaying for the day or the season when everything would hit just right. With the establishment of the shop and securing of equipment and property, Ted was broke. On paper, no; in the pocket, yes.

Little Dandy ran hot at the season's opener in Reading. Mark Light won the feature. Light repeated the next week at the Grove, but at Langhorne Horn took down everything in sight. Then came Indianapolis.

Ted set the Miller on the pole in the second row. Beside him was Mel Hansen and the Hartz-Miller, with Bergere on the outside. Old friends all. Mays and Shaw were in the front row. It was an uneventful race.

The Miller was performing beautifully. Mays and Shaw traded the lead and Ted kept within striking distance. With two pit stops behind him Ted was set for a charge to the finish. So were Rose, Mays and Shaw. Then it rained.

Shaw was leading when the rains came, with Mays second, Rose third and Ted fourth. The caution light remained on the last 150 miles, and after the first three cars finished the grind the field was flagged. Ted completed 199 laps and again a fourth place finish. Ted wrote White:

> Am putting my other engine together which will not be run till a National Championship race comes along. How about some of those new Decals? I'll put one on each side of the cowl if you'll send them. Well, take it easy and I'll be seeing you. Best of luck always.
>
> Ted Horn.

Second to Vic Nauman at Union, and to Nalon at Langhorne in a 100 miler; 4th behind Willman at the Grove; then 5th to Holland at Thompson; 3rd at Allentown with Willman and Snyder in front, and a blank at Thompson to Holland again. Nalon took the short way home at the Grove, and again Ted was out of the money; 3rd to Andres at Milwaukee, then a feature victory at the Wisconsin fair.

September opened with a second to Chitwood at Syracuse; then a clean house at Dunkirk ahead of Walt Brown. Ted then wrote:

> Just a line to let you know I won a race at Dunkirk last Saturday. I didn't wire you when I won that race at Miluwakee because it was close in to the factory, and I was in kind of a busy spell, trying to run my other car at Springfield the same day. Darn near won another at Rutland, Vt. last Friday, but the way it ended up guess I'm the big chump. I sat on the pole with the fastest time of the day and won the first heat hands down. Led the 30 lap main until the 27th lap, when I was about to lap two cars and they tangled. To me it looked like I couldn't get through, so I stopped. All the rest of the field came along and having to slow down to get by me, they made it through and

finished the race. I got what the little boy shot at when it was all over—NOTHING. Well, anyway, hope I can pay off a few more times this season. Anyway, I'll try.

Best of luck.

Ted Horn.

At Allentown Ted made good his wish. Took Holland, and won the feature, breaking Nalon's track mark. Second and third to Nalon at the Grove and Richmond; then took down the Hankinson Championship at Columbia, S.C., in a blaze of glory, broken records and in front of Chitwood, Saylor and Willman.

Again the familiar Paterson postmark on a letter:

I am now running two cars. One being driven by myself and the other by no other than the great Bobby Sall of Paterson, N.J. Bob will drive the first race for me at Shelby. N.C. this weekend, and we hope to have good news for you. I knocked another one over last Saturday at Allentown, setting a new track record for the distance. Best of luck always—Ted Horn.

Just returned from what I consider a very successful trip into the south. It was successful financially anyhow. Bob Sall has not been doing too bad. One remarkable thing that has happened on the car he has been driving for me is that I put the engine together right after Syracuse, and he has been running it ever since, without the engine ever being taken down. That was eight races ago, and the compression right now is as good as it has ever been. That's a pretty good record for running in dirt all the time.

Took both cars to Raleigh. Bob finished third and I got fifth. Both of us crippled in with the wrong gears. At Charlotte I finished second and darn near won the race. Sall had a little trouble again (saving it for High Point the next day).

At High Point I let Tony Willman drive my car, as the boys couldn't, or wouldn't get it up (appearance money). He walked away with every event he was in, including the main event, and Sall in the other car finished third. At Columbia I drove myself and won everything, in one car and Joie Chitwood drove the other one and finished second. I'd like to do as good next year. Guess that's all for this time. Take it easy and I'll be seeing you. Best of luck always — Ted Horn.

PS: Am sending you the rings from one of the pistons that was in the motor I told you about. Thought you would like to have them to see for yourself.

This was correspondence to one firm. Champion Spark Plug, Montgomery Ward, and others were getting the same type. The one finger typed letters that took so long and said so much were not necessary, but Ted knew such companies were the ones that kept racing alive. Ted Horn was serving as public relations counsel for racing. The American Automobile Association published the recognized records at the end of the 1940 season. Those listed under the name of Ted Horn were:

ONE, ONE-EIGHTH MILE TRACKS
Altoona, Penna. .... 10 Laps 7:19.96

ONE MILE TRACKS
Columbia, S. C. .... 1 Lap :42.6
Columbia, S. C. .... 15 Laps 11:47.5
Imperial, Calif. .... 1 Lap :38.14 (World Mark)
Imperial, Calif. .... 40 Laps 28:35.1

FIVE-EIGHTHS MILE TRACK
Phoenix, Ariz. .... 5 Laps 2:47.8

ONE-HALF MILE TRACKS
Danbury, Conn. .... 1 Lap :26.9
Danbury, Conn. .... 10 Laps 4:37.5
Danbury, Conn. .... 25 Laps 11:44.5
Dunkirk, N. Y. .... 1 Lap :27.42
Dunkirk, N. Y. .... 10 Laps 4:42.22
Dunkirk, N. Y. .... 30 Laps 14:18.8
Hughsville, Penna. ..... 1 Lap :25.8
Hughsville, Penna. ..... 10 Laps 4:36.2
Raleigh, N. C. .... 1 Lap :27.3
Raleigh, N. C. .... 10 Laps 4:46.2
Richmond, Va. .... 1 Lap :24.44 (World Mark)
Richmond, Va. .... 10 Laps 4:32.3
Rutland, Vt. .... 1 Lap :28.1
Rutland, Vt. .... 10 Laps 4:48.2

Ted had three important conferences scheduled for the winter. The first took him to Indianapolis and his friend Cotton Henning. Jimmy Snyder's death had left the Sparks six cylinder job open for a driver, and this was the car Ted always wanted to drive. Cotton gave his consent and best wishes.

The second was with a Paterson lawyer, and here Ted incorporated himself. Another small piece of business was attended to. The legal news contained the terse notation that Eylard Theodore Horn was petitioning to change his name to Ted Horn. This announcement differed from others so inserted with the following attachment: "Without anywise desiring to be considered as employing flattery to himself, the petitioner feels the name of 'Ted Horn' has developed a commercial value in auto racing, and to return to the name Eylard would not only cause confusion, but have no commercial value in the auto racing field." Ted had insisted on the statement although the barrister had declared it unnecessary. His modesty was becoming a trait.

The third conference was again held in Florida, and the result was the formation of the "Ted Horn Racing Team." Ted was on the prowl for additional race cars, and when he found what he liked his business was over, and he was broke again.

That winter Ted worked. His little machine shop was humming with his own business. The additional cars were called, "My Little Gems," and Ted was doing the work. On April 17th, just three days before the opening race of the season, the entire racing fraternity was rocked to its very foundation with the news, "HANKINSON BOLTS AAA." The most powerful single figure in American racing had joined forces with I.M.C.A. in a precedent shattering move to unite the fair circuits of the mid-west and east under one independent banner.

To Ted, this was a move he couldn't understand. Torn between two loves, Hankinson on one hand, and his beloved Cotton Henning, Indianapolis and AAA on the other, it was too big a personal problem to settle without some thinking. He decided to await developments.

Jimmy Wilburn cleaned house at Reading as Ted and others sat in the grandstand. Then to Langhorne, where two races were held in May under the AAA banner. Ted's Little Dandy, rested after a long winter, responded to come home in front of both races. The first before 43,810 people, and the second with a new 20 mile record. Nauman and Holland trailed. Then he left for Indianapolis.

The Sparks-Thorne job was fast and Ted knew it. Still the old feeling of confidence was not there. Snyder had encountered too much hard luck with the car. Ted wondered if his luck would be the same. It appeared to be, as Ted couldn't get qualified. 124.247 was the mark he finally turned in, and it placed him in 30th starting position. Almost a repeat of the 1937 race.

Shaw was again the heavy favorite, and it looked as if he would win as he took the lead with only a hundred miles to go. But here Fate stepped in, and a wheel buckled on the swift Maserati, placing Cliff Bergere in front, with Rose second, Mays third, Hepburn fourth and Ted fifth.

Ted had trouble getting up in this race. The car had speed but to Ted was treacherous. He nursed it into a money spot midway, then started a careful climb. He was still climbing when Rose passed Bergere for the lead. Ted too passed the tiring Frenchman, who in this race had become the first driver ever to complete the entire 500 miles without a stop in a gasoline powered race car.

Ted was third at the finish, three minutes after Rose had scored his first Indianapolis victory. Ted was tired. The car had been a hard one to handle — so great was its speed — and although Ted might have thrown caution to the winds in a mad dash for victory he was reluctant to take the chance.

That night Ted sought out Cotton Henning again. As a father, kindly Cotton listened, then shook his head. "I don't know how to advise you Ted, but the rumors are very strong this speedway will be sold to a real estate development. That means it will never be replaced. It might mean the end to speedway racing in this country. The big fire this morning won't help any. Lots of good cars burned up and it doesn't look too promising for me."

Ted made his decision. He would join Hankinson and return to the dirt tracks and the county fairs he loved so well.

His wire to the Florida promoter was the second bombshell to explode in racing circles that spring. Baby, or little Dandy and the Gems took care of the rest of it. Victories at Dunkirk, Reading, Allentown, Columbia, Spartensburgh, Raleigh, Shelby, Greensborough, Richmond — all victories. Sall took care of Batavia and Flemington. The pair were running one, two in as great a double punch as had ever been seen on an American track. It was all the old master Hankinson needed. 563,064 people turned out in just 17 meets to watch the holocaust. Racing was booming on the Hankinson circuit.

CSRA was sanctioning the amalgamated forces, and at Richmond on September 9th, Ted took the point lead. At Charlotte, November 2nd, the championship was his. The first recognized, undisputed, national title.

There hadn't been a single fatality all year, but the midgets were having their baptism. On October 12th, Tony Willman had sacrificed his life to the little thunderbugs, and Ted took on a decided hate toward them.

Ted's stationery now listed four names as team drivers. Bob Sall, Tommy Hinnershitz and Rex Records, besides his own. Late in November he was a little tired as he sat humped over his office desk at the Ted Horn Engineering Company, figuring out his result statement for the year, to send to his sponsors.

He did a painstaking and thorough job. Attendance marks were included as well as a short description of the racing. Results were broken down for each car and driver, qualifying heat, first, second, third, fourth, and features. It revealed that car No. 1, driven by Ted Horn participated in 15 meets, scored a total of 10 feature victories, 14 heat wins and 8 qualifying marks. Car No. 7, Bob Sall, in 14 meets scored 2 feature victories, 9 heat and 2 qualifying marks. Car No. 5, Tommy Hinnershitz, 14 meets, 3 seconds, 6 thirds, and 3 fourths — and car No. 34, Rex Records in 8 meets, 1 second, 3 thirds, 2 fourths, and 2 fifths.

NOT ONE CAR WAS RETIRED FROM ANY RACE DUE TO MECHANICAL DIFFICULTY. This was entirely due to the mechanical genius of Ted Horn.

Ted grossed $18,000 that season and when his expenses were met, overhead paid, and outstanding obligations met, he was broke again.

Broke and tired, with a mountain of work to do, he punched out a short letter:

> I had a very good season. Won the championship with two of my other cars — second and third. I expect to be in Chicago sometime before the first of December and will come to see you. Maybe we could find something to talk about. Guess that's all now. Best of luck.
> Ted Horn.

Gone was the affix "always" to the best of luck, and missing was the "I'll be seeing you." Ted was planning a trip and his mind was elsewhere. He was trying to discount a hunch he just had. A terrible hunch.

The trip took Ted to Akron, Toledo, Rockford and Chicago. Calling on sponsors of racing, and in his own mild mannered style, trying to sell racing to the sponsors of his business. It was a self-subsidized good will tour. Not for Ted Horn, but for racing, and the business of which he was now a titular spokesman.

In Chicago Ted and Mr. White had a long conversation. It wasn't all business, but an exchange of thoughts on the problems of the day. Ted didn't speak of his hunch, but he gave credence to his pessimism on the future. On December 7th, it happened, and Ted knew his hunch had been correct. The Japs bombed Pearl Harbor.

Ted locked the door to the Paterson machine shop and packed his grip. For a week he was gone, and when he returned, in his pocket were rejection slips from the Army, Navy, Marines and Air Corps. Not even as a civilian instructor would they take him. Ascot, Lewistown and Nashville was the reason. The last recruiting officer had told him, "That machine shop of yours will kill more Japs than you could with Washington red tape."

RACING BANNED FOR DURATION

Ted wrote a long letter this time:

> Dear Mr. White ... Been a couple of weeks now since I had my pleasant visit with you. Can't get it out of my mind how we were talking about the very thing that happened since, namely, war with Japan. If we only had gotten the warning to the Navy a lot of boys would have been saved. I figured it was bound to come but couldn't get many to agree with me. Funny we had that dinner conversation on it and never knowing how soon it was to happen.
>
> I intend to go down to Florida immediately after Christmas for a conference with Mr. Hankinson. In talks we had before on this matter he told me that he didn't think it would affect fairs, as it didn't last time — although Indianapolis and the still dates might suffer. Take it easy and I'll be seeing you ... Best of luck — Ted Horn.

Then in January Ted wrote again:

> I guess maybe you too are interested in what's to become of auto racing this year. For me it means a lot, even in war time. I have about $25,000 in racing equipment and have to keep it working ... The President's stand on sports is very encouraging, and I myself have on hand enough tires, and fuel and parts to operate my five cars for two years at least, and maybe three ... I'm not fit physically to enter the armed forces — auto racing having exacted its toll in that direction ... Best of luck always — Ted Horn.

Then later:

> I am at present working on my cars and trying to get everything in best possible shape for a strenuous season. At the present time it looks as if we are going to have just that. I've been making all the fairs' conventions, and will be in Albany the 9th. Mr. Hankinson is setting up more fairs and dates this year than he has ever had before. He is an old-timer in this business and has been through all the situations before, and I'm putting all my faith in his judgment, and giving him all the help that I can ... I will have five cars this season, all under his banner exclusively, and they will not be raced elsewhere without his consent and approval ... I'll keep you posted from time to time on what is going on ... Best of luck, always — Ted Horn.

In February, AAA announced it had ceased sanctioning for the duration. The Indianapolis Speedway was for sale. Hankinson and Roy Richwine formed a big car circuit, and racing opened at the Reading Fairgrounds on April 19th. Ted set a new track record with Baby of 25.79, but Chitwood won the final. At the Grove, before 31,347 war workers, Ted edged Holland in each event. At Langhorne, Wilburn won with Ted second, and at Milwaukee he was second to Chitwood. At Davenport the Indian continued his mastery in the Peters Offy., and at Birmingham, Ted sunk to fourth as Chitwood continued on the warpath.

As suddenly as the raid on Pearl Harbor, the Government announced a ban on racing, the only spectator sport to be so affected.

August 19th, Ralph Hankinson, stormy petrel of auto racing, czar in his own domain, and benefactor of Ted Horn, passed into eternal sleep at his Florida home. Fate had stepped in where mortal man couldn't decide and gathered a great being to his ethereal domain.

Ted attended the funeral, and returned to Paterson. Lines of responsibility and worry were beginning to show on his face. His heart was not in his task and he quit to write a letter — the last for more than two years:

> I have just finished getting my house in order so that I can get busy on the task at hand. Don't know where you might hear from me next... it might be from a long way off, and then again it might be from right here, if I can get some defense work for my little shop. I took all the engines apart and have them on a bench. The chassis are all stacked against the wall with the front and rear ends laid out along the floor and the bodies tied up against the the roof. If you don't think that five race cars apart makes an awful mess, you ought to see this. Don't know of much to say — guess there isn't much. Take it easy and I'll be seeing you. Best of luck always — Ted Horn.

The task at hand was fishing, hunting and some thinking. Ted spent a lot of time away from Paterson that first year. A lot of it was in Washington and to a specialist, a doctor. One trip he took was to Dayton, and to the Wright Aircraft factory.

When he returned, he had a sub-contract for his shop. Milt Marion, former Indianapolis driver, and now car owner, had a shop similar to Ted's, and it was as a sub-contractor to Marion that Ted Horn Engineering lasted out the war.

Sept. 5, 1945 ... Dear Mr. White ... Been a long time since I wrote you a letter, but must say it makes me happy to have the occasion to do so again. First, I want to tell you I won the first big car event to be run after V-J Day. Aug. 26th at Essex Junction, Vt. I had the fastest time, heat and won the main event. I only had one car together which I drove myself. On Labor Day I had two cars together and Tommy Hinnershitz drove the other. I won and Tommy was second. The race was at Hughesville and they had a wonderful crowd. Burd Piston Rings were in both these cars and I had them since before the war. Don't look like aging did them any harm.

October 4, 1945 ... So far I haven't lost a race unless you want to count the one where I dropped a valve at Leighton, Pa., warming up. Tommy and I ran one-two again at Hughesville, and the same at Kutztown and Williams Grove. We are now on our way to Gratz, Pa., which is a new track I've never seen. I'm not worried as the "Little Dandy" is hotter than ever. I'm running three cars tomorrow and shooting for one-two-three. Ain't I the hog though?

November 26th ... I'll be leaving for out west right after the fair conventions which run the 3rd, 4th and 5th of December. Looks like AAA is really going to town next year. I haven't seen the bulletin yet, but it is supposed to read not less than $3,000 for half miles, $8,000 for miles and $12,500 for championship races. I figure to be ready to get my share of this. I am working over all my cars and also a championship car. I'm spending quite a little bit of dough, and I think before I'm finished I'm going to have to have some help. Anyway, I'll drop in and see you when

Best of luck always.

Ted Horn.

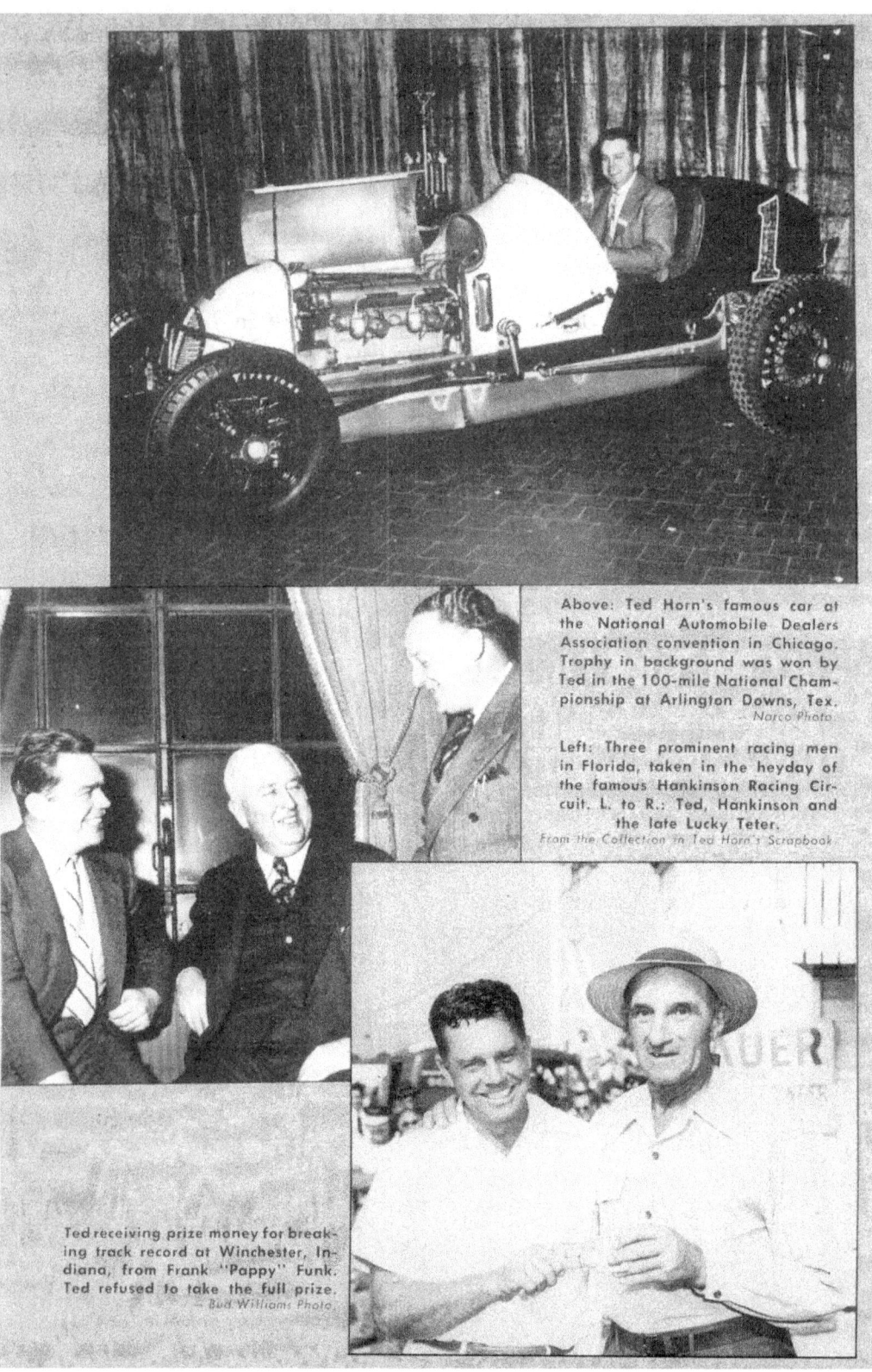

Above: Ted Horn's famous car at the National Automobile Dealers Association convention in Chicago. Trophy in background was won by Ted in the 100-mile National Championship at Arlington Downs, Tex.
— Narco Photo

Left: Three prominent racing men in Florida, taken in the heyday of the famous Hankinson Racing Circuit. L. to R.: Ted, Hankinson and the late Lucky Teter.
From the Collection in Ted Horn's Scrapbook

Ted receiving prize money for breaking track record at Winchester, Indiana, from Frank "Pappy" Funk. Ted refused to take the full prize.
— Bud Williams Photo

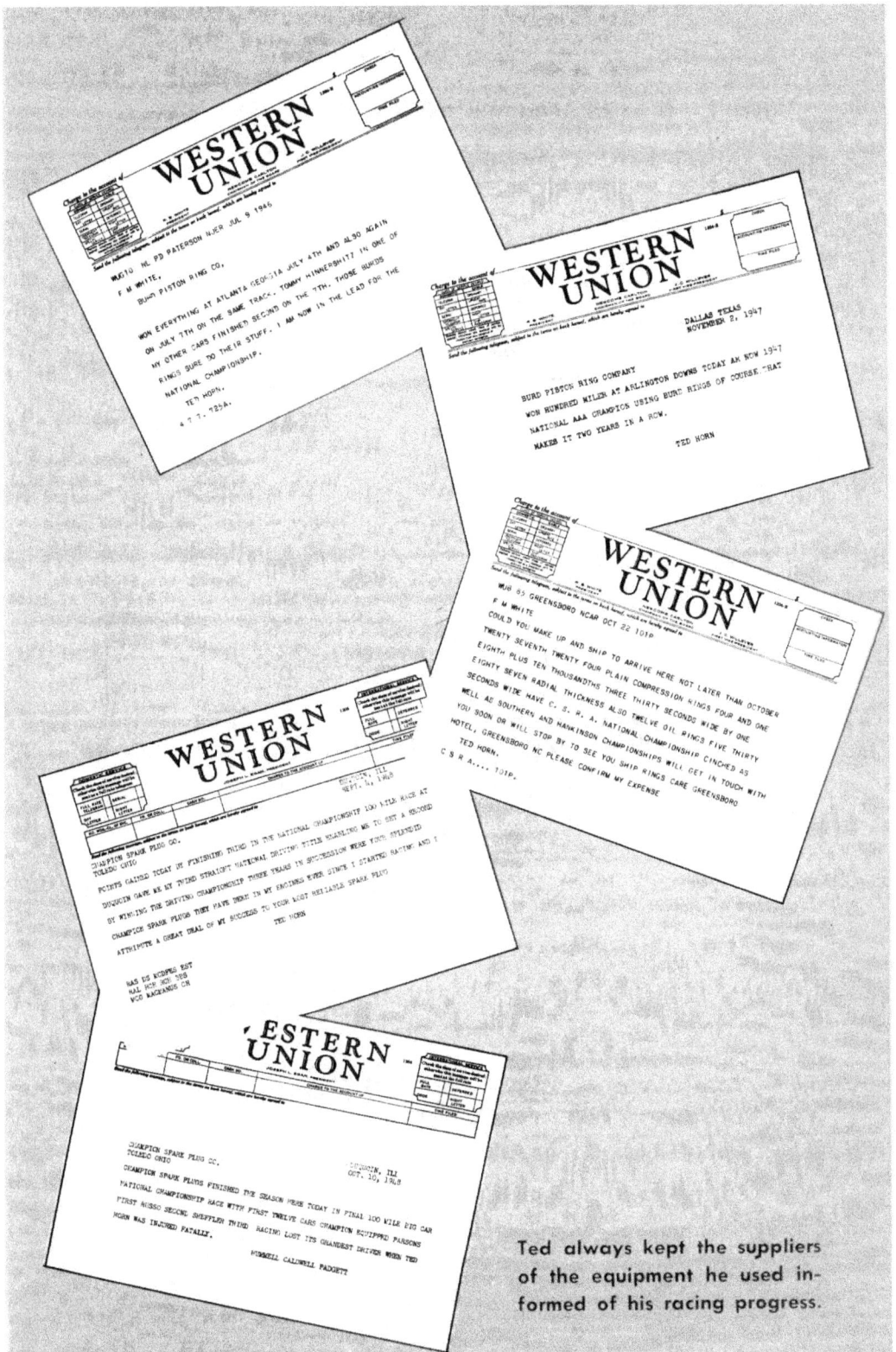

Ted always kept the suppliers of the equipment he used informed of his racing progress.

CHAMPION
100-MILE-AN-HOUR-CLUB

THE WORLD'S MOST EXCLUSIVE CLUB

Members
BILLY ARNOLD
GEORGE BARRINGER
CLIFF BERGERE
BRUNO CONNOR
BILL CUMMINGS
DAVE EVANS
FRED FRAME
CHET GARDNER
TED HORN
LOU MEYER
REX MAYS
CHET MILLER
LOU MOORE
KELLY PETILLO
FLOYD ROBERTS
MAURI ROSE
WILBUR SHAW
RUSSELL SNOWBERGER
LOUIS TOMEI
"HOWDY" WILCOX

Board of Governors
T. E. ALLEN,
SECRETARY, AAA CONTEST BOARD
H. C. DEWITT,
V. P., CHAMPION SPARK PLUG COMPANY (BONEUR)
T. E. MYERS,
VICE PRESIDENT, INDIANAPOLIS MOTOR SPEEDWAY CORPORATION
E. V. RICKENBACKER,
GENERAL MANAGER, EASTERN AIR LINES

Mr. F. M. White
Burd Piston Ring Co
Rockford Ill.

Dear Mr. White:

Sorry I have no more wins to report at the present time but hope to have a couple more this season yet. There are no other races scheduled but half milers. If I win a few of them that ought to be equal to a miler shouldn't it? Fact is, it's a lot harder to win one on the halfs than it is on the miles.

This year I am the high point man or champion or what ever you want to call it for the MidWest district. This is two years in a row as I won it last year too. Will carry #1 on the little dandy again next year.

Am enclosing the slip out of one of the boxes of rings you sent me. Am also sending you the rings off one piston that I took out. It was a shame to take the old rings out, but I had to rebabbit the job so put new ones in at the same time.

The rings I am sending you are the ones that I won at Hamburg. They also were used at Flemington where I got a big fat fourth. But they won three out of four so that isn't so bad I guess.

Am getting a new block so need some 4-1/16 standard rings. 1/8 compression and 5/32 oil.

I'll be a seein you, Best of Luck,

Ted Horn

Broke the track record at Hughsville Pa. last Saturday.
Former record 27.3 by Frank Bailey, my record 25.8 with Burd Rings
In winning at Hamburg N.Y. set new record of 26.02 for that track with Burd rings.

To qualify for membership, drivers must complete the Indianapolis 500-mile Race without relief and average over 100 miles an hour.

A characteristic example of Ted's modesty and also his attention to details.

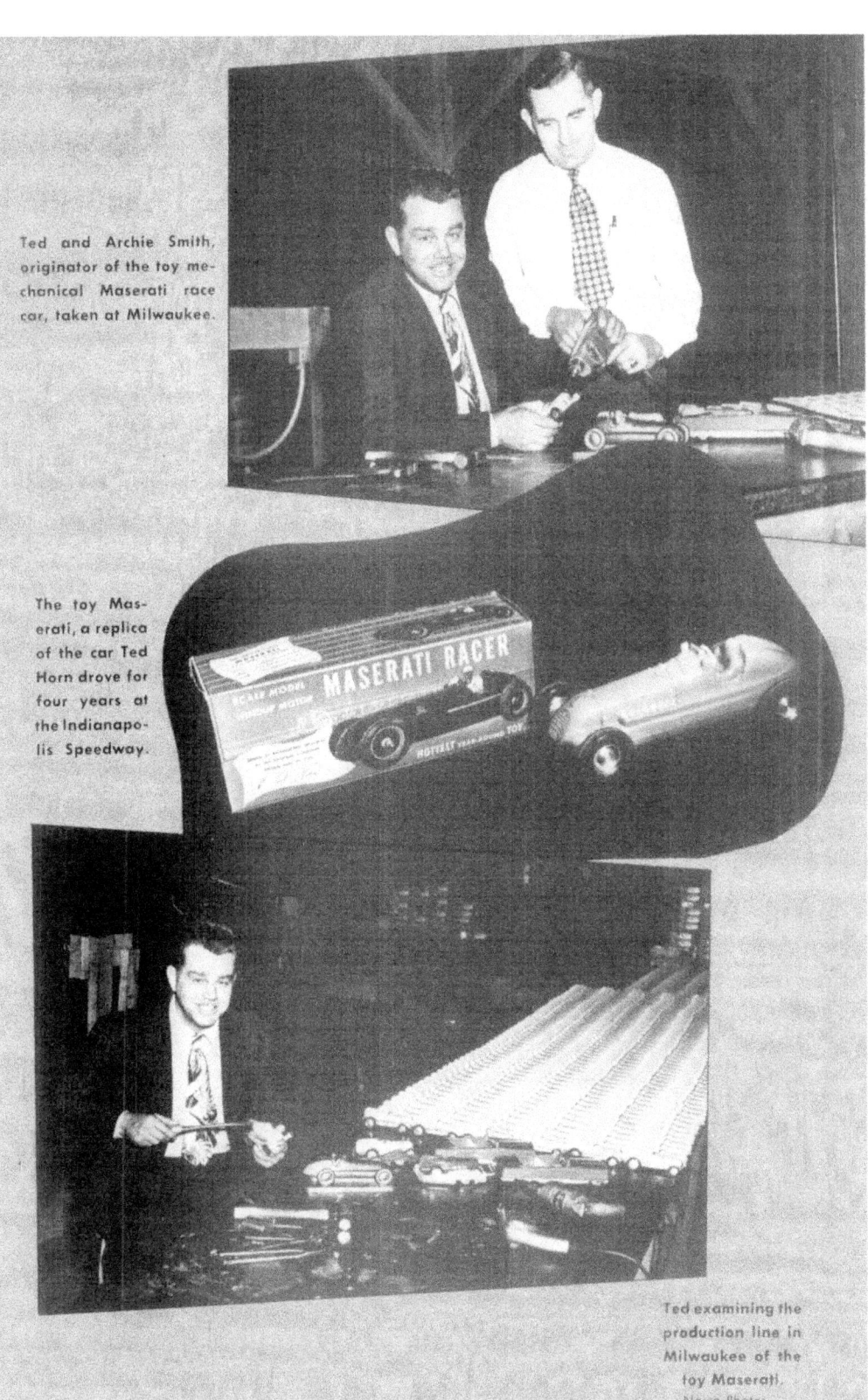

Ted and Archie Smith, originator of the toy mechanical Maserati race car, taken at Milwaukee.

The toy Maserati, a replica of the car Ted Horn drove for four years at the Indianapolis Speedway.

Ted examining the production line in Milwaukee of the toy Maserati.
Norco Photos

Ted Horn — the business man. This photo taken in his office January, 1948, shows him admiring the toy Maserati. Papier-mache model belonging to Cotton Henning is shown on top of box. This model was insured for $5,000. — Narco Photo.

CHAPTER V

The Champion

IN seven race meets in 1945, the Ted Horn team scored seven clean sweeps, bowing only to each other. Bobby Sall had retired and the team was now composed of Hinnershitz, Walt Ader and Lee Wallard.

In December Ted stopped on his way to the coast and saw Cotton Henning in Indianapolis. Cotton was bubbling with enthusiasm. "Ted, my boy, Wilbur did it. Sold the track to Tony Hulman, and we race next spring. Wilbur is General Manager, and it's you, young man, who gets the Maserati."

On the coast Ted bought a new motor and the championship car was ready. Ready for the biggest and busiest season Ted would ever experience.

The last day of March Ted was at Atlanta for the first of three big race events he was to run there this year. Back under AAA sanction and the field was eager and hungry. Ted was no exception. Baby's motor had put Ted well into the red and before the season was well advanced the Little Gems were to go, one by one.

34,362 Georgia Crackers lined the confines of Lakewood for the big event. Ted and Chitwood hooked into a match race to start the festivities. After four grueling miles Baby had a half length advantage on the Cherokee in the Peters Offy. Jimmy Wilburn won the main all alone, as again Horn and Chitwood dueled. Again Baby was the winner for second spot.

The Grove opened April 15th, and 41,753 watched as Walt Ader put a Gem into first with Chitwood besting Ted for the "place." On the 19th, the positions were reversed. Horn, Chitwood and Ader. May 5th, Chitwood was in front at Trenton, Ted second, and the next day, back at the Grove it was Chitwood, Ader, Horn. Here was hard riding and competition in the raw, and Ted loved it. No crowd was less than 20,000 at any of these races and the payoffs were in astronomical amounts.

Then Ted arrived at Indianapolis. The war years had taken its toll of the big plant. Workmen were busy right up to the time the first car rolled over the starting line race day, putting paint on newly laid lumber.

The Henning garage was a bee-hive of activity. If there was a garage anywhere that equaled Ted's own in Paterson for cleanliness, it was the Henning garage, now known as Henning's Hash House.

Ted found the Maserati more car than he had dreamed. It was smooth and effortless. Day after day Ted roamed the long stretches, getting the feel, and his 123.980 in the time trial was made with no particular effort. Not too many cars were ready for this race, the announcement had been made so late, but up in front and certainly contenders were Rex Mays, Paul Russo and Sammy Hanks. Mays, now National Champion two years in a row, was not only gunning for his first Indianapolis victory, but for the championship again — to be the first man in its long history to turn the trick.

The long race got underway in a blaze of speed. Mauri Rose grabbed the lead on the first lap, and drove as if he intended to stay there all day. On the first lap, cars started to come into the pits, and the first one in was number 29 — Ted and the Maserati. Before the race had started, Ted's magneto had gone out.

Everything happened in the early part of that race. Lap 5, and Mays passed Rose for the lead with a blinding pace. Ted was still in the pits. Other cars were coming in, the speed too hot for them. With a new magneto installed Ted took out after the field — SEVEN LAPS BEHIND THE LAST CAR.

Hepburn, in the first of the Novis screamed into the lead by the 11th lap, and on the 15th the caution light went on. Russo hit the wall, and shortly afterward, Mauri Rose.

Lap 25, and Mays went out. Hepburn continued to roll up a big lead. On the 55th lap he too headed for the pits and Robson took over. Little George Robson, born in England and never able to hit the big time until this year, driving a Thorne-Sparks 6 cylinder entry.

Ted came in for fuel, then off again. Hepburn too was running, and all were gaining on little George. At the 225 mile mark Ted entered the first ten, and traffic was thin, nearly half the field was out — tired iron giving away after the long war years of non-usage.

The 400 mile mark was reached and Hepburn was done. Grinding away in front was Robson, and chasing him was Jimmy Jackson. Ted was still climbing. It was hopeless. Like two tired gladiators, Robson and Jackson struggled toward the finish and Ted was miles away in third. Robson got the checker after a race of almost complete exhaustion of the field — only nine cars still running, and one of these Sheffler, crippled on the inside. Twelve minutes after Robson, Ted gave Klein the familiar salute — the 13 minutes in the pits at the start, costing him the race.

Ted didn't wait for the banquet. The next day he had the "Little Dandy" at Reading, getting between Ader and Holland at the finish. Atlanta again and a victory, after trailing Indianapolis winner Robson for 49 laps. Langhorne, the Grove, Dubois, Flemington — three wins and leading the fourth when a tire blew, and Ted crashed the fence. Robson won that one.

Second to Holland at Washington, Pa., and Robson at Columbus, Ohio. Wins at Uniontown and Hamburg, then second to Holland at Batavia. A trip up to Skowhegan, Maine and Baby showed her fine colors to the sea people. Back to Rutland, Vt., and second behind Wallard. Victories at Altamont and Bedford.

At Altamont, the fans were given their choice for a match race. They picked Ted and a six foot four, slim blonde giant, with a mile wide grin—Freddy Carpenter. To Freddy, this was a signal honor, to be singled out for battle against pre-occupied and busy Ted Horn. It was the laurel wreath in advance.

As their cars were pushed to the starting line, Freddy, not too sure of the procedure, approached Ted with a grin and a question, "What do we do in a case like this, put on a show?"

Ted's returning grin froze, his eyes snapped, and his usual mild voice sounded guttural as he responded, "I drive to win — ALWAYS. Don't forget that, but if you want to split the purse, it's all right with me."

Freddy took his licking on schedule, but was puzzled.

As he was loading up, Ted approached with an explanation. "Look Freddy, many years ago I asked that same question, and I remember how I felt when I got my answer. We who make our living from those people up there, never let them down intentionally. The race may be poor, but we're honest. I'm sorry I gave you the answer I did out there, but that's the score."

A friendship was born that day. One that would never end.

September opened with a big 100 mile championship race at Atlanta. Over $14,000 was in the pot, with first place paying better than $3,000. 38,000 fans packed every inch of space around the big mile track. Indianapolis pilots by the score were on hand, and Ted qualified for the big event. So did Billy DeVore, George Barringer, Steve Truchan, Gaorge Connor, Bud Bardy, and George Robson. Smiling George, winner of his first big race in 1946 at Indianapolis.

Always willing to cooperate, George was the target of the camera hounds. Ted didn't like it. Here, he developed the habit of remaining away from his car until the event was ready to start. In that manner he escaped refusing pictures.

Austin Shay, long time AAA starter, lived in Lebanon, Pennsylvania. That was near Williams Grove, and the field was scheduled to appear there the following Sunday. Shay owned a popular filling station in Lebanon, and as a delay in the starting ceremonies occurred, Shay walked to the car containing the smiling Robson.

"George, do me a favor," asked Shay. "When you come to the Grove next week, how about parking your car in my filling station for an hour so's I can invite my customers to come over and meet the Indianapolis winner?"

George looked up, studied a minute then countered, "I'll

Top photo taken June 8, 1948 at Milwaukee prior to championship race. L. to R.: Tommy Thomas, Harry Hartz, Ted Horn, Chet Barnekow, Ike Welch, Norm Olsen and Jim Lamb, Secretary Contest Board, A.A.A.
Lower: Start of championship event at Milwaukee. Horn in "Beauty" leading on outside, Dinsmore on pole. — Bud Williams Photos.

Ted on a record run at Lakewood Speedway, Atlanta, Georgia. —W. P. Dodd Photo.

Action at Salem, Indiana. Chitwood in the Nyquist Offy leading Ted.
—Bud Williams Photo.

A start at Dayton. No. 91 is the Iddings Special driven so spectacularly at Indianapolis by Lee Wallard. L. to R.: Shackleford, Horn, Walt Ader, Johnny Fredericks, Jackie Holmes. —Bud Williams Photo.

Ted and "Baby" on the record run at Dayton, Ohio. —Bud Williams Photo.

go you one better Austin. If you have a pair of overalls handy, you can tell your customers the Indy winner will fill their gas tank." That is championship material.

The field got under way. Before five circuits of the oval were made, red clay dust followed the field. Ted forged to the front, now he was lapping the slower cars, he looked at his pit and got the steady signal. The dust was now meeting him — getting thicker — reminded Ted of that day back in Nashville. Then he did some mental calculating; it was the odd years that he always had trouble, and this was 1946. Ted felt better and let it out some more.

Now Ted was "flying blind." Watched the tree tops to keep his course, but in the third turn there were no trees. A big "No Fishing" sign on a bank was his signal to turn. Ted was watching for the sign when a car loomed out of the dust, cruising on the inside. Ted just missed it — then again it happened — the pit signaled two more laps — thank goodness this one's ending. Ted was looking up for the fishing sign and a car came down out of the dust and landed on his hood. Ted skidded and ground to a stop. It was Nashville all over again, the tearing of metal, timber and blinding dust.

Ted vaulted from his car. One was down through the fence in the lake, just like Gardner. Another lay crumpled near the rail, no, Nalon isn't here, a figure was sprawled on the track — no, it couldn't be Howdy Cox — that was nine years ago. Ted ran to the water's edge and a figure was emerging. More cars winding down the stretch — Ted ran up the track waving his arms, but they couldn't see him.

The dust settled and the broken body of little George Robson, still champion, was lifted into the ambulance. So was that of Barringer. Ted was uninjured but DeVore was hurt. Robson and Barringer had made their last lap, a victim of the dust, and —"It always comes in pairs. Damn those cameras."

Ted was given first place that day, and a big jump in championship points. Little George, who had led the point standing from the outset due to his victory at Indianapolis, would never carry the national title of his adopted country.

Championship events were coming up fast now. Big crowds — the biggest yet seen — were turning out for the jousting. Records were going right and left. Ted sold one of his Gems to Chitwood, and the car paid for itself in a month. At the Grove, in the race Robson was to have appeared, Ted won followed by Andres and Hinnershitz. A championship event was on tap for Indianapolis, Indiana, Fairgrounds — the first to be held there in over ten years.

Ted needed victory in this race. His lead in the big chase was not large. Mays had the Bowes Seal Fast job humming again, and was very much in the running for the title he owned. Besides Ted and Rex, there were Mauri Rose, Al Putnam, Tony Bettenhausen, Floyd Davis, Russ Snowberger, Elbert Booker, Eddie Zalucki, George Connor, Emil Andres and Spider Webb to take time trials.

Little Al Putnam never completed his time run. A skid, crash and a drop into a concrete abutment ended his life before he had qualified. Little Adelbert, the curly topped veteran who had started back on the coast in Ascot days, and always wanted to be a race driver, and who had sold caricatures of himself to finance his first race car. Little Al, the joiner. He no longer needed to race. He was an honored engineer in industry, a member of the Society of Automotive Engineers, The American Society of Tool Engineers, The American Society for Metals. A 32nd degree Mason, member of the Speedway Masonic Lodge, Scottish Rite and Murat Temple Shrine. Al joined a higher lodge this day. "That completes the cycle," Ted said, "always in pairs."

The race was a thrill producer. Mays led from the outset, trailed by Rose and Ted. Near the 80 mile mark, Ted moved up on Mauri, then slowed. A horseshoe nail, souvenir of the horse racing that had been held on this track for many seasons imbedded itself in a tire. Ted's crew — Jughead, Woodenhead and just plain Head — were the picture of perfection in the change. Thirty seconds and he was away.

Mays averaged almost 80 MPH to win. Rose was second, Andres third and Ted fourth. The scene moved to Milwaukee, and another 100-miler.

Mays and the Bowes job duplicated the Indianapolis results of a week earlier. This time he had Tony Bettenhausen to vanquish. Tony, the blonde smiling Dutchman, the Tinley Express. Ted took second, almost a lap behind.

Goshen, and still another 100 miler. The big kite shaped track on which the Grand Circuit annually holds its "Kentucky Derby" of the harness sport. No crowd was any larger than the one which turned out early for the auto events. Ted now had the Peters Offy. The Little Dandy needed an overhaul and there wasn't time. Rex beat Ted in a match race, then threw a rod. Out for the day. To Ted, any kind of a decent finish and the title was his. The big one. The hard one to win.

The Tinley Express roared into the lead on the first turn. Ted trailed, then moved slowly forward, picking up stragglers and slower cars. Andres was chasing Bettenhausen, and as the half way mark was reached, the pair lapped Ted. At the three-quarter mark, Jughead hung out the "GO" signal, and the big Peters job leaped. In one lap Ted had unlapped himself. Andres was slowing. Ted went by, driving with one hand and waving with the other. It was the wave of a champion. Second place made the title his. They coasted to the finish.

At the finish line it was bedlam. Jimmy Frattone, the young war time pilot and now promoter, had elaborate ceremonies awaiting. Miss America greeted the victor with a big hug and a kiss, and blonde Tony blushed way back to Saxony. It was a happy throng, but in the Horn pits another kind of a celebration was going on. For the first time, Jughead was showing some enthusiasm. Laconic, tight-mouthed, always dependable Wallace J. Cornforth, Ted's stooge, was happy. The boss had the title sewed up tight now, and the boss was pleased.

Jughead was one of Ted's admirers. Somewhere along the line, he had stood out from the milling mob of youngsters that always hung around Ted's pit. He followed the "big one" everywhere he went and soon Ted had him in his crew. Jug was efficient, quiet and obedient, with a will to learn. Ted liked Jug.

Those names were part of the nomenclature Ted always attached to things close to him. Baby, The Little Gems, The Little Dandy, Woodenhead, Aighead, Squarehead, and now Jughead.

Ted's crew was now taking his race car to the tracks on a truck. They formed an efficient working staff. Ted burned the highways in his Mercury. So tight was his schedule, it was the only manner in which he could meet it. Back at the shop the mechanics were busy re-boring, re-ringing and re-building spare motors. But never, never did they go into a chassis until Ted himself had given them the once over. Attention to the little things — that was Ted's creed. No part was so minor, or no part so insignificant as to be slighted. Ted was the master craftsman. His had been the hard school, and he knew in his own mind that this was the reason he was living today.

Appearance came next. Ted's pit crew and himself were always uniformed. The truck carried fresh clothing. It was a cardinal rule that one hour before the race, the entire group would don clean apparel. Not wrinkled, not the cleanest of that worn during the week, but spotless white coveralls. Pressed, clean and untorn.

Jughead had emerged from his beardless days into a Sergeant in the armed forces. Ted was racing near Fort Bragg. Jug went A.W.O.L. to see his idol, and lost his stripes. Ted wrote Jug and asked what he could do to make amends. Jug said he only wanted to be Ted's mechanic. So, Jug now was learning. Not just a plier and screw driver mechanic, but one in Ted's own shadow, one who could make his own pistons, tune his own motor and mix his own fuel. It was a long school and Jug had years of study ahead, but his was a will to learn.

Another rule that was cardinal — Ted's reluctance to pictures before a race was well known to the photography boys and they respected his wishes. But once a race was over, Ted would pose until every camera had its fill. The first of these shots showed Ted with the race track dust (or dirt) on his unshaven countenance. That wasn't in keeping with his creed, so, as Ted swung into the pit row at the end of a race Jug would toss Ted a towel. Ted would hurriedly wipe his face, in case any picture takers were on hand, then leap from his car and disappear. Minutes later he would be back, freshly shaven, clean clothes, and his big smile showing the even white teeth. The workman's countenance became scarcer and scarcer on picture plates. Ted was standing out from the mob, and there was reason besides his victories.

Back to the Grove, and Bedford, Flemington, Trenton, Reading. Now the papers were recognizing the fact Ted was the coming champion, and the well-wishers and autograph seekers increased. Ted remembered — back at Ascot he was just one of the boys on the program, pushing poor cars, and watching as Gordon and Spangler and Triplett — there never would be another Ernie Triplett — and Shaw, and Roberts, and Gardner — a lump came in Ted's throat as he thought of the good and kind man who had lived true to the code of the track, and had given his life to spare that of a child's. They were the ones who had been asked for autographs in those days and now it was Ted's turn — twenty long years later.

At Williams Grove one person remained after Ted had signed his program. Stood a little back from the crowd. He had a drawn face, but a kind face. Ted wondered what he wanted, but gave no recognition. The crowd thinned a little, and the two men's eyes met. Ted read honesty there and he smiled. The man smiled back. "See you in a minute," Ted called, and he waited.

Finally they were alone and Ted offered, "Darned if I can remember your name, but I've seen you somewhere." "Back in Richmond," was the answer. "I always go to see you race Ted. Been doing it for ten years now. I was there the day you broke the world's record on our track."

Ted smiled. That was long ago, and he had secretly felt a little proud that day. Proud of Baby and the work she was doing. "Yeah, I remember that time," Ted returned, "hope to get back to Richmond. I always was lucky there."

"That's what I want to see you about," the visibly nervous man answered. "There's a new track being built. It's a half mile and will be used for the fairs. I got it in my head to promote an auto race there this fall. I'm the tennis pro out at the Country Club in Richmond, but racing's in my blood. I think races at this new track would do well."

Ted studied a minute. "Yes." he agreed, "they should. Richmond is a good town." "Well," after a minute's reflection, "what can I do to help you. How are you coming?"

That was the answer Jim was waiting for. It was Jim Mitchell who was meeting Ted for the first time, and he now poured out his mind. "I've seen to everything. I can get the contract and line up everything necessary. The newspaper boys are friends of mine and they'll help. But Ted, I'm new to racing, and I don't know how to get the cars and drivers. I thought maybe you could do that for me. If you do, half of all I make will be yours."

To Ted, it was Fate speaking. Ted was tired, that was true, and he longed for a rest, but here was an idea he had never thought of. The promotional end. He still would be in the racing game and in a position where he could teach the ethics he knew were so necessary for the continuance of the sport. "I'll do it," was the answer, "get back to Richmond and start the wheels rolling. I'll fly down there as soon as I can finish a few more appearances, and we'll go to work. I'll get the field together, and you call me at the shop in Paterson if there is anything you need."

Thus it was that Ted Horn Enterprises started, and Strawberry Hill in Richmond got its first race meet.

True to his word, Ted flew to Richmond. Put his entire heart and soul into the new venture. He and Jim worked as a team. Ted gave out interviews, and told of his experiences from a great store of memories. Entries poured in. Ted was promoting, and the respect his adversaries on the track had for him was being manifested. Bill Holland, Walt Ader, Mark Light, Joie Chitwood called. "What's this I hear about you turning robber on us?" the Indian asked. "Get me a car, get me a car, this is one time I'm getting some of that Horn dough without having to run over you." Hinnershitz, Earl Johns, Lee Wallard and Ted grinned. Ted told Jim, "Now that darn Chitwood can't stay away from the track. Quit driving this summer to start his own thrill show, and doing right well too, and now here he is, leaving the show to race. Just goes to show you—once a race driver, always a race driver."

But Ted was wrong, and he knew it. Joie wasn't returning just to get a race out of his system. He was coming to help his friend Ted, and down deep Ted knew it, and he was pleased. Al Fleming, Otis Stine and Lee Wallard—it was going to be a mighty field, those descendants of the Confederacy were going to see, and Ted was pleased.

Jimmy was the worrier. When Ted was gone he felt lost. This was new business to him, and he watched as Ted swung through the ritual. "O.K. Al, the deal is a hundred bucks for you, and have that Offy winding," he had heard Ted say. So, as the mild voice came over the phone to Jim he answered, "the deal is a hundred bucks."

Ted swung into the room, hunting a pad to make some notes. Jim had never seen him happier. "So and So just called Ted, and he said he would be here." "Good," Ted shot back over his shoulder, "guarantee him fifty bucks. He has a flathead."

Jim's face fell. He didn't know the difference. "I told him a hundred Ted," Jim finally mumbled, then brightened, "but I'll call him and tell him the difference." Ted stopped. Laying a hand on Jim's shoulder he smiled. "No Jim, a hundred it is. You gave him your word, and never break it. Now you know what a flathead is and it only cost you fifty dollars to learn. I paid a good many times that amount to learn some of the things in this game."

Jim studied the face in front of him and thought, "Man has made him a champion in name, but there's something bigger than man that has seen he is champion in everything." Jim didn't know about Destiny and Fate, and their meeting back in Cincinnati thirty-six years before.

Richmond is used to the unusual in November. Sometimes it rains, and then again it pours. This November, in 1946, was no exception. Pappy Hankinson would have known it, but Pappy was gone now, and there was no one to tell Ted and Jim. In Jim's business, when it rained, you worked in the shop and re-strung rackets and mended nets. You didn't lose much when it rained during a tennis tournament, just postponed things a few hours, then when the sun returned, the sand of the tennis court dried in a hurry and the clay underneath absorbed the moisture, and you put on heavy soled tennis shoes and played.

But rain on a race track on race day is another thing. It's clay on top, and it gets gooey, then slippery and sticky — then just plain mud. The clay holds the moisture and the cars can't run. A race track on a rainy day is the most lonesome, forsaken, cheerless spot on the face of the globe — outside of Siberia. Promoters can do nothing about it. The old timers do watch the almanac, and they make periodic calls to the weather bureau, and they can tell pretty well whether to order their perishables or not. The worst thing that could happen would be just a slow drizzle in the morning, stopping at noon, but threatening clouds overhead. A promoter would sooner it rained in cloudburst proportions and washed out the entire program. He could then write off his bills of the moment and come back another day when the sun did shine. But an experienced promoter doesn't put all his eggs in one basket. He plays it easy in the spring and fall when the rains are more apt to come, and he takes rain insurance. But Ted and Jim were new promoters and they had this to learn.

Ted went back to the Grove to race on the 28th. It was the big 50 lapper that carried the trophy and ended the season. Ted was the favorite, as he set the fastest time and gave every evidence of continuing his winning streak. But on the first lap a skid, and Ted stalled, off the track.

It was three laps later, that Ted got back in the race. From there to the finish, he drove phenomenally. Time after time he passed cars, and made up one, two; then the three lost laps. But the finish was coming up, and Holland's lead was too big to overcome, and Ted took fourth behind Bill, Ader and Chitwood.

At the payoff, Ted came in for much ribbing. Rebel, they called him, "Get that rubber band off that cabbage Ted," Chitwood warned, "I'm coming after it next Sunday."

On November the third it rained. It wasn't just a drizzle, but a cloudburst. Ted and Jim stood beneath the empty stands and watched the little rivulets of water seeping through the cracks. "Well," Ted said, "Come again next Sunday. Can't win 'em all."

By the tenth it was still raining. Now, however, the kind of a rain all promoters fear. Just a little drizzle that made you too hot with a raincoat, and too wet without one. The well-planned publicity had backfired too. Beamed, as it should be, to reach a climax the day before the race, and it all had taken place the week previous. Jim and Ted, new to the game, didn't think of making the statements of how the postponement had helped the field. More cars and drivers were available, and how they were all looking to Strawberry Hill to get those final all-important points in the sectional championship, and a bigger slice of the point money.

Ted and Jim had to share their publicity with a football game, where the week before they had it alone. Then too, the drizzle was perfect for football. Fumbles, and sliding, spectacular tackles.

The crowd was down, but the racing up. The track was slippery, and the knobbys digging, as race after race slid through to a finish. Wallard, spinning and skidding hit a light pole, and broke his leg. Al Rogers slid out in the feature, then blocked the track as he bounced back from the wall. The race was declared over with Hinnershitz the winner, Holland second and Chitwood getting the third out of "the cabbage."

As close as they could figure it, the two men lost around $1,800. "The postponement did it," Ted said as he climbed on the train for the return to Paterson, "We'll do better next time." Looking Jim squarely in the eye, Ted sobered, and added, "You sure that's all we lost? You aren't holding out on me are you?" Jim's eyes searched the pavement, and Ted reached in his pocket, "I thought so, here, take this hundred and if that doesn't do it, call Paterson and I'll send more."

That ended the Strawberry Hill promotion, and Ted's last chance to escape the rigors of almost daily competition.

Ted went back to the shop and to work. It had been his busiest season. Almost 60 race meets and his books were in bad shape. Wanted to re-build Baby too, and the championship car. Now, Baby, the championship car and some of the Gems were all one. Parts were intermingled, until only Ted knew which was which. Motor failures were negligible and he was determined the following year would be the same.

Ted wasn't hungry, and he wasn't broke. As he sold excess equipment, his bank account mounted. He gave up trying to list events and finishes. Just the feature, that's all, and how much they paid. Expenses were higher than they had ever been, but so too was the gross. The corporation now took care of the big income bite. Hankinson had been right. Parlay everything you get back in your equipment, and someday the bucket would be full, and then the overrun would mount until you had that security you wanted. Ted filled a paper out. It was a publicity questionnaire AAA sent every year. Rapidly he wrote in longhand. Name, address, birth, age, height, weight, hair, occupation (other than race driver), and Ted hesitated. Then slowly scrawled, None. Hobbies? His face lit up. Hunting yes, fishing yes; swimming yes, others? Ted wrote, boating.

What type racing you like best, National Championship, Banks, Dirt Track, Midget? Ted placed a firm X after Dirt Track. What do you carry as a good luck charm? Ted stopped, then felt in his watch pocket. There was seven cents there. Seven letters in his name. He had thought of that back in '41 when his name was changed, but he hadn't mentioned it after the lawyer kicked up the fuss over his wanting everyone to know he changed his name for business reasons, and not for publicity. He wanted to add that the seven letters in Ted Horn matched the seven cents in his pocket, but he didn't. He looked over at Baby, and in the corner of her dash he could see the St. Christopher medallion. He left the space blank and went to the next question.

What is your ambition? Ted glanced at the papers on his desk. The one unfinished, and the task he had interrupted to fill out this form. Slowly and deliberately he wrote in a firm hand, as if a decision had been made, "Make enough money to retire."

What was the most outstanding event in your racing career? Ted chuckled, then hastily drew a big question mark, signed the form and sealed the envelope.

Ted was going to Washington and then south. A banquet was coming up in the Capitol, and Ted was to get his medal. That meant speeches and being very formal. Ted wished he could speak better in public. There was so much he wanted to say, so much he could say. He wanted to tell the young drivers, just coming up, how important it was to keep their equipment up and how important it was to handle the public as was their due, and to keep their word —oh, a million things he had to say, but he knew he would never say them. When the time came, he would just grin and say thanks and sit down. Someday they would get said however. Maybe if he just kept practicing his golden rule and setting the example, someone would say the things for him. Set an example? The thought sobered him. Yes, now he was champion, and he would be looked up to; to set an example. Ted accepted the responsibility.

He had other plans too. Would stop in at the Specialist's again. The back bothered him; then he would stop in Richmond and see Jimmy and Butch. Maybe Jimmy would have the books of the Strawberry fiasco ready and he could tell if that hundred covered it or not. Then Butch, Jimmy's youngster, was making a Ted Horn scrapbook now. Just like kids, Ted thought, always looking up to someone. But he liked the thought. Will stop in Warrenton too and see Tom Frost. Tom was a member of the Contest Board, and one of the real pillars of racing, but it was Tom Junior Ted wanted to see. Junior liked racing, and that time Ted took him along on the trip to Raleigh the youngster's face paid him ten times over for his troubles. Got to take care of these kids, Ted thought, it's they, not us old bucks, who will be the lifeblood of racing and see that it continues. Maybe Butch will grow up to be a promoter like his Dad wanted to be. Butch would be honest, like his Dad, and racing would need that type. Tom Frost Junior could very well inherit his Dad's post on the Contest Board. Got to see that he knows all about it, Ted thought. That's the champion's duty.

Ted went to the Specialist in Washington the afternoon of the banquet. He was thinking of what he was told as the fine speech was made and the medal given him. Ted mumbled his thanks, forced a grin and sat down. The guy with the white coat and short cropped mustache had told him, "It's just the same as a blood blister you get on your finger when you pinch it. Only this one is near the base of your spine, and extends through that member. No, no particular danger right now, it's small, and although its position makes an operation inadvisable, rest and proper care of yourself will tend to reduce it somewhat."

Rest and proper care? A bouncing, rough race car was hardly that, Ted thought, but the Sawbones had a pretty nice way to make a living himself, and he just didn't understand race drivers.

At Richmond Ted studied the final statement. "Phew," he said, "So that's what it takes to put a race on, eh?" Then with a grin he added, "Guess we bought us a race track that time Jim." "By the way Jim, this medal I got carries a little bigger guarantee for appearances next season, and I just can't afford to try any more promoting as long as I have this." Jim knew. It was Ted's way of saying that promoting was another man's business, not his. He was a shoemaker, and would stick to his last.

Ted fished that winter. Fished with his friend Fred Peters, the big car owner up east, whose car he would drive when Baby was laid up. Fred hadn't been looking too well, and the two men took their full measurement of the Florida sunshine, boating and fishing. Fred told Ted he had an operation coming up, and after that, felt he would feel better. Ted said, "You're lucky. Mine can't be operated on, but the only way I can be cured is by fishing. Tough isn't it?" and Ted grinned at his home-made joke.

Ted glanced in a mirror. S'funny, how some men, when they get old, their mustache turns white, and others gets blacker. Ted's once referred to as platinum blonde, was now darker. That newspaper guy probably had a case on

Jean Harlow when he called mine platinum. Great bunch, those newshawks. Always interrupting a man at work, and asking the darndest questions. Cold blooded creatures too, nothing seemed to faze them. Would look at a broken and bleeding body, then ask, "What was the stiff's age, anybody know?"

It wasn't human, the way they did it. But wait a minute. They're just guys making a living same as myself, and it's part of their job. Some guy in a swivel chair tells them what's wanted, and if they didn't get it, some guy in a bigger swivel chair would raise the roof over the smaller swivel chair, and then the "What's the stiff's age" would get it too. Maybe the gate. Certainly they weren't hardened to it. That was a trite statement. No one got hardened to death, or misery. The boys in the war could tell you that. Oh yeah, you got used to it, and when you saw a Jap you liked him better dead, but you never got entirely used to it.

No, these newshawks had an angle too. That was just a front they put on, Ted reasoned, just like race drivers. Pappy Hankinson could never understand it either. How, when a bad wreck happened, they could go right on with the race, when maybe you had the guy's socks on. You don't speak of these things, but the one that went would have wanted it that way. He just pulled the short straw this time, and when it was over the drivers would put on an act too.

Maybe that's why some newshawks hit the bottle, Ted thought. Well, some do anyway. That's the reason. They have to put on a front too, and Ted made a mental note he had to take care of these guys too, next time around the circuit.

It was a big load a champion had to carry. George Robson would have made a great champion. His friendliness, modesty, and commoness; just folks, that's the way to be.

Ted stopped in Warrenton on the way back north. Ordered a new car from his friend Tom Frost. A Lincoln Continental, Ted said, then apologetic, "Could you have some lettering done on it for me? On the back I want "TED HORN, NATIONAL CHAMPION RACING DRIVER."

That, explained Ted, was his way of publicizing the sport, and as people read it on the highway, maybe they would want to come see the races. That helped the promoter and the sport. Secretly, Ted was a little proud of his title too.

Then he ordered uniforms. Lots of them. Some maroon, and some snow white. The same lettering, with crossed flags on the back, and on the front, over the pocket, a miniature insignia. Just part of the show he would say publicly, but he liked this too.

It was well along towards spring when Ted opened the AAA bulletin he had been watching for. It read:

AAA NATIONAL POINT STANDINGS
1946

Position	Driver	Address	Total Points
1	Ted Horn	Paterson N.J.	2,250
2	(x) George Robson	Maywood, Calif.	1,484
3	Emil Andres	Chicago, Ill.	1,208
4	Bill Holland	Bridgeport, Conn.	1,115.6
5	Jimmy Jackson	Indianapolis, Ind.	800
6	T. Hinnershitz	Reading, Pa.	769.8
7	Walt Ader	Benardsville, N.J.	721
8	Joie Chitwood	Reading, Pa.	623
9	Rex Mays	Long Beach, Calif.	613
10	Duke Dinsmore	Osborn, Ohio	454

A long way from that first listed sectional point award. 75 and 83rd position, Southwest Pacific Standings in 1931.

Trenton, New Jersey, 1948. Ted is being congratulated by promoter Sam Nunis after winning his final victory before going to DuQuoin for his last race. —Kozub Photo.

Williams Grove, Pennsylvania, 1948. Starter Austin Shay gives final instructions to Horn and Hartz. Second from left is Ted's loyal friend and mechanic "Jughead."

Springfield, Illinois, August 21, 1948. Governor Dwight Green at microphone, at left Ike Welch and John W. Hobbs, representing A.A.A.

Williams Grove, Pennsylvania, 1948. Another triumph, and picture of Ted Horn, always a colorful winner. —Kozub Photo.

Start of feature event in Indiana. Ted on the outside, Chitwood on pole. Horn won this race, after losing a heat race to Chitwood. This feature was hub to hub for twenty laps, and Horn's margin of victory was about the width of the radiator shell.
—Bud Williams Photo

Action on the Indiana dirt with Ted and "Baby" leading Holmes.
—Bud Williams Photo

Ted and "Baby" at Reading, Penn. This unusual shot shows Ted's reaction to losing a close heat race, as he is being given the "razzberry" by "Jug" and his pit crew.
—Kazub Photo

At times Ted Horn was a comedian. Few people knew that he had a flair for making faces, and his friend, Charles Lytle, was able to get these humorous shots at various times in Indianapolis.

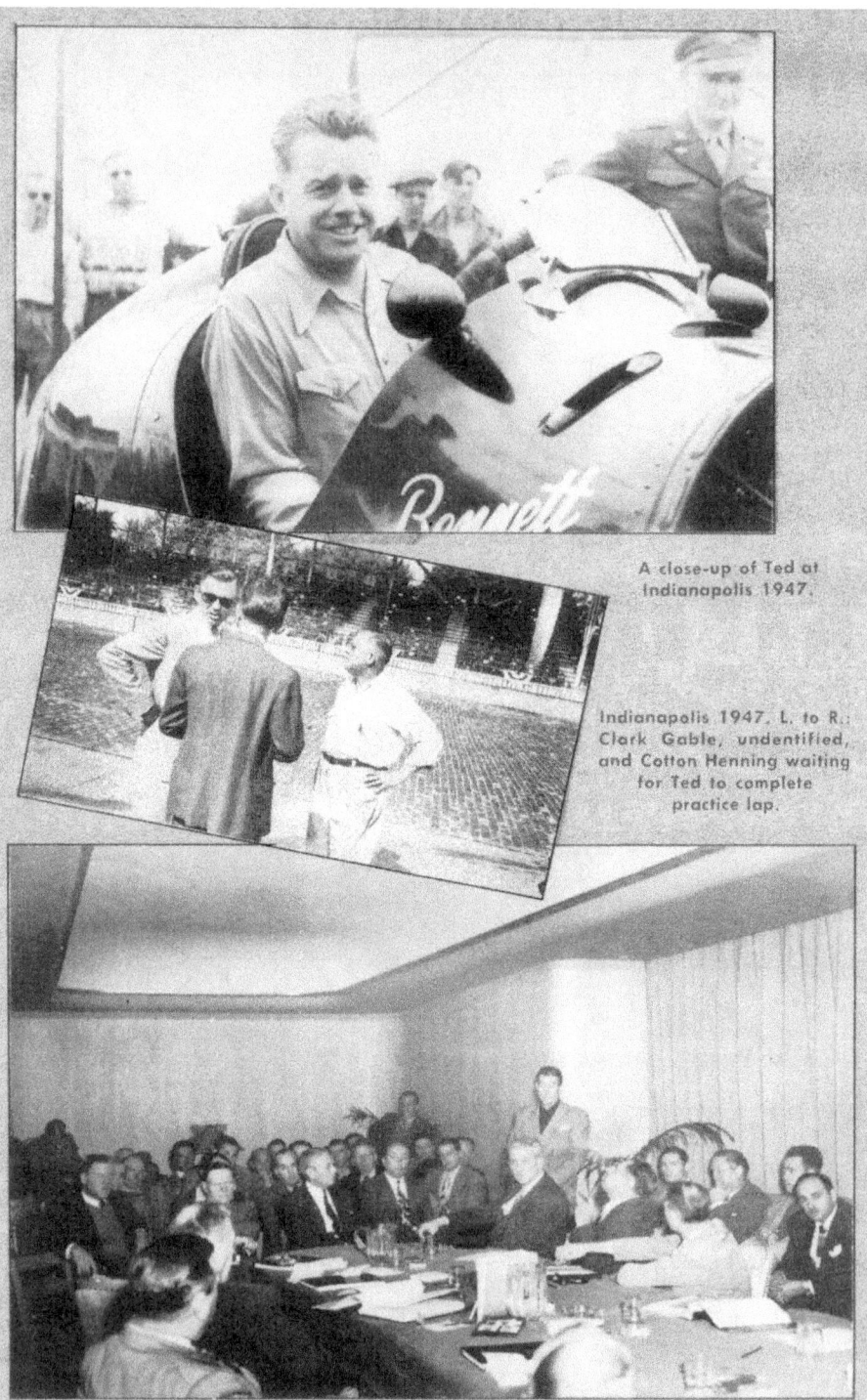

A close-up of Ted at Indianapolis 1947.

Indianapolis 1947. L. to R.: Clark Gable, undentified, and Cotton Henning waiting for Ted to complete practice lap.

The open house session of the annual meeting of the A.A.A. Contest Board taken at the Ambassador Hotel in Los Angeles, Tuesday, December 16, 1947. Horn is seated at the right of Sam Hanks, who is standing and speaking.

At Indianapolis 1947. L. to R.: Clark Gable, Tom Frost, member A.A.A. Contest Board, and Ted Horn. Cars shown are the Maserati and Ted's Lincoln Continental.
—Tower Studios Photo.

At Indianapolis in 1947. The drivers in the first row were Ted Horn on the pole, Cliff Bergere in the Novi Governor Special, and the eventual winner, Mauri Rose, in Lou Moore's Blue Crown Special.

Indianapolis 1947. L. to R.: The late Harry Bennett, Assistant Chief Steward, Horn in Maserati, and Ike Welch, Chief Observer.

A late posed photo of Ted Horn taken for the Decatur Herald-Review.
— Jack Ericksen, Staff Photographer.

CHAPTER VI

Horn and Holland

DESTINY had fulfilled her part of the deal made 36 years ago, and Fate drew the cards from here on in. The hand she now dealt was one of the strangest and most unique in all auto racing history. It held three aces, a deuce and a joker. Then, as if to dare contradiction, Fate handed the joker, two spot and one ace to Destiny, and said, "I'll stand pat with this pair." It was a strange game.

Ted was the overwhelming favorite in the winter book for the Indianapolis Classic. Not because he was the defending champion, but because racing itself felt Ted could no longer be denied this race. Long ago he had surpassed Hartz's great record for consistency, and now held a string of finishes that probably never would be equalled, and still not a win.

Ted, too, felt this was his year, and depended on it. He was rebuilding his championship car completely for the defense of the title, and it included a gleaming white and blue color scheme. Baby kept the traditional maroon and white, but both now sported a gold numeral one. Only the National Champion wore the gold numeral and Ted proudly displayed the honor.

His plans changed drastically from the headlong pace he had been setting himself. As the schedule of championship events was released, Ted charted a program with a minimum of travel. Personal appearances and sponsorships were more numerous, and this was the medicine Ted decided to apply, as the Doctor had suggested.

He was to change his plans as the season progressed.

In March the activities opened in Atlanta with a non championship affair. Ted used the big car and bested Holland in a match race. Then, while running second in the feature, developed trouble and withdrew. Holland was the victor.

April 21st opened the Grove, and this time Baby romped. Holland was second and Ader third. Baby broke all existing records from 1 to 30 laps before 47,682 screaming race-hungry fans. Then back to Richmond the next day and a second to Holland. Five days later and Baby scored a victory at the same track with Ader and Holland in that order.

Back to the Grove as May opened and another victory when Baby erased her own 30 lap mark. Dinsmore and Hinnershitz trailed. Holland was in Indianapolis looking for a car to drive. Ted followed. Fate chuckled and wrote the score—Horn 2, Holland 2.

Mike Boyle quit racing. Owner of the Henning stable, and producer of innumerable winners, he sold his cars. The Maserati was bought by Cotton, and in turn sponsored by the Bennett brothers of Texas, oil drillers. Ted was now a sponsored driver, but had plans of his own. The championship car was entered, with Hinnershitz named as the driver, and car owner with a contract driver.

Ted found Cotton happy and contented. "This is your year Ted," the jovial Henning remarked as they greeted each other. Ted smiled and shrugged.

For the first time in the nine years Ted had raced at the Speedway, he shot for the pole. Bergere, Doc Williams in the Novis and Rose in Lou Moore's Blue Crown were the opening day contenders. The Novis were dangerous. Speed to spare, their trouble was the need to harness the horsepower, once released. Bergere drifted to almost a 125 MPH average. Rose shot his bolt with 124, then Ted set sail. 125 on the first lap, 126 on the second, near 127 on the third, then a tremendous 127.80 on the last. It was good for the pole, and America's number one driver, in car No. 1 sat in number one position, for the nation's number one race.

The turkey at the 100 mile banquet was especially good this year. Ted ate with relish, and applauded loudly as his old nemesis, and the man he had unseated as National Champion, Rex Mays was elected president. Possibly the fact Ted noted that he and Wilbur Shaw stood alone in the listings for those having qualified the most times for this honor. Seven listings for each, with Shaw retired to the front office of the world's greatest Speedway, and Ted on the pole for the world's greatest race.

ANOTHER "500" GRIND

This year Ted was treated with a reserved respect at the Speedway. As he went about his daily practice rides, more and more attention was paid to his every move. Ike Welch, the very exacting and efficient Chief Observer had asked Ted to check drive many of the new pilots for him, on their driver's test. Ted did, as he always did, a thorough job. He liked this assignment for two reasons. First, he enjoyed having the confidence of the officials, and secondly it gave him a chance to advise and help the younger drivers.

The honored guest of the Speedway this year was Clark Gable, the movie actor. One of the first he met was the champion. The pair were attracted to each other at once. Later Ted said, "He made me feel as if the honor was all his at our meeting." Ted didn't mention the fact, but he did think of the time Gable was honored at another track—Ascot, and he was running far down on the B list.

But the two had one common like. Both avid hunters and sportsmen. Ted asked Gable to autograph his helmet, and they exchanged signatures.

Holland secured a car to drive. The twin sister to Rose's entry, and his first qualifying run produced a breathless 128.755. The world stood open mouthed. Not only was it the fastest in speedway history by a first year man, but the fastest of the entire field. From this point on Holland was on everyone's lips. Fate erased the score and rewrote, Holland 3, Horn 2.

It was a beautiful day for a race. Ted felt fit and the Maserati purred contentedly as Ted warmed the oil. Among the officials and celebrities making last minute checks, was one who walked towards the serious Ted, now setting in the car and checking his oil pressure. Clark Gable wanted to wish his new friend luck. "How about a picture?" the movie actor asked, and Ted's grin faded, but only for a moment. Then out came the big flashing smile and the picture was taken.

The pit crew looked at one another. "Let's race," said Ted.

Ted brought the field to a flying start, then dropped into second place as Bergere shot the big Novi to the front. For four laps they traveled in this manner, Ted trailing by 25 yards. On the 7th circuit, Cliff and Ted were lapping cars, and Holland had pulled into third. Then Ted signaled Cotton. The old familiar clenched fist with one finger raised.

The crew was ready as Ted braked to a stop. Ted was covered with oil. They looked for a leak. In two minutes and 3 seconds Ted was away, with no leak apparent. Now Ted was cruising, and Bergere four laps in front. Lap 16 for Bergere and Ted again pulled up. This time Cotton had it. Pressure was building up in the reserve oil tank, blowing the black gold everywhere. Two minutes more and the trouble was corrected entirely. The Maserati now had seven laps to make up.

Lap 23 and Holland led as Bergere stopped for a tire. Ted was flying now and the caution came on. Shorty Cantlon, the Ascot veteran, and whose motor Baby first housed, drew the short straw against the south wall.

The race settled into a Holland-Rose-Mays strategy pace, and Ted edged into the first ten. At the half-way mark, they were 6th and still gaining. 22 laps later Ted challenged Bergere for fourth. It lasted for eleven laps and as Mays dropped out, Ted won the duel and was now third, and two laps behind the flying Holland.

Eight laps later, Ted had to stop for fuel. As the machine was being serviced, Ted jumped the low wall, flexed his hands, then rubbed his back. Seconds later he was away, now fourth.

50 miles to go. Cotton had his watches out. Holland went by and and one watch started. Rose flashed past and the second watch began to hum. The third watch ticked as Number 1 hit the line. Cotton picked up the first watch. Holland appeared. He reached for the second. Then came Rose. The third watch stopped as Ted came up. Then he read them. Holland, 112.899. Rose, 113.565. Ted, 118.741.

Rose completed his first extra lap as Ted got the checker. For the eighth year, he had qualified for the 100 mile club, and still had his first 500 to win. Holland was second, Ted third.

Tommy Milton was toastmaster at the victory banquet. Entertainingly blunt and to the point, Tommy, the first of the double Indianapolis victors had a difficult job. The feeling was high that the famous "ezy" signal mixup of the Lou Moore team which saw Rose nose Holland for the victory, would break out at this gathering. Tommy was not one to shirk his duty. With a few well chosen words, he paid his compliments to both the Blue Crown drivers, then raising his voice, Milton shouted, as if he dared any one to contradict him, "But every one of you here knows who drove the greatest race yesterday." All eyes turned towards the driver sitting with bowed head alongside Cotton Henning. Ted blushed and tied a shoe string.

Ted and Cotton shook hands that night and bade each other good-bye. Then Cotton cleared his throat. "Ted," he said, "I would like to ask you a question," and continued as he saw the look of respect in Ted's eyes, "That picture."

It wasn't a question. It was a statement. Ted answered, "I know Cotton, but what could I do? He was SUCH a swell guy."

Ted drove his Lincoln over the highway like a madman. He had wired Jug to meet him at Reading with Baby, and Ted was heading back for the dirt and the circuit he loved. The races were underway when Ted arrived, and he had to start last in the consolation. Then Ted's sense of humor returned. "The World's Champion last in the consy. Well, here's where I started back at Ascot, and those boys were a pretty good bunch too. Let's race." Ted won the event.

Hurrying to Paterson, Ted found the big car was not ready. In spite of all the Ted Horn Engineering skill, it did not make the 500, and now had to be built for dirt. That meant start from scratch again. Milwaukee and the first of the 100 mile championship event was hours away, and Ted said, " We'll sit this one out."

Those who witnessed the Milwaukee race, saw a great display of great driving. They also saw a determined man, Bill Holland. Bettenhausen grabbed the lead, followed by Holland 25 yards in the rear. Mays started late, then opened up. The Tinley Terror went to the pits, and out of the race on the 37th lap and Holland was leading. At this point Mays unlapped himself, and began drawing away from the easterner. Nip and tuck it was, and at the three-quarter pole everyone knew Mays could catch Holland. Near the finish he did, and as the flag fell, Holland was three-quarters of a length in front.

In Washington, Tom Smith, AAA statistician, marked up the standings in the title race. They read: Rose 1,000; Holland 1,000; Horn 700.

On the 15th, Ted and Baby were at the Grove. The pair now felt this was their home track, the last in a long row of famous speedways to play their host; Ascot, Hohokus, and now the Grove. On the 14th lap, Baby started to sputter, and Ted understood the language. The magneto had gone elsewhere, so Chitwood romped, with Light and Goss trailing. Langhorne coming up and the second championship 100 miler.

This time the big car was ready. Ted took a laconic 35.08 time trial. It placed him fourth. More and more the railbirds were to notice the Horn Offy not too impressive in the time trials, but actually outrunning the mark set up in the big event to follow. Ted started fourth.

Andres and Dinsmore dueled for the lead, after Mays had blown his motor. Then Dinsmore pulled in with an eye injury, and Bettenhausen took Andres for the lead. Holland was moving up fast, and Ted trailing in seventh spot. At the half way mark there was no change. The big blue and white No. 1 was not extending itself. Lap 69 and Tony Bettenhausen was done. It was Holland's race by two laps over Andres and Brown. Ted got the flag third, but a recheck of the tape showed him 5th.

Fate changed her board to read Holland 4, Horn 2 and Smith listed Holland 1,200; Rose 1,000; and Horn 800, in the AAA offices.

July was to be an exciting month. The big car got another overhaul in Paterson, then journeyed to Atlanta and the third 100 miler. The big track around the lake, the "No Fishing" sign, little George Robson and Barringer.

Rain entered the proceedings before race day, and Ted wondered if it was raining in Richmond, and on Jim's tennis courts.

Holland went to the front at once, and by the time Ted reached the backstretch, he knew he was in for another licking. The big car didn't have it, and Ted had a hunch. On the 75th lap Holland came in for a tire, and Brown forged to the front. Ted still cruised and as cars dropped out moved into fifth position. One lap was all Brown led, and then it happened. Ted watched from the backstretch as the car exploded and caught fire. He knew his hunch had been right.

Brown escaped injury, but the race was halted. The winner was Walt Ader, the former Horn team member, with Holland second and Eddie Zalucki third. Ted was a poor fourth. Fate wrote, Holland 5, Horn 2 and Smith recorded Holland 1,360, Rose 1,000, Horn 920.

This time the pair hurried to Paterson, and the midnight oil burned and the cops on the beat brought sandwiches and coffee to the always lit garages. All Paterson was holding its breath. Their champion was going down in defeat.

July 15th, Bainbridge in Ohio held the next event. It was the first titular AAA big car race in the Buckeye state in over ten years. Not since Ted and Baby had run well down the list at North Randall, back in the mid thirties, and before that the immortal Frank Lockhart.

Not many people were on hand. The rain bugaboo had put the race in the doubtful class, but those that were there, only had eyes for Holland.

The flag dropped and Brown assumed the lead. Holland had qualified in third spot and Ted fifth. Brown was winging, but Mays dropped out and Holland was second, with Ted yards behind. Lap 23 and Brown was done, Holland took charge. The gold No. 1 started to move. Four laps later the champ was in front. Paterson, the police and Ted's patience had paid off.

As the half-way mark was reached, the crowd rose to its feet. No. 1 was peeling a front tire. Jug was ready. So, too, was Mauri Rose. The little 500 winner was everywhere, helping everyone. Like the thoroughbred he is, the excitement of the competition had him its its grip. Ted slid to a stop and the Indianapolis winner grabbed the hammer in

Jug's hand and went to work. 18 seconds later he and Jug pushed the car on its way and Mauri looked up. "Who was that," he said.

Holland was leading, but No. 1 gaining. Ten seconds, nine, eight behind. Could he pass Holland? Mays couldn't, back at Milwaukee. They met and a white nose inched to the front

The track was heavy. Once out in front, the champ called on all his experience. Hard into the turns, then as the car drifted to the outside fence, a burst of speed, wheels spinning, and the last minute, before the inevitable crash, the knobbys would catch and the car jump forward. The master was teaching class that day.

Eight laps later the rains came. Horn first by a quarter lap, Holland, then Van Acker and Bettenhausen. The official scorer made out his report. Under speed average, he wrote 89. Under remarks, "Horn clocked 94.7 on 83rd lap."

A thoroughly tired and drenched reporter trudged into his office, wet, hungry, and empty handed. The editor looked up. "Get that interview with Horn?" he asked. The Cub hung his head. "Couldn't," he said, "It was raining buckets, and in five seconds there wasn't a person around," he lied. "What kind of a newshawk are you anyway?" came back the man sitting in the swivel chair, "You tired of your job?"

The reporter slumped before his typewriter. He was thinking. Yes he could have gotten the interview. The track did empty in five seconds—that is, all but for one man and about fifty youngsters. Just urchins they were. Probably sneaked in anyway, but they had discarded programs, slips of wet paper and wrappings in their hands and the man was standing alone in all that downpour, shaking the water out of his bushy blonde hair, wiping his eyes, and signing his name.

Not until the last youngster had clutched his soggy shred of paper to his breast and run for shelter did the man leave the track. And the reporter tip-toed down out of the press box, and spoke in a whisper to himself. There is a great man —a Champion.

BEAUTY HAS TROUBLE

Fate erased the clean spot after the name Horn, and wrote, Holland 5, Horn 3, and Smith scratched Holland 1,520, Horn 1,120, Rose 1,000, and in the fire house at Paterson, a sleepy guardian of the night chalked the standings under the work schedule for the week.

Milwaukee was coming up for its second championship race. Holland had the pole and Ted was back in the field. The two men were now eyeing each other out of respect. Both were determined. The challenger, and the Champion.

Holland traveled only 25 feet, when the Peters Offy ground out its gears in the Wisconsin soil. No. 1 was moving. 27 laps and the low qualifiers had the lead. He set a blinding pace. Cars trying to catch him blew apart. Mays, Dinsmore, Fohr, Ader. The field dwindled. Four laps to go and the blue and white beauty was two laps ahead of Van Acker. Then the motor stopped.

Two gallons of oil and water spilled onto the track. Beauty opened up her sides and got sick all over the track. Ted rolled into the pits. The official finish, Van Acker, Nalon, Russo. Ted was awarded sixth.

Fate shook her head as she wrote Holland 5, Horn 4. Smith doodled, Holland 1,520, Horn 1,200.

Ted was glad to get back to Paterson and take Baby to Dover. In 30 laps Ted had passed the second place driver, Light, and won handily. The day before Goshen, the pair faced the starter at Middletown, but Brown couldn't be handled that day, and they had to be content with second. Holland was elsewhere.

Horse running Goshen was overfilled. The Horn-Holland duel was now taking on the aspects of a blanket finish. Bill's car developed trouble before the racing started, and Duke Dinsmore gave up his chance to drive in order that the duel might continue.

Ted again had a miserable time trial, and was far back as Andres and Hansen traded the lead. Holland dueled Bettenhausen for third place, then Hansen gave up the ghost. Soon Andres followed Hansen and it was Holland ahead. Ted got the go from Jug and opened. The starter had just signaled with crossed flags — the half way mark — when Holland slowed, done for the day. This placed Ted third behind Bettenhausen and Brown. The white car was eating up the distance—a half mile on the leader now, and Brown fell out. Now Ted was second.

That was the standing at the finish, with Steve Truchan third. Bettenhausen had again scored at his favorite track, but this time did it in world's record time. 1.04:51.08. 92.54 MPH. Holland was awarded 10th. Fate and Smith went to work. The former wrote Holland 5, Horn 5, and the latter, Holland 1,560, Horn 1,360. Getting closer.

The Grove was running night races. Baby liked her sleep, but Ted and Baby stayed up this night. After leading for 18 laps, a Cherokee came out of William Penn's woods and went on the warpath. That path was at the Grove, and Baby paid silent respect as Chitwood flashed to victory. The pair saved their scalp with second.

The third Milwaukee championship race was next, and it highlighted the annual fair. Here it was that Ted first ground the dust for Pappy Hankinson. There were MacKenzie, Billy Winn and Chet Gardner in those days. Ted was just another name on the program, but today it was different. Locked in a death struggle with a challenger who wouldn't give up was Ted, the defending Champion, and to this point a beaten one.

The Horn Engineering Special went to the front. The mercury hovered near the 100 mark, and soon it seeped into the cockpit. 11 laps and Andres pushed in front, with Ted trailing. The heat was unbearable, and Ted kept looking for Holland.

Rain clouds came over the grandstand, and Jug looked up. Before the race Ted had told him, "I'll pace this one, unless you think an emergency is coming." Jug looked at the clouds. He knew the boss would move when ready but back at Bainbridge, sudden rain had helped. This, Jug thought, was the emergency. The "GO" came out.

Almost effortless, the white nose edged towards the outside. In the turn it slid even farther, then as the backstretch unwound, cut sharply to the corner. The white car laid its ears back and flew. Midway of the stretch it was leading.

Ted raised his right arm to Andres, then flew to the finish flag.

Order of finish was Horn, Nalon, Connor. The clutch on Andres' Belanger had given out on the 90th lap.

Ted sunk to the ground and used the wet towel Jug threw him to wipe his face. He was hot and tired. Never had he felt so all-in. Andres congratulated him, then Holland, who had gathered his share of bad luck that day of heat.

Ted dressed slowly. He was thinking as a friend approached. "Why the wave back, Ted? I thought you were having trouble." The grin came out as Ted spoke. "I knew it was hot. I had seen Ike Welch throw a bucket of water on Holmes as he came in, and I was really suffering. I figured Emil was too, and I didn't know if Beauty could take him in one lap or not. So, I held on with one hand and waved with the other. Kind of thought maybe he figured I was pretty fresh and wouldn't give me trouble. But really I was hanging on and praying."

The old Tommy Milton Indianapolis trick, when he and Roscoe Sarles had hooked into such a duel on such a day. Milton won that one too. Only a veteran and a Champion would remember it.

Smith was deluged with telegrams as he answered each, Holland 1,560, Horn 1,560. The Champion had fought back.

Thompson closed the month with a big event. Again Baby was panting at the finish, and Holland looked back and waved. The finish was Holland, Shackleford, Horn.

Only Fate changed the score. Her board read Horn 6, Holland 6.

August opened with the tie-breaking championship scheduled for Springfield, Illinois on the 20th. Ted was nervous. The back was bothering anyway, and dozens of races were on tap. He ordered Baby groomed for the job, packed and headed for Flemington.

Wallard couldn't be held that day, and Ted saluted the spot along the rail, where so many years ago a little child ran onto the track, and Chet Gardner through the fence. Holland worked hard to get third behind Ted. Fate noted the race.

At Rutland, Vermont, Baby struck her gait after dusting off Hinnershitz and Mattson. That was the finish. At Port Royal, two days later, Brown Mattson at the checker; otherwise it was the same.

At the Grove, and the Robson Memorial race, the pair met Holland again before 24,841 people, and it was Holland's race with Mattson following Horn. Fate was still recording.

Four days later, before 40,000 partisan people at Reading, Ted and Baby gave their all, with Holland trailing. Earlier, in the heats, Baby had to be content with second. A tall race driver, pushing No. 4 Burd Piston Ring job, had stuck his long leg clear out to the radiator, to keep ahead of the little gold No. 1. This driver had it, and as the cars pulled in, Ted went over to where the blonde giant was removing his gloves, and shook hands, laughing, "Well Freddy, you can stick with any of them now. Just beat the champ. How about a match race and let me look good?" Freddy grinned, jerking his thumb over his shoulder towards the stands said, "OK Ted, now were even, but thanks anyway." Deep down Freddy knew they weren't even, but he felt Ted wanted him to think so, and he paid his respects in this manner. "Always looking out for the other fellow," he remarked to his stooge, "none of us coming up will ever draw even."

Springfield drew the same championship field and the same unfavorable weather. After the usual lead changing, the race settled down into Beauty chasing Bettenhausen. Lap after lap the pair reeled off in equal time, the Chicagoan always in front. Holland had again dropped out.

Many watched from the pits, and Nalon joined that of his fellow townsman, Bettenhausen. Only these veterans knew how demanding the struggle had become. Lead-footed Tony and sure-footed Ted. Finally it came, the familiar "GO" from the spotless Horn pit. Inch by inch Beauty closed the gap, then inch by inch dropped back. Again the two cars drew close, and again they separated. It was the competition Ted had always loved, and Bettenhausen was giving his best.

TIE BROKEN

Nalon, The Iron Duke, was the first to spot it. The colorful veteran of hundreds of such duels, who had catapulted into that dust cloud at Nashville ten years ago, when only a youngster. He watched No. 1 intently as it rounded the turn—then glanced at the driver's face, and he knew. Almost reluctantly he scratched on Bettenhausen's board, (HORN'S TIRED—R. U.?)

Bouncing Tony sunk a little deeper in the seat, grabbed the wheel just a little tighter, and grinned. He had the race and he knew it. So did Nalon, and so did Ted.

Had Ted known, he would have little cared that an ethereal and a mortal being were writing his name at that moment. Fate wrote Horn 9, Holland 7; Smith wrote Horn 1,760, Holland 1,620. The tie was broken and the champ was in front with only one race to go, but what had been the cost?

Ted drove slowly back towards Paterson. At Pendleton he stopped to see his old friend George Burch. Twenty years before, he and Ted had hitch-hiked to those first races Ted drove—back in the early California days. More often than not they were hungry and dirty, but twenty years had worked lots of changes. Ted now was the Champion, and well on his way to financial independence. Burch was a prominent jeweler in his community. The pair talked of the old days and laughed at their misfortunes.

Johnny Hyland was there too, George's photographer. Johnny had a ready smile, so Ted liked him. Ted wasn't smiling too much these days, but he liked those who did.

Out in front of the jewelry store, the Lincoln was parked. On the back was the familiar "Ted Horn, Champion Racing Driver." Dickie Dyer saw it, and before his timidness hit, found himself inside the store, looking for the Champ. Ted spied him at once, and dropped his conversation. Dick was a newsboy at the tracks, and had often hoped to see the Champ.

"Hiya," grinned Ted, and the youngster's face lit. He bolted from the store to tell his friends of his fortune, and Ted Horn was the immediate god of Pendleton's younger set.

Ted rose to go. "I'm going to Dayton in a couple weeks, but first I'm going to get a little rest. Getting lazy I guess. I'll see you then, but sure hope you and Johnny decide to go along to Texas," was his parting shot.

The couple weeks' rest seemingly did Ted worlds of good. Baby too knew it. At Dayton, Spider Webb had held for many weeks. In fact was far out in front of the point standings, and headed for the mid-western title Babe Stapp once had held. There was no denying, he was king and he looked for another clean sweep at Dayton, this Sunday.

Glancing up from his work, Spider spied an unfamiliar truck and race car heading towards the infield and the pits. His eyes followed its course, as did everyone's. There were no words spoken and the strange ensemble neared pit row. Spider broke the silence, "Brother, er, er . . . it's gonna be hell 'round here today."

It was Jug and Baby.

Spider had one word for it, but the papers told it differently.

"Tramping Ted Horn gave the accelerator of his Offenhauser Special an extra kick as the field of 10 cars went into the first turn and for the next 20 laps sprayed dirt and burned rubber into the faces of his fellow chauffeurs, scoring a quarter length victory in the big car feature at Dayton Speedway.

"Terrible Teddy, the national racing king, was just out for a Sunday afternoon 100 mile-an-hour joy ride as he captured the feature, shattering the track record which was marked up just a month ago by Spider Webb. Yesterday, Webb was literally tooted off the track by The Horn, finishing a sad second.

"In the qualifying heat, Horn set a new track one lap record of 21.84 for the half mile plus 289 yard track. And in his eight lap qualifier, he cracked a third record, touring the distance in 7.36:63.

"Jackie Holmes was third, Walt Ader fourth, Freddy Carpenter fifth, Johnny Shackleford sixth, Norm Hauser seventh, George Metzler eight, Jimmy Lynch ninth, Billy Cantrell tenth."

Spider Webb had the word for it all right. It was the same manner in which Sherman once described war.

On October 19th, the Grove ran its big trophy race of 50 laps. This was the race Ted wanted to win the year previously and lost, but this time Baby was not to be denied. At the finish they had a wide margin over Hinnershitz and Holmes, and another record—one that Nalon had set.

On the 26th, Ted appeared at Charlotte for the final two days of the Exposition. Every track now was closed, and following this event would come the final big championship race in Texas. The one that would end the Horn-Holland point duel and settle the national crown.

Baby scored both days of the Exposition. Chitwood was second and Rodgers third the first day, Brown and Carpenter the second. Then, with the good wishes of Joie and Freddy ringing in his ears, Ted set the wheels of the Lincoln towards Arlington and Texas.

The Texas race was important in many ways. First, it was being promoted and underwritten by Babe Stapp and Freddy Lockwood. Remember Stapp? Ted did, very well. The heavy footed Indianapolis veteran, and Ascot luminary, when Ted was first starting. The same Egbert Stapp who, on Ted's first trip east, back in 1934, had given him his car. The one that went for the world's record at Salt Lake. Who, along with Harry Hartz, had first tabbed the hungry kid with the platinum mustache as potentially a great driver.

Then too, this race, the first AAA national point affair to be held west of the Mississippi in over ten years, was to tell if the west, and in particular Texas, would support big time racing. In many ways it was important.

To the nation, it held the long awaited decision whether Horn would successfully defend his title, or whether Holland would succeed. Horn could cinch the crown with a fifth or better in the race, regardless of Holland's fortune, and many were betting that was the plan of action the Horn stable had mapped.

But those people didn't know Ted Horn. To Ted it was the return of a Champion, back home. In it he saw the chance to return and score his greatest triumph in the land he had failed before. The chance to return many favors he felt unpaid and the chance to advance the sport he now headed and loved so well.

Race day, it rained. Ted remained another week and helped the Babe. He visited newspaper offices and gave interviews. Appeared at luncheons in his honor and all told, distributed much good will for the sport.

November 2nd dawned cloudy and cold. Ted's heart went out for Babe and Lockwood. Only too well did he know the experience of watching those skies, through a promoter's eyes. Nevertheless, he dressed in a uniform he had worn only once all year. It was the spotless whites, with Bennett Brothers inscribed on the back. Wasn't Texas the home of the sponsors of Henning's cars, and if Ted won, wouldn't lots of pictures be taken? Well, he reasoned, it might make Texas folks a bit happy if the winner, and National Champion was in the livery of one of their own citizens. Then, too, that would make Cotton happy. Yes, Ted thought of everyone.

Beauty protested little as Ted qualified with an average of 95.56. It was third fastest as Nalon scored 96.28 and picked up the first trophy. Railbirds' eyes opened a bit at Ted's performance. Earlier, Holland had been declared out of the race with a sick car. Ted could very easily back into the title, but this didn't look like it. A champion didn't back into anything. At least, not a champion in Ted's book. In spite of the threatening weather and cold atmosphere a goodly crowd was on hand. Some gave it as 25,000. George and Johnny were there and greeted Ted as he changed shoes for the race. Ted had a dime in his hand and was placing it in the shoe.

Babe Stapp drove the pace car and Seth Klein served as starter. It was truly a second Indianapolis and well it should be. Notables of every station in racing attended, as this was the payoff race. There could be no appealing the decision.

Nalon shot to the front, closely followed by Bettenhausen, then Beauty. As the pack hit the backstretch, Nalon moved away, while the rest strung out in order. By the 25th

TWO STRAIGHT CHAMPIONSHIPS

lap, Nalon had lapped all but Ted and Tony, and on the next lap, edged past the blue and white No. 1. "Stroking for a finish," said the railbirds as the big car carrying No. 1 flashed by. But, they were wrong, very wrong.

Lap 42 and Nalon was done. A wheel, then the motor quit, and again it was Bettenhausen one, Horn two. The big Beauty did not gain, but Ted kept glancing at his pit and for the familiar signal.

The halfway found the Tinley Express pitted, and the railbirds gave in. "Horn can coast now," they said, and Jug seemed to agree as he watched every circle of the big car through half open eyes.

But speed was picking up. Not the field but the lead car. It looked as if all cars were being drawn towards No. 1. Soon the field was lapped. Then the same illusion all over again. Now Horn had the field lapped twice. Jug was standing straight, with both fists clenched. Again No. 1 was drawing them in, and just as Klein waved the white flag, passed Russo in second place — the winner by three laps.

It was Ted's greatest hour. His greatest triumph. The fruitful ending to a long hard fight. The fight of a Champion, a real Champion. One who never gave up. When the sky was the darkest, he fought the hardest. That was the manner of a Thoroughbred and a Champion. Ted had repeated, and now was not just a Champion, but a Great Champion. Rex had repeated, and he was great. Wilbur had repeated and he was great. Lou had repeated, and he was great. Now Ted had joined that circle — his spirits were high.

Babe grabbed the smiling Champion and almost single handed lifted him from the cockpit. Jug, with the ever ready wet towel, was pushed into the background. A milling, surging mob surrounded the car. Half dragging and half lifting, the eddy of human bodies surged towards a platform. Ted reached right and left grasping hands. One was that of Bill Holland, and Ted watched as he too was swallowed up in the mass of humanity. It was a cheering and gesticulating mob and as the camera bulbs flashed, Ted reached down to help the Iron Duke to the platform, and his trophy.

Tears were in George's eyes as he perched on a truck and watched the demonstration. There he was, after all these years, waving and smiling down on the rest of the world. Alone, at the top of the pile. His face was drawn and his hair was darker and the lines on his face, he had noticed back in Pendleton, a month before, were still there, but Ted was smiling. It wasn't the same smile exactly, the eyes didn't narrow as they used to. The lids were physically tired, but it was a real smile.

Jug too gave up the fight and languished at the edge of the crowd. The boss had done it and the boss was happy, and that was all that mattered. Ted's eyes searched for those that were close to him, but there were too many people. So he nodded and smiled and waved some more, and he was happy.

Destiny rose from her chair. The cards were all face up now. No longer was there a question of Fate's choice at the beginning. The two aces Fate held, were Horn and Rose. The discarded ace with the two spot was Holland. Second at Indianapolis to Rose, and second to Horn in the championship. The joker was Fate's manner of indicating her play.

George and Johnny rode back to Indiana in the Lincoln with Ted. That was his wish, and Jug loaded the big car on the truck for its trip back. Ted wanted to talk. He had a lot inside he had to get out, and it was this friend of twenty years standing that he wanted to tell. Johnny sat in the back seat, held the huge trophy and just listened.

The two talked of many things. First, they re-lived those heart breaking California years. Names Johnny had never heard. Stanyer, Balmer, Smith, Rienke, Boyce, Hafferly. Then they became familiar; Gordon, Stubblefield, Spangler, Triplett—let's see, wasn't he some sort of a Champion too? The voices droned on and Johnny got drowsy.

Suddenly, the car lurched as if in trouble. It was snowing slightly and they were heading into it. Here and there ice spots appeared, and Johnny knew they had been traveling 80. Ted righted the car without slowing, with his left arm. Always he drove with the one arm. Johnny wondered,

Arlington Downs, Texas, 1948. In a happy mood, Ted is shown here holding the Whelan Memorial Trophies after winning for the second time the 100-mile American dirt track championship. — Acme Photo

Famous Indianapolis personalities 1948. L. to R.: Ted Horn, Jack Mehan, Chief Steward, Wilbur Shaw, President Indianapolis Speedway, and Seth Klein, Starter.

Coming in from a practice lap, Indianapolis, 1948. — Lytle Photo.

was it Lewistown that did that, or Nashville. Ascot maybe. Ted was laughing and his voice came back clear, "You know George, Mother Nature is no respecter of World Champion drivers. In this ice and snow I am just as lost as any novice." Johnny glanced at the illuminated speedometer. It said 95. He glanced at the oncoming traffic. He didn't drowse anymore, and the huge trophy shrunk a little at the grip that was around it.

George was asking about the dime in the shoe. "Just a habit I formed," Ted answered. "Anytime I find a piece of money at a race track, it goes in the car with me. Lucky, you know."

"Ted," George asked, "Tell me, you didn't use to be superstitious. Some people think only the ignorant are superstitious." Ted thought a long time before answering. Johnny held his breath. He knew this was the real truth that was coming. Only two people who had climbed the long, hard road these two had traveled could talk without the apologetic explanations that only rang half true.

"I don't exactly know, George," the words were coming slow now, "but I do know that the people who really are ignorant are those who pass judgement on matters of which they themselves can't explain. Jimmy Murphy's last ride was a puzzle. His kind of a driver didn't ask for it. I had the same thing at Hohokus once. Then those peanuts at Nashville and the green truck. Red Campbell and Robson with the pictures, and the regular cycle things happen. You can almost tell when it will be. Then something inside me doesn't just click right. Some call them hunches, and I've always found mine right. I can't tell what it will be, but it always is something. Truthfully George, I can't say that this stuff has any bearing on happenings, but I find if I perform them my mind is free for the race, and that's one thing I learned long ago. Never, never race unless your mind is perfectly free. Not only your life but others depend on it."

There was a long silence. "Is that the reason you never eat before a race Ted?"

"No, definitely not." Ted continued. "That's the way things get changed. One time I was heading back to the coast. I hadn't won a race all year and I was too proud to borrow money to get back. The season had closed and I read of a race in Phoenix. I counted my money and thought I had enough to get to Phoenix, if I didn't eat. So I filled the tank and left. Then in the race I found my reactions sharper. I won it by thinking faster than the other fellow, so I've never eaten since on race day."

George laughed. "I wondered what you were going to tell me. I heard that one before, only I heard that when you got to Phoenix you had fifty cents left. Instead of eating, you bought a can of polish and cleaned your car. Right?"

"Yeah, that's right and that brings up another thing George. A lot of young fellows today forget their appearance, especially here in the east. You remember that time I drove the Puckett Atlas Chrome Special at Ascot, and it got the cup for being the best appearing car? I was awfully proud that night, but it was Puckett who really won it. That taught me a lesson, 'cause Puckett got 32 bucks, and in those days that looked to me like enough to retire on."

"Now, you said it Ted. When you gonna retire?"

"I don't know. Not this season anyway. This winter I'll know how much I made this year and I think it was quite a lot. Probably enough at least to take care of my family if anything happens to me. But when I do no one will know it in advance, and I assure you, once I hang up the tack, I won't be back, ever. First Ernie, then . . ." and he didn't finish the sentence.

Then he continued. "I have a couple of goals set. When I reach them, maybe I'll quit. If I don't reach my goals, then I'll quit when I no longer feel I can win races—when I lose my touch. There's De Paolo, Meyer and Shaw. It can be Horn too."

"My God Ted, you're the Champion, what higher goal can you set? Indianapolis?"

"Indianapolis? Yes, I guess that is one, but it doesn't matter too much now. My record there ought to be good enough to trade in for one victory. Next year I'm going to set a 120 average, and if that doesn't do it, I don't know what will. My goals George, may sound funny. Once I wanted to be a Champion. Then to repeat. Now, it's to keep it. That, you know is a lot harder. No one has ever kept it, and no one ever took it three years in a row. I'm even with Rex now, and if I can get it again it will be the first time I ever had a margin on him. He's a great competitor George, the toughest. We don't talk much but we understand. Rex is still a champion in my book.

"But George, I think my biggest goal is to do something for the kids. The little underprivileged urchins that haunt every race track. I don't know how I'll do it yet, some sort of a fund or something, but its gotta be done. I went over fences too, once, and sometimes a kid gets the feeling that is the way to go through life. Those kids George, are the life blood of racing. Ten years from now it will be they that are paying the admissions. We have to do something for them. Baseball has their "knot hole plan" and we have to do it too."

"But Ted, you're only one person. How can you do all this and besides, baseball has the newspaper backing, and we don't."

The Lincoln picked up speed now as it sensed the driver had a point to sell.

"I'm the Champion, aren't I? If I don't do it, who then? And as for the newspapers, that's our fault. You remember back in L. A. the time of the big kidnapping? We were wrong George, in that we didn't recognize the fact it was just one man's campaign to sell papers. We fought him like a bunch of wild Indians and we couldn't win. We didn't try to tell our story, we just got mad and fought. Today a different bunch is writing sports, but we don't play ball with them. We lie to them, tell them anything and don't really let them know this sport is as honest and as good as any they write about. Those guys are just trying to make a living too, not hurt us."

"But Ted, even if they are new—the fatalities!"

"Has anyone ever pointed out to them the lack of fatalities? Look at this year. More championship races than ever before, and not one fatality. All new records too. George, if the truth is really known, football kills more every year than we do, but ours is more spectacular. That's why it gets the headlines."

"You counting midgets, Ted?"

"Midgets—you know my thoughts on them—let's skip it."

"This plan Ted. Any ideas at all?"

"No, only to talk to some friends who know of such things. Roy Richwine for one, and Pappy—say, Pappy Hankinson would know how to do it. He'd have the kids selling tickets or something, or patching the fence and he'd get a big bang out of it." Ted had a laugh, then continued, "Some guy over in Milwaukee phoned me about a mechanical race car of some sort he wanted to make. I told him to go see Cotton, but think I'll stop and see him this winter when I come to Chicago. The NADA convention . . . you going?"

It was getting light now. The two friends had talked the night out. George never answered the question, "Darn it, you aren't racing today Ted. When we gonna eat? There's a lunch wagon up ahead, let's get some coffee. Awake Johnny?"

Daylight came and traffic thickened. Now they were in a big city and weaving from light to light. Suddenly a panel body truck pulled alongside. Ted was pocketed next to the curb. Traffic moved forward but the truck kept the car in the pocket, and the driver was grinning and pointing.

"You gonna let that lug keep you here Ted?" George asked.

Ted grinned. "He saw the sign on the back I guess, you know the one, World's Champion Race Driver? Now he has the world's champ in a pocket and he's happy. Yeah, I'm gonna stay here. If that's what it takes to make one person happy, pocket the champ, then I stay pocketed. There'll be one happy person today," but George knew there were two.

Back in Paterson a celebration was waiting. Civic honors had been prepared, and the affair was to be held at a big open air gathering, but it rained. Ted left for the races in Florida, and for a bit of fishing before winding up the season. When he left, however, he wrote a letter to the local Editor. The Editor then wrote a column entitled, "Ted Horn Extends Thanks to Old Timers and Friends."

"Ted Horn, Paterson's National Auto Racing Champion was never one to be unappreciative of any favor or any honor bestowed upon him. As a result he was deeply disappointed last Friday night when the program, at which he was presented a plaque by the Old Timers A. A. of Paterson was rained out before he could express his thanks.

"Having engagements that will keep him out of town for several days, Horn has written to us to relay his thanks to his many local well-wishers. His letter follows:"

> I certainly consider it a great honor to receive this beautiful plaque from the Old Timers' Athletic Association, Inc., of Greater Paterson. The presentation was marred by the rain which also stopped the full program.
>
> In accepting this token of good will from the Old Timers of Paterson, I don't want to accept it for myself alone but want to include also the many friends and associates without whose help and cooperation I couldn't have accomplished what I did. It isn't possible for me to remember every detail over these years nor each individual, but those I can't forget are my immediate crew at my shop—Dick Simonek my chief mechanic and shop manager, his son Charlie who works with us, and Wallace Cornforth, whom everybody calls "Jug," a nickname he acquired from Ronnie Householder when he was just a little fellow; my close personal friend the late Fred Peters, "Pappy" Hill who helps us out at his machine shop with work we can't handle in our own shop, and always forgets to send a bill, and all the many friends that I have all over Paterson, who have helped me time and again with various favors.
>
> And I have to include the Paterson Police Department. They've been very considerate and lenient when we had to fire up a car at 4 or 5 a.m. after working all night to make a race the next day. I don't know how they quieted down the neighbors but they did, and even brought coffee and hamburgers when I had to work all night making a crankshaft and couldn't leave the shop while the lathes were running. I'll try to back up this great honor by winning the AAA National Championship for the third consecutive year which so far has never been done. And I'm going to keep trying till I win that Indianapolis race too, so we can have an Indianapolis winner in Paterson. And many thanks to you too, Bob.

Ted won at Macon and Jacksonville, setting new records both places, then bowed to Chitwood at Atlanta when Baby gave out — too tired from too long a season.

At Indianapolis 1935. Ted and Bo Huckman in the Ford entry.

At Indianapolis 1936. L. to R.: Hartz, Wolf and Ted.

At Indianapolis 1937. L. to R.: Harry Hartz, Dean and Ted.
Tower Studios Photos

At Indianapolis in the Thorne-Sparks car 1941.

At Indianapolis in the Maserati 1946.

At Indianapolis in the Maserati 1947.

At Indianapolis in the Maserati 1948.

Tower Studios Photos

Above: Indianapolis 1938. Shown alongside the car are Ted Horn and Harry Hartz (in cap). At Hartz' left is Riley Brett. Ted won 4th Place.

At Indianapolis 1939 in the Boyle-Miller. — Kirkpatrick

At Indianapolis 1940 in the Boyle-Miller.
— Bell — Tower Studios Photos.

Candid shot at Indianapolis, 1948. L. to R.: Tom Frost, member A.A.A. Contest Board, Floyd Clymer, Motor Book Publisher, and Ted Horn, American Racing Champion.

Ted Horn and Bill Holland exchange congratulations as Pop Myers (extreme right) announces awards. Man with pipe and hands on hips is Mauri Rose, famed Blue Crown Special winner. Taken in 1948.

Left to right: Jimmy Jackson, Ted Horn, George Connor, Gordon Schroeder, Peter DePaolo, unidentified, Mrs. Rudi Caracciola, Cotton Henning, Otto Wolfer, Curly Wetteroth and Ray Howard. Photo taken at Indianapolis Speedway, 1948.

— Lytle Photos.

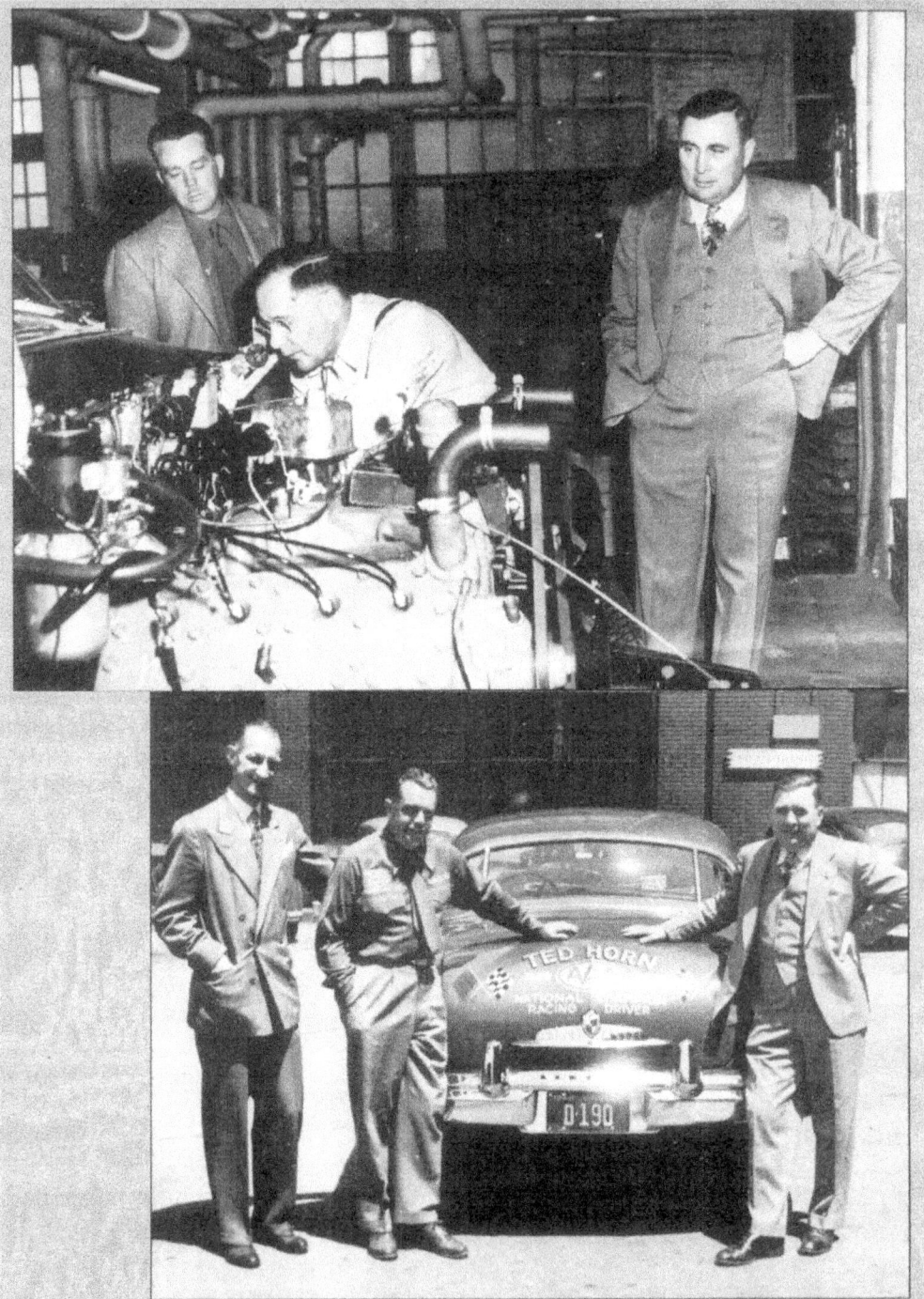

Top photo shows an employee of the Ford Motor Company, Lincoln-Mercury Division, giving a final check-up on the Lincoln Cosmopolitan being delivered in 1948 to Horn. L. to R.: Ted, Ford employee, and Frost.

Lower photo shows Ted Horn taking delivery of 1948 Lincoln Cosmopolitan purchased from Tom Frost. Ted considered the sign on the rear of the car important as a contribution to popularizing automobile racing. L. to R.: Mr. Mackey of the Ford Motor Company, Ted and Tom Frost.

— Photos from Frost Collection.

CHAPTER VII

The Year of Fate

There was little time for fishing, this winter. Following the Jacksonville race, Ted sent Jug to Paterson while he stopped in Virginia to see Tom Frost. Now that the excitement at winning the title for the second time was over, inwardly Ted showed the effects of his hard campaign. Outwardly, the Florida sunshine and salt air had made a temporary change.

Ted had ordered a new highway car, and expected to pick it up in Virginia. This time there was no need for his apologetic explanation for the lettering on the back. It was changed slightly—now reading, TED HORN, NATIONAL AUTO RACING CHAMPION DRIVER, 1946-47. Modest crossed flags were included.

Eventually, the conversation led to the inevitable question. "What are your plans now Ted, going to keep on?"

"Can't say yet," Ted answered, "I want to see the schedule first. Of course I'll make Indianapolis, and all the championship events, but I do believe I'll cut down some on the small races. I'll make the Grove of course, and Reading and places like that, but I have so much other activity now that I believe I will devote some time to it."

"What, for instance."

"Well, I'm heading for a convention right now, then there's a radio program for Firestone and I want to take some part in the Soap Box Derbies. There are a lot of places that need me for personal appearances, and racing needs that too. I feel it is the duty of the champion. Along with the testimonials, it all pays me about as much as racing, so right now that is my mind."

That was the opening Tom wanted and his next question was not hurried.

"Ted, I heard that you turned down some testimonials. Is that true, or don't you want to say?"

Ted looked up, and in his straightforward manner answered, "Yes, I did. They were for cigarettes and liquor. I don't use either you know, but I felt there were too many youngsters who look up to me now, and I would be setting a pretty poor example for them, advocating liquor and smoking."

A year ago a cub reporter had said it. Now a business man said it, but to himself. "He is a Champion. A great Champion."

Ted stopped in Paterson, and put the finishing touches on Beauty. The big car was going on the stage now, and her every crevice was spotless. The NADA convention in Chicago would display the car which had twice won the National Championship, and its owner would be part of the display. Here was the first of those all important appearances Ted spoke about.

Ted stopped in Milwaukee and met Archie Smith. That was "the fellow who wanted to make a mechanical race car toy." Ted liked what he saw. It was to be an exact duplicate of the Maserati, and it wound up on the side and glided silently on its real rubber tires. "Just what the kids like," said Ted, "I'll have papers drawn at once. If you need help in any manner, money or publicity, let me know. You can always get a line on me by calling Paterson." That was the Ted Horn Speedway Special, which made its appearance at many track concessions. Ted knew he would like it because the man smiled. Then too, it was for kids.

At the convention, all of the Horn enthusiasm was unleashed. Displays lined both sides of a great hall, and the crowds surged from side to side, examining each object, and offering themselves as targets for the displayer's sales line. Ted was selling too. He was selling his sport. "Yes, that is the car . . . Oh, it'll do quite a bit over a hundred . . . No it hasn't run at Indianapolis, but it could . . . Yes, the championship is won at Indianapolis, as well as other events around the country . . . Well, I was lucky enough to win it . . . Oh, I'm old enough all right," and Ted showed his white teeth . . .

That was the way it went. It was a tiring ordeal for ordinary people, but Ted seemed to get stronger as the time lengthened. Other booths worked in shifts, but the Champion stayed on his feet, behind the felt rope, explained and answered questions by the score.

Ted was giving a technical description of a Meyer-Drake motor at one end of the display when another group surged to the opposite end. Just looking. A high pitched feminine voice called out, "Oh look, what is it, a midget?" Ted halted a sentence mid-way. Turning his head slightly, and with a look that would do justice to any insulted person said, with emphasis on the first and fifth word, "THAT, ma'am, is a RACE car" . . .

Ted flew to the Contest Board banquet and gracefully accepted his second championship medal. It was a beautiful thing, in gold, platinum and diamonds. On the reverse side was lettered:

1947
FIRST PRIZE
Awarded to
TED HORN
Contest Board
AAA

The medal hung from a red, white and blue ribbon, held by a bar lettered, "Championship Award." The medal itself, represented an automobile tire and wheel surmounted by the torch and wings of Mercury. From the wheel, wrought in gold, was suspended the National shield in which set a blazing diamond. Curled about the shield, a wreath of green gold. In the center of the wheel, covering the hub and portion of the spokes, the National Emblem of AAA, worked in platinum.

As Ted gazed at this thing of beauty he thought, Resta, Cooper, Mulford, Wilcox, Chevrolet, Milton, Murphy, De Paolo, Hartz, Meyer, Arnold, Schneider, Carey, Cummings, Petillo, Rose, Shaw, Roberts, Mays—all had worn it, and now he, the hungry kid that was stopped by a cop back in California, was wearing it, and he filled with humbleness.

The Specialist this time seemed gruff and hasty. In school, Ted had seen the teacher display the same manner when one of the pupils disobeyed. "Rest does a lot of good," Ted said, half begging for some word of encouragement, "This year I don't intend to drive as much." The Specialist merely mumbled a reply and never looked up.

Back in Paterson, the shop was again burning lights at night. Ted himself was working. Always, when any part was to be replaced, it was Ted who made the final decision. Even back in the days when dollars were scarce, if anything new had to go on Baby, it would be the best money could buy. Now sometimes even the best was not good enough, and when that happened, Ted made the part himself.

But, as if he knew, this was to be the big year, Ted groomed both cars minutely. He grinned when he thought of the scuttlebutt around some tracks, of his secret formula for fuel. Someone believed that, too, because at one track a man had offered him one thousand dollars for his barrel on hand, and ten thousand if he would include the formula. "Just Lynnfuel and some bug juice mixed, and good common sense setting a carburetor," Ted said. Yes, the bug juice, plus the knowledge of a carburetion genius, and the slide rule. Ted had taught himself the use of the rule, and now his clearances and ring sizes and such were set, only after careful study.

About the rings. Ted was still writing letters, but now they contained much technical data that he had found the answer on in racing, as well as plugs and other sponsors' products. Once he had taken Beauty to Indianapolis, when the snow had just been cleared, and ran a tire test. This, Ted thought, was the real reason racing had been established, and he was doing his unsolicited part to the hilt. He frowned when he thought of the companies not using the Speedway. "They're really missing the boat," he said.

In February, Ted went to New York to be interviewed during the "Voice of Firestone" program. A script was prepared with the stock questions and answers. Much had to do with his career and he did all right for the first few questions.

JAMES: This evening, we have with us one of the most colorful and most skillful race drivers in America. In 1946 and 1947 he won the national championship by compiling more points in American Automobile Association competitions than any other man on the track. It is an honor and a pleasure to introduce to you the National Champion race driver of the United States, Ted Horn.

HORN: Thank you Hugh. It's a real pleasure for me to be here.

JAMES: Ted, I understand you have been racing ever since you were fifteen years old.

HORN: Yes, I have been at it for twenty-three years.

JAMES: Have you driven on the dirt tracks as well as on the paved speedways?

HORN: Yes, I've driven about every type race that's run.

JAMES: Isn't it a fact Ted, that it takes years of experience to acquire the skill necessary to win the national championship?

HORN: That's right Hugh. And it takes more than skill. It takes the very best of cars and the very best of tires.

Ted had jumped the script. He was so anxious to do his part, execute his right to advise, that in return for one of racing's benefactors, Ted was launching right into a tire selling campaign.

Baby and Beauty were both ready. Not only spotless on the outside, but under the hood, every part inside and out of the motor was gleaming. This year Beauty and Baby would be on display more than ever. They had to set the style.

Beauty went to Atlanta, late in March, for the season opener. A program of sprints, not the championship title chase. That would come later. A phone call was waiting Ted when he arrived at the track. It was a frantic man. His son was ill, and for days now had been talking only of when the Champ would come to Atlanta. Wouldn't Ted please come to see him?

Ted was scheduled to the hilt. Another radio interview. Then the cardinal rule, race day, only business until the race was over. Ted suggested the youngster be brought to the track. It was arranged and Ted saw to it that the car was to be placed directly behind his pit.

The Pettillo family arrived on schedule, and Ted's heart swelled as he saw the youngster. His first act was to purchase one of the little race cars, made in his name, and give it to the boy. At the end of each heat, Ted would go to the car and romp with the feverish Eddie. It was this that Ted was enjoying, and not the clean sweep victory he scored that day.

Baby took over in April, to score wide margin victories at both Reading and The Grove. Beauty again at Trenton, and the Champ had another. Four events, and four straight victories. Then came the first of the Championship events— back in Texas again, and Babe Stapp's Arlington Downs.

It was a fresh and undefeated Champion Texas saw this time. But the waving and happy Horn of the fall event was missing. In its place, Texans saw a deadly serious man going about his work as a master craftsman. Early morning rains turned the track into a quagmire, yet as usual, the Champ made his annual trudge around the oval.

Ted was fourth in the qualifying. Russo won the pole, and went to the front at once. Harold Ratliff sent the results, under his by-line, over the Associated Press wires:

Ted Horn, the National Champion, repeated in the 100 mile Arlington Downs race here today, finishing in front by three laps.

Returning to the dirt track he last year clinched the AAA title, the handsome blonde did a sprightly tune up for next month's Indianapolis 500 mile race by taking the lead on the 47th lap and never relinquished it the rest of the way.

Duke Dinsmore was second and Duke Nalon third, four laps better than Joie Chitwood, the hard luck man of the race. Chitwood had led for 46 laps when he developed trouble with his steering wheel, but stayed doggedly in the race.

Paul Russo led until the ninth lap. In winning his race, the fifth straight this year, Horn averaged 81.25 MPH which was 11.75 MPH slower than he averaged last year. However, a heavy rain last night had made the track heavy, and even the daredevil driving of the field, failed to dry it out at the finish.

Again the A.P. wires carried a story. This time it was a Ted Horn interview:

Handsome Ted Horn, kingpin of the dirt track racers says, "This is it," about the Indianapolis Speedway Classic next month.

The Paterson N.J. blonde is undefeated for the season among the daredevils of the roaring road, his latest victory being in the 100 mile Arlington Downs race here yesterday.

"I think the 500 mile race at Indianapolis is going to be mine this time," he said after finishing the gruelling grind three laps ahead and picking up $2,478, "I'm getting old you know, and I need to win it pretty soon, if ever." . . .

Ted drove direct to Indianapolis, and Cotton, following his Texas romp. At the big speedway he founds things humming. More cars entered than ever before. Many new ones, and new drivers galore. As usual, Cotton had the big Maserati ready and waiting, and Ted spent his time again check-driving the new lads. If a newcomer made mistakes, Ted would have him follow the Maserati for a few laps, then Ted would follow and observe. Finally, the joined thumb and forefinger signal to Ike Welch would come from the track, and another driver had made the grade.

Ted drove to Reading to continue his string with Baby, and the following week to Trenton. Now the victories stood at seven straight, and neither Beauty nor Baby had been extended.

First day for Indianapolis qualifiers—the day the pole position would be decided, and again Ted was favored, along with Nalon in the Novi, Holland and Rose in the Blue Crowns, and Mays, in the white, black and red Bowes Seal Fast. All were impressive, but Mays again gave a demonstration of his educated heavy foot with a tremendous 130 MPH. Nalon wasn't ready, and Ted faced the line. First lap at 127, second, 126, third, 126 and last, 125 . . . an average of 126.365, far off the pole pace. What was wrong? Cotton and Ted smiled to each other—just as planned. Not too impressive but good enough. "120 this year Cotton," Ted said, and hustled off for Salem, Indiana, and the eighth straight clean cut victory, of which four were Baby's.

The habit was too strong, formed over so many years, for Ted to take it easy. The dust of battle was in his eyes and the smell of victory in his nostrils. One week before the big 500 Classic, Ted wired acceptance of two dates to Richmond and the Grove. The week he should have been resting, his decision was made because a new promoter needed help. At Richmond, on Saturday, Baby showed a clean pair of treads to the field and it became victory number nine.

Ted helped Jug load Baby for the Grove the following day, then prepared to leave in the Lincoln. He was in a hurry, but as he loaded the last of his gear into the trunk, he became aware of a bespectacled youngster, standing in awed silence, yards from the pit. Ted eyed the youngster, then spoke, "Hiya, what can I do for you, Sonny?" No answer. Ted advanced and smiled. Then, the boy held out his hand. In it was a piece of wrapping paper and the stub of a pencil.

Ted knew then. As he signed the wrinkled piece of paper, his eyes roamed the almost empty grounds. Finally he spied what he was looking for. Still holding the paper, Ted waved an itinerant photographer his way. "Take our picture, will you?" Ted asked, then placed his arm around the apparently paralyzed youth. Out came the famous Ted Horn smile, and the picture was taken. Digging a crumpled bill from his pocket, Ted gave it to the man with the camera, "Get his name and address, and send him the picture."

The whole procedure took five minutes, but Ted was the lone speaker. Today, a copy of that picture probably holds an honored place in some household, but a copy, which the photographer made and sent to Ted, reposes in the Ted Horn scrapbooks.

Baby still had the combination and the Maroon and White of the Horn stable flashed to number ten.

Back at Indianapolis, Ted found consternation in the Henning stable. Following Ted's qualifying run, Cotton had discovered abrasive in the oil. That meant a complete tear down and rebuild. "I don't know how it will come out," Cotton said, "We can just do the best we know how, and hope we get it all." Ted was noncommittal.

That night was Ted's seventh consecutive Champion 100 Mile Club turkey dinner. Ted loved to eat, and if there was anything he liked better than turkey, it was more turkey. He listened politely as president Rex Mays spoke, then announced balloting was in order for the new officers. He was still listening when his all-time adversary spoke the words, "I want to be the first to congratulate our long time

"Ted" Horn is National Champ*

"THANKS TO BURD PISTON RINGS"

*A steady string of dirt track wins . . . at Flemington, N. J.; Atlanta, Ga.; Bedford, Pa.; Skowhegan, Me.; Williams Grove, Pa.; Harrington, Del.; Duboise, Pa.; Greensboro, N. C.; Hamburg, N. Y.; Uniontown, Pa.; Altamont, N. Y.; etc. . . . earned sufficient points for Horn to be declared National Champion.

● Ted Horn is the most respected man in racing today. He won the 1946 AAA National Championship in spite of the fact that he did not win the 500 Mile Race at Indianapolis. Turning to the AAA dirt ovals, in a car designed and built in his own shop and equipped with Burd "Graf-Flox" Piston Rings, Horn won practically every "big car" race he entered. Time after time he telegraphed his appreciation for Burd's dependable performance; some of these messages are reproduced at the right. Put Burd's reliability to work for you . . . re-ring with Burd "Graf-Flox" Rings.

BURD PISTON RING CO. ● ROCKFORD, ILLINOIS

Ted liked to endorse the products that helped him win.

This photo was taken at the Champion's 100-Mile-an-Hour Dinner at Indianapolis in 1948. Ted is being congratulated on his election to the presidency by former president, Rex Mays. Harry Wismer, famed radio commentator, in center.

— THE INDIANAPOLIS TIMES —
FRIDAY, MAY 28, 1948

Horn, AAA Champion, Heads 100-MPH Club

Members of World's Most Exclusive Group Honor Earl Twining as 'Mr. Champion'

BY ART WRIGHT

Rugged, reckless auto racing kings who will battle it out for the world's richest speed prize next Monday, proved last night at the Indianapolis Athletic Club that they're as sentimental as the average fan who will attend Monday's "500."

They got together for the annual dinner of the "world's most exclusive" organization — the Champion 100 Mile-An-Hour Club.

They stood reverently with enthusiastic applause for the introduction of T. E. (Pop) Myers, vice president of the Speedway. It was their way of "showing Pop" that he had been "daddy" to most of the 37 members of the club.

For "Pop" was managing the affairs of the Indianapolis Speedway when most of them were wide-eyed youngsters yearning for the glamour of speed.

They bowed their heads in a moment of silence out of respect for one of their fraternity, Ralph Hepburn, who lost his life in a crash during practice this year.

"Mr. Champion"

They "whooped it up" when Earl Twining, racing representative of the Champion Spark Plug Co., whom they had selected for the honor — was presented with a plaque designating him as "the individual who had contributed most to racing." Sentiment that gripped the evening was reflected in Mr. Twining, who choked back tears to tell "the boys" of his gratitude . . . a gratitude founded on 33 years of devotion to their problems with racing engines.

And finally, they acclaimed one of their own group who will be out there on the Indianapolis Speedway Monday trying to beat every one of his "buddies" to the finish line. They crowned Ted Horn, National champion, as their new president.

Rex Mays, retiring president, was presented with a plaque.

The dramatic evening was attended by famous personalities of the sport, by some of the biggest names in speed who no longer race, and by newspapermen.

friend on his election to the presidency of this great club, Ted Horn."

Ted was dragged to the platform. Earl Twining was there. The man everyone called Mr. Champion, and who in the years gone by had been sought by Ted for advice on plugs for Baby, and Beauty and the Little Gems. Harry Wismer, the sportscaster, posed a dummy microphone and Ted was asked to say a few words. Again, words failed him, but looking Mays straight in the eye, as he still held his hand, Ted managed to say, "This is the greatest honor I have ever had."

Were he a speaker, he would have told them of his first disappointing ride at this great race, when his hopes were so high, and his determination to succeed in that Ford, so that California would welcome him as a famous son, and how he had come home almost unnoticed. And of the lift Harry Hartz had given him, and of their great disappointment. Then of Cotton and that work of Fate with the magneto in '46, and the oil in '47, and of their discovery of the morning. But he didn't. He merely held to Rex's hand and swept the room with his eyes, noting the smiling and happy faces before him.

The Henning pit was the acme of orderliness race morning. Cotton's trusty watches were wound, and a table was set up to keep a private account of the running of the race. One pit hand crossed to the far side of the track and made a mark on the wall. There would be no guess-work this time. Ted was going to pace himself at 120, and that was the plan of execution.

The Maserati was placed in the middle of the second row. The sandwich spot again, after so many years. "Right back where I started," thought Ted, but there were no Weatherlys or Seymours today. Jimmy Jackson, the tobacco chewing ex-footballer was one, and wise-cracking veteran Doc Williams, the other. A microphone was placed in front of Ted's lips and he was urged to say something. The voice came soft and high, almost boyishly, "I'm going to try and do it."

It was a perfect day for a race. Fast cars were sprinkled

all through the lineup. Besides the front row of Mays, Holland and Rose, Jackson shared Ted's row, then Nalon in the fourth, Miller and Hellings in the seventh, Bettenhausen the eighth, Carter and Wallard in the tenth. All had as fast or faster time than Ted.

Anyone could have predicted the start. Mays, the leadfoot on the pole, then Rose, the new strategist, and Holland who wouldn't budge, Horn with a date with 120. That is the manner they turned the first lap, with only Holland in front of Rose.

Single file they came again, and the only change was the black car an inch closer to Rose. Third lap and now Horn was right on Rose's tail—the speed unbelievable, and even Holland had no thoughts of catching the flying Mays. Two more laps complete. Lap six and Horn makes his move—Rose offers no battle and the black car moves right up on Holland. Will Bill give way? Before they made the turn at the end of the stretch, the great crowd had their answer—the black had passed the blue and now was winging for the white lead car fifty yards in front, as they disappeared around the turn. One lap with the black behind the white—now two, and they were picking up the tail enders—three laps.

It must have happened on the backstretch. Suddenly the stands at the north turn let out a concerted shout. The black was ahead at last, except for one brief period, the Horn colors leading this race substantially for the first time in 12 years. This was the year. Now for a glance at the pit—it's there, a big 121 on the board, right on schedule. Horn doesn't slacken and the 50-mile mark slips past—so does the 75; then Horn picks up Nalon driving a steady race in the big Novi. It seems impossible, but the black leads the cream—Nalon is sticking to Horn's rear, but a lap behind. 100 miles is history and again Cotton holds the board aloft—"121.789," picked up almost a half mile in average, and well over the scheduled speed.

Nalon right behind, a lap to the rear. Only three other cars on the same lap, but far behind. Almost monotonous, as the big, low black car with the gleaming golden No. 1

stayed in the groove, the driver sitting ever so straight, even leaning forward a bit with everything coming into eye focus at 150 MPH. This was the Champion, and the veteran who was leading, and he had a date with 120.

Cotton started a watch, then stopped it as two cars went by ... the board comes up as No. 1 came into view, "Mays 30 Sec" it said with an arrow pointing back. Mays is 30 seconds behind now. Ted had lost two of these races by less margins. 150 miles now and the Henning board reads 121.876, still picking up. Oh well, that extra will be needed now as Cotton flashed an unnoticeable hand signal to the black car. Ted nodded. "He's coming in," Cotton said quietly, "Alcohol."

The car glides silently to a stop and Ted gets out. New goggles, a drink and he returns as the new tire is pounded into place and the gas cover replaced. It was almost as if they were deliberately slow, but it was haste without waste, as only a well-trained, veteran crew would act. Away, and the AAA observer in the pits clicked his watch. "Twenty-five seconds for Horn," the observer spoke, as the scorer recorded the time on his chart. That observer was Harry Hartz.

Horn fourth behind Mays, Rose and Nalon at 200 miles. Ted's pit stop was over and their's still coming. Speed, 120.453. Right on schedule.

250 miles now—the half way mark. 120.337, and out comes "A Little Faster" on the Henning board. Nalon coming in and that puts No. 1 in the third slot on the big board. 300 miles and Mays is in, Rose leading, Horn second and Rose has a pit stop to make. Average 120.337 again. Ted hopes Rose will make his stop at the same time he does. The Maserati can't make the full distance on one extra filling, but if they pit together, Ted feels he has the speed to best the Blue Crown. Mays is done. Holland only slightly faster than Rose, but not as well placed, and Nalon puzzling with his lack of a move. Oh, well, Cotton will let him know in time. Cotton looks at his watch, then at Ted as the car moves into view. Ted is sitting just a little more forward now and not looking around. If nothing happens

now Ted will win it. Cotton knew it as well as he knew it the time little Pete De Paolo posted the first 100 mile victory for him. But the 350 mile mark was 119.135. A new record for Ted, erasing Wilbur's, but certainly Ted had lifted for a reason.

Finally it came—Ted still was looking straight ahead as his left arm came over the side, fingers straight out. That meant coming in for gas, and the last stop—then as the car was even, Cotton saw the fingers slowly form a tight fist with one finger still out. Cotton turned to the crew and quietly said, "Ted will be in next lap for gas. Have tires ready too, and there is some trouble."

Rose had the lead as Ted ground to a stop and the crew went to work. Hartz watched, and inside prayed just a little as he went about his official duties. Ted and Cotton were talking. "Wait until we start it," Cotton said. The big motor roared to life and Ted gunned. Cotton listened, and didn't say a word. "O.K, let 'er go," he finally said, almost a whisper, and the new tires screamed as Ted shifted into gear. Turning to Ed Metzger, as the car rounded the turn Cotton said, "It's the rod bearings. That sand. We didn't get it all. Ted caught the pressure dropping all right, and he lifted to save my car. What a Champion."

Ted was fourth now, but just cruising. High speed and the pressure went down. At a hundred it stayed almost normal—Oh well, it just wasn't to be I guess—did kind of think this was the year, but something decided differently. I guess the Champion has a right to stroke to the finish this time.

He never looked at the pit again. He felt sorry for Cotton, and all those fine people back in Paterson, in the Fire House and Police Station who were listening on the radio. Oh well, I'll make it up someway.

Those were still his thoughts as Klein waved him into fourth place again. "That makes eight times for the club for me. That ought to be worth something. It is. That's why I am president." But Ted Horn was wrong. That was part of the reason, but not all. The main reason was because he was a great Champion.

Cotton was forcing hilarity as the crew headed for the garage. "Not bad Ted," he said. "I fully expected those bearings to go any time. Say, I've got some news for you. We got a little combine together, and I'm going to Europe this fall to get a new Maserati. It will be yours Ted, next year you will have the new car." Ted looked up almost frightened. "Guess he's a little tired," thought Cotton.

The Indianapolis results unseated Ted from the National point lead. Rose and Nalon were in front, and Holland tied with Ted. Milwaukee coming up the next week with a 100 mile race, and Ted had planned to stay in his trailer and rest before making the Wisconsin city. Therefore, he again attended the victory banquet, and sat beside his beloved Cotton. The pair had a good time. Ted recovered quickly and was again his jovial self. Now, the champ was behind and had to come fighting. It was the breath of competition down his back again, and he loved it.

Suddenly, in the midst of another conversation, Ted broke in, "Sure great about the new car Cotton. If I remember right, the old one was for Bill Cummings, wasn't it?" "Yeah," Cotton answered, "but he never drove it. Died that winter, if you remember. That accident was the same day I landed in New York with the car too. I sure was lucky to get Wilbur then. Just he and you drove that car Ted, and I guess it has the greatest record of any in the history of this track."

Milwaukee turned out 30,000 strong for the Indianapolis field. The spirit of extended celebration prevailed, and Ted found himself in the mood of the day. Once when he pulled in from a warm-up he noticed a large group of youngsters lined in back of his pit. The next time he pulled in, they were still there. This time he pulled in to stop, and got directly from the car towards the rear of his enclosure.

Looking at the ragtag band, Ted removed his helmet and goggles, then spoke, "What do you kids want?" About half the bunch fled, but a few remained stationary. "Nothing, Mister Horn," the spokesman returned, "We just want to watch." Ted grinned; then with a twinkle in his eye added, "Bet you fellows want my autograph. Tell you what you do.

When the race is over, I'll meet you here and we can sit down then and take it easy. Save your programs or hats you want signed, and I'll do my best. O.K?" Naturally, it was; then Ted grinned again as he had another idea. Turning to Jug, Ted drew a bill from his pocket. "Here Jug, go over to the stand and get a case of coke. Let those kids split it up."

There was an organized Horn rooting section as the big race got under way. Ted had fifth spot as usual in the qualifying. He was a bit uneasy, but it couldn't be Beauty; she was purring and surging and anxious to run.

Mantz took over on the first lap as the field strung out. Ted fell in behind Mays as they streaked down the backstretch—'round again, and positions drew out a little more—down the backstretch they came, and then it happened. Duke Dinsmore, the veteran who looked like a collegian, slid a little high on the front turn—just like Ted slid back at Bainbridge, only this time the track was fast—the car drifted. Suddenly the back end clipped the wall, and end over end it went. On the second flip Duke was thrown to the track—right in the middle, like a sack of salt. Directly behind came Mays. It was split second thinking, but Rex, true to the code of the track, never hesitated. His car headed straight into the wall and struck with a loud crash.

Ted right behind had inched between Mays and Dinsmore. He made it and the field came on. An official ran onto the track and straddled the unconscious Dinsmore, waving cars right and left. It was a brave thing to do, but auto racing is a he man's game; the other kind like other sports.

Dinsmore was seriously injured, but Rex unscathed. Harry Hartz was the AAA official who stood by Duke's bedside until danger had passed. Meanwhile the race proceeded. Mantz continued to lead until the 75th mile. At this point Beauty moved into the first five. Andres challenged Mantz and they staged a beautiful duel until Mantz blew a piston.

It was Andres race by almost a full lap. Then three cars flashed over the line, only four seconds between the first and last. Scorer Christy, pencil in each hand, correctly recorded: Hellings, Horn, Fohr. A thriller from start to finish. A fan in the stands was heard to remark, "Wow! Baseball might be the national sport, but I'll take mine right here, and keep the mustard."

Beauty now rested and got ready for Langhorne, while Ted and Baby went on one of those killing barnstorm hauls. Mineola, N. Y. on Saturday and Dayton on Sunday. Baby stayed undefeated, making it victory number 12, a third and a fourth.

Langhorne Sunday and a point race. Ted was now second to Rose, 60 points away. Nalon and Holland were close, and a victory for either would mean the lead. 40,000 people sensed a spectacle. It came at the start. Four cars engaged in a qualifying duel and at the end it was the Colton youngster, Rex Mays, who held a new track mark of 106.82 MPH.

Mays started the race in the same groove, heading a blinding pace. The fourth lap, Russo crashed in a horrifying accident. His car left the track, catapulted over parked cars and landed in trees bordering the track. The race was stopped and rescue workers took an hour to dislodge the car from the trees. Many felt the Russo luck had caught up with Pudgy Paul, because it was at this same track, many years before, that his famous brother Joe had taken his last ride. But Paul was only slightly injured.

Mays again broke on top, turning the track in competition under 35 seconds, followed by Mantz and Nalon. Lap 25 and his heavy foot took its toll—done for the day; and now the first three were Mantz, Nalon and Horn.

Lap 35. Mantz gave up to the terrific pace. Now it was Nalon and Horn. Lap 44 and there were no cars in front of Beauty. Nalon had taken a final pit. For 33 circuits Beauty kept the lead, then slowed and headed in—a broken throttle. Brown came from nowhere and took over, and at the finish had seven laps on Hellings. Andres was third.

Ted was right. Keeping the championship was the toughest. This was raw, courageous competition of the mightiest. Never in the lush Ascot days had he seen driving any harder, but he breathed it and loved it. Only, now the back hurt a little.

Baby continued her rampage at the Grove the following week, and two weeks later repeated, to make it victory 14 out of 17, and still undefeated on the halves. On the 18th, the pair journeyed to Charlotte to make it win number 15.

Now Ted had an understudy. The big blonde youngster he had first taught the facts of racing, back at Altamont, was an unofficial member of the Horn contingent. Ted liked the big man's ready smile, but more, he liked the manner in which he had developed. Clean and hard driving —with attention to appearance. Freddy liked kids too and it was only natural that the two were attracted to each other.

Ted suggested Fred and he ride the Lincoln back north together, and that they wait until traffic cleared before starting. So the two languished in the hotel. Fred was talking, "Ted, some of the guys have been criticizing you— said you won't take appearance money. That true?"

Ted's eyes narrowed and he answered, "Yeah, it's true, but only once recently. That time it was a new promoter, and he got rain. Freddy, he was an honest man and I wanted to help him. His kind makes for better conditions in the sport, and I felt he had taken enough of a loss."

Fred thought a long time, then added. "I know Ted you aren't flashy or big headed, but those dollar tips you always leave in restaurants?"

Again Ted was serious as he answered, "I know what it is to be without money, and now that I have more than people waiting on table, I want to share it with them. That's all."

The conversation ended right then. From somewhere came a car out of the darkness. There was a rending crash and Ted flew out the door of the Lincoln. Behind him came Freddy, to land in the road with a shattered leg, and unconsciousness. When he woke he was in a Washington hospital, with Ted at his bedside and tears in his eyes.

Six months later Freddy was still in a cast, his shattered leg having failed to heal. He wrote a friend:

> "Once a week, Ted flew down to see me. He sent me books and wrote me letters. He called when he didn't think he could make the trip. He sent me money to pay the bills

TED MEETS GOVERNOR GREEN

when mine was gone. From the first day I was hurt, he left orders at the shop that in case he wasn't there when a call came in from the hospital, they were to send out immediately whatever I asked for. He made it known this summer at all the tracks that he was going to see me through this—come hell or high water. Ted never got over the fact that I had been hurt riding in his car. He always blamed himself for the accident, although it wasn't his fault. Many times I have seen him standing by my bed in the hospital with tears in his eyes. Ted couldn't believe he had hurt a friend. I have had letters from car owners offering me their cars to drive at Indianapolis this year. In every letter, there is always the phrase, 'Ted talked to me about you last summer.' He was always looking out for the other fellow."

Winchester; Harrington, Delaware; Martinsville, Virginia, and the victories stood at 18 out of 21, with Baby still undefeated, and Ted close to Rose in the national standings. Milwaukee could change it on the 15th, and it was to be Beauty's job.

Myron Fohr looked like the man to beat, as he sat on the pole and took the lead into the first turn. Never better than fifth, Beauty stayed close to Mays as Mantz followed Fohr into the lead, Andres trailing. The afternoon wore on and the finish was near when Ted got the usual "GO." Go Beauty did, and for one of the few times in her career left Mays behind. Ted was moving up on Andres when he got the checker, the winner.

A recheck of the tape proved Ted had received the finish flag one lap too soon, and the revised standings gave Mantz the victory, Andres second and Beauty third. The Champion now back in front by 80 points over Rose; Nalon third, 160 away.

One week later, Springfield, the state capital, was to hold the next championship race. It drew a huge throng and many notables. One was Governor Dwight Green, the white haired, self-made executive head of the great state. He sat in his box, watching the activity with much interest. Ike Welch, AAA official in charge that day, asked the governor if there was anything he could do for him, and the executive answered, "Yes, I'd like to meet your Champion, Ted Horn."

Welch introduced the two, trackside. The Governor was impressed with Ted's modesty and sincerity. The governor asked, "Ted, you've been racing a long time now. When are you going to retire?" There wasn't a second's hesitation in Ted's answer. It came with a suddenness that shook the governor. "Mr. Governor, I always felt a man was designed to do certain things. Lucky is he who is able to do so. You were to be a great politician and as such have reached the top of your profession, the Governor. I always felt I was to be a race driver and now I am at the top of my profession, the Champion. Now at my age it would be kind of foolish for me to quit, and say take a job sweeping out your office at eighteen dollars a week."

All through the afternoon, Governor Green was to ponder that statement. It rang with a sincerity and a philosophy the governor never dreamed a race driver would possess. It made food for thought and auto racing had another friend. The Champion had seen to that in his own manner and honesty. Six weeks later the governor was to remember the words and he said to himself, "He never finished. He didn't tell me the rest of his feelings. He knew; he was a great man; he was a great Champion."

Ted won the race. Ted and Beauty, in near record time, after Mack Hellings had emulated Dinsmore and crashed. Injuries that were serious and painful, but not fatal. Ted gave an interview and answered a question to a scribbling reporter: We have had two bad accidents this year, but no fatalities; in fact, none for two years. These boys are the best, and they don't have accidents on purpose. All racing accidents are unavoidable. Always, they are either the result of the failure of some part, or mistaken judgement, never deliberate. We do not take the chances highway drivers do. But if a wheel comes off at 100 MPH that is an unforseen and unavoidable accident." A wheel was to come off in an unforseen and unavoidable accident—or was it?

Baby had a field day at Dayton, setting more records. The score now read 20 out of 24 and still undefeated on the half miles—the events that were hardest to win.

TED MEETS AN OLD FRIEND

At Dayton, Ted met his old friend, Pappy Funk. In lots of ways Pappy was like Hankinson, and Ted loved him. From the old school, Pappy had differed from Hankinson in that he had stayed at the tracks he built. Winchester had materialized in the midst of a farming community, yet the straightforwardness and honesty of Pappy Funk had made it successful. Earlier, Ted had made a token appearance and set a new record just over 20 seconds for the banks. This bettered the one painted at the end of the grandstand and so elevated because no one thought it possible to erase.

That day Pappy had presented Ted with $500 for his feat. At the microphone, Funk had said, "Ted, it gives me great pleasure to give you this $500," and Ted came right back, "Pappy, it gives me great pleasure to take this $500." The crowd ate it up. Later, in the office, Ted had come to Pappy saying, "Pappy, I don't feel right taking this money. Let's you and I split it."

Now Ted was talking, "Pappy, I only had Baby at half throttle when I set those records. I felt you were paying me to come out here and set records, and I wanted something left the next time I came out." Pappy looked up and countered, "But Ted, you wouldn't take the money." "Looks like rain," Ted lied, gazing out of the window at the bright sunshine.

Back to Milwaukee and a 200 mile race. The first time such a distance had been scheduled on the Championship circuit. It was a gruelling race, and many drivers sought relief. Yet Ted and Beauty stuck it out. Never in 23 years covering Indianapolis and circuit racing had the Champion asked relief. This was no exception. Fohr won before hometown fans, with Bettenhausen as his partner; Parsons second and Beauty third, a lap away. Previously Mantz had crashed and was unhurt, but this time Ted had a pained expression on his face as he slowly crawled from the cockpit. It was as if he shouldn't have done it—gone the whole trip alone. He was in pain but only he knew it.

Du Quoin, Illinois was next, and the Championship season drawing to a climax. The title wasn't clinched yet, but Ted was in front. Du Quoin was holding its annual Southern Illinois fair and a big crowd jammed the beautiful plant to watch the race.

Ted hadn't recovered from the 200 mile beating, but once the feature started, gave Beauty her head and drove with all the skill he possessed. It was grim nerve alone on which he finished that race, third. He had many things to do and his job was only half completed. He helped load the big car on the truck, and saw his entourage head for Atlanta and the next championship race, two days later. Then, both tired in body and spirit, he performed the duty he felt so necessary to a Champion. He visited the telegraph office. To his friend and advisor of many years, Earl Twining, he sent the following wire:

POINTS GAINED TODAY BY FINISHING THIRD IN NATIONAL CHAMPIONSHIP 100 MILE RACE AT DU QUOIN GAVE ME MY THIRD STRAIGHT NATIONAL DRIVING TITLE ENABLING ME TO SET A RECORD BY WINNING THE DRIVING CHAMPIONSHIP THREE YEARS IN SUCCESSION YOUR SPLENDID CHAMPION SPARK PLUGS HAVE BEEN IN MY ENGINES EVER SINCE I STARTED RACING AND I ATTRIBUTE A GREAT DEAL OF MY SUCCESS TO YOUR MOST RELIABLE SPARK PLUG.

—TED HORN.

It was not the telegram of a braggart, nor the wire of a favor sought. Ted was beyond the sordid pale of commercialism. He was wealthy and financially secure in every respect. It was his way of being a Champion, and sharing his triumph with those he felt had aided him to his victory.

At Atlanta, Ted led in the early stages of the race, but a broken crankshaft retired Beauty. Somehow he was almost glad, he was so tired. Mel Hansen swept to victory, but the Champion had already sent Jug on his way, back to Paterson. More work was ahead, and the Champion set out to complete his job. In a Macon paper the following item appeared:

> Ted Horn, national AAA auto racing champion will be at the Sport's Center Store across from Central Park at 1:15 tomorrow. Horn will give autographs and meet any local racing fans who wish to drop in.

Still performing the ritual, in his interpretation of the code of ethics of a Champion. Then Ted did something he had never done before—stopped to see the Specialist during the racing season. This time his steps were sure, swift and determined, after leaving the office. His mouth was set in a hard, straight line as he headed for his car. He didn't stop until he arrived in Paterson, and his orders were direct and to the point: "Load Baby; we're making that New York trip, then New England. Pick up Beauty for Springfield, Trenton and Du Quoin, but keep Baby with us. See you in Hamburg on the 10th."

It was like the olden days—Hohokus, Flemington, Harrington, Richmond, on successive days. Sleeping by the side of the road, up at dawn, racing all day and working all night. Never stopping to eat; always on the go. "Ships that pass in the night."

On Friday, Baby won at Hamburg, N. Y., Saturday at Port Royal, Pennsylvania; then the Grove on Sunday, and Baby's first and last defeat. It was a tired pair that finished second to Hinnershitz. Before leaving for Springfield and the next Championship race, Ted told his old friend Roy Richwine, "I'll be back in a month for the Cup race. That is one I want to win. I have one leg on that trophy, so go ahead and advertise my appearance." He was to break his word, but not of his own choice.

At Springfield, Ted hurried to a newspaper office. A request had come that he furnish a photograph so he took time to appear and pose for an original print. When they were developed the photographer mailed a copy to Ted. Back it came in the next mail, autographed to the sender. Still selling auto racing "to those guys who are just trying to make a living too."

Beauty took third at Springfield, then headed for Trenton, while Ted and Baby made a five day haul to Massachusetts. Here Ted wanted to see another old friend, Lou

Vollmar. Lou, the Bosch magneto man, who had secured these valuable parts from Nazi Germany and who helped the boys at Indianapolis and other races with their problems. They talked of many things other than racing, and Lou wondered.

Baby made short work of the field at Springfield, taking the features both days. This made 19 wins in 20 starts for Baby, and 24 out of 33 for the stable. Was there any question to the right of Ted Horn to the title "National Champion"?

At Trenton, so near to those memorial years; Hohokus, Flemington and Union, Beauty led the parade. The car beautiful, which three times had taken down National Championship honors, been displayed at a great convention as the prima donna of a great stable. This was her day and she reflected the pride of her owner in the manner she did her work.

The big scoreboard in the Fire House read:

BEAUTY:		BABY:	
13	Races	20	Races
6	Wins	19	Wins
5	Thirds	1	Second
2	Out		

It was Fate's year and her hand guided the chalk as it wrote, "NEXT RACE — DU QUOIN."

Ted's name was familiar in national advertising.

Start of the tragic event at DuQuoin, Illinois. Rex Mays is on the pole, Mel Hansen is on the outside. 2nd row, Andres and Horn. 3rd Row, Fohr and Mantz. Extreme right, Russo and No. 7, Parsons, the eventual winner. 90 sec. later, Horn's fatal accident occurred.

Involved in the tragic accident that cost the life of Horn at DuQuoin, was Johnny Mantz. Due to a broken spindle, Horn's car went out of control and hit the Mantz car. The wrecked Mantz car, badly damaged, is shown here, Mantz was only slightly injured. — *Bud Williams Photos*

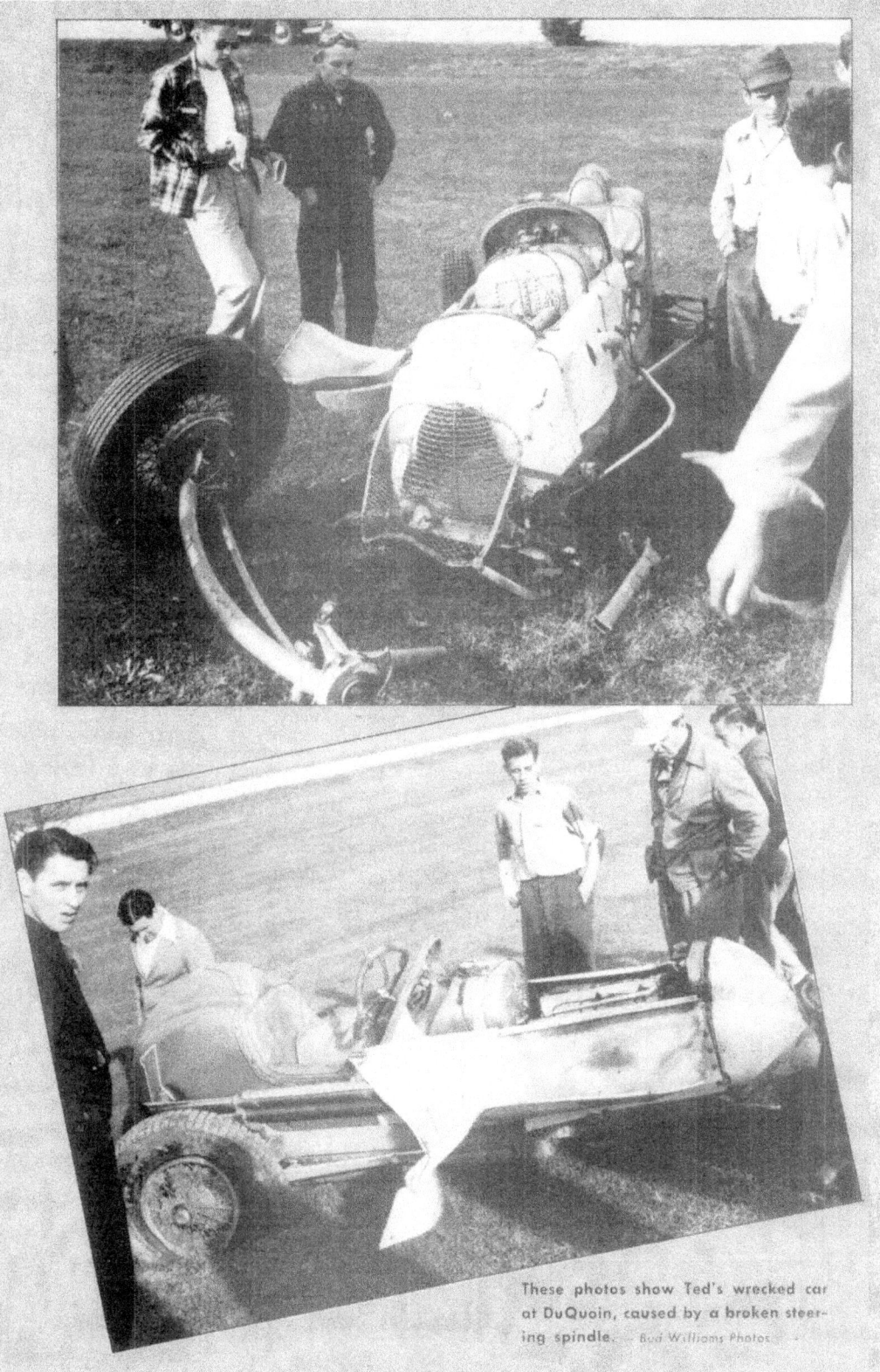

These photos show Ted's wrecked car at DuQuoin, caused by a broken steering spindle. — Bud Williams Photos

Ted Horn Fatally Hurt in Illinois Race Crash

DU QUOIN, Ill., Oct. 10 (AP)—Ted Horn, 38, national auto racing champion and one of the most consistent money winners of all time at the Indianapolis Speedway, was injured fatally today in a 100-mile race at the Du Quoin Fair Grounds.

The veteran driver from Paterson, N.J., was injured when his car went out of control on the second lap of an AAA-sponsored race and careened into another racer. Horn died at Marshall-Browning Hospital.

The other driver, Johnny Mantz, of San Pedro, Cal., was injured slightly in the crack-up and released from the hospital after treatment.

Token Appearance

The race was more or less a token appearance for Horn, who already had clinched the American Automobile Association racing championship for the third straight year.

Illinois State police said Horn was on the second lap of the 100-mile AAA contest when a wheel spindle broke, throwing his car out of control.

Horn was thrown out on the track just before his car struck Mantz's machine. Both drivers were taken to the hospital and Horn was pronounced dead 20 minutes after arrival. His injuries were described as "a concussion, crushed chest and fractured left leg."

Parsons Wins

The event was won by Johnny Parsons of Los Angeles, driving a Kurtis-Kraft Special. His time was 1h. 11m. 47.7s. Paul Russo of Kenosha, Wis., was second and Bill Sheffler of Los Angeles, third.

Horn's car was running fifth at the time of the accident. Horn's wife, Gerry, was among the 5000 spectators who witnessed the race and the crash.

Horn, although he never won the big 500-mile Memorial Day race at Indianapolis, reportedly won more than $55,000 since his first start in the classic in 1935.

Horn failed to finish in his first Indianapolis start in 1935 but he was never farther back than fourth in nine subsequent races.

Horn was a veteran of motorcar racing. He began his career at the age of 14 in 1925. In 1928 he was seriously injured in a race at Ascot Speedway and retired for two years.

In 1930 he returned to the track and competed regularly thereafter. He was rated one of the top drivers ever to compete in the 500-mile race at Indianapolis and nine times he finished the Memorial Day classic with average speeds of more than 100 miles an hour.

For the last three years at Indianapolis he drove an Italian-built Maseratti in which Wilbur Shaw twice won the race. Horn finished third twice and fourth once in the last three years.

Previously he had finished second once, third once and fourth three times. A heavy-set, genial man, Horn was expert at timing himself in a race and rarely was caught out of position.

He was highly regarded by racing drivers, mechanics and car owners.

The Associated Press dispatch

CHAPTER VIII

Du Quoin

SPIRITUAL demands sometimes reach the point of human exhaustion. Ted had now reached this point. He knew it and neither a specialist nor an advisor had to tell him. Therefore he submitted to a rest from his self-appointed schedule. Ted loaded the house trailer and drove to the beach for a week's vacation.

He rigged himself a camp stool, with a little canvas back, so that he could rest while watching the waves. He didn't take fishing tackle. He knew he wouldn't fish, but he did want to be near the water that had afforded him so much enjoyment; fishing, swimming, boating.

Lee Wallard visited him as he was preparing to leave. Lee had made the grade this spring at Indianapolis, and to Ted, Lee represented probably his closest friend of the Championship Circuit. Lee, too, had that inborn love for the sport that Ted embraced—his whole life wrapped around its activity.

Lee noted his friend's camping preparations; he was pleased. "Glad to see you aren't going to Du Quoin, Ted," he offered. "You've won the Championship again now and there's no point in your making the trip. You certainly don't need the money."

Ted reflected, then answered slowly, as if he had no choice in the matter: "I'm going Lee, but first I'm going to rest a little. They expect me out there and I can't let them down. No, I certainly don't need the money."

The inflection of the last sentence was on the I. It was a puzzling statement.

Ted packed a handgrip of unanswered letters. "I'll get caught up on my mail at the beach," he thought, but after almost a week all had remained unanswered. One he held in his hand as he watched the horizon meet the big white fluffy clouds. Slowly and carefully he rose from his home-made camp chair and opened the typewriter. Then he returned, balancing it on his knee, and inserted a sheet of paper.

"Hi Walt," he wrote. Walt Woestman, 'way back in his beloved California. Walt Woestman, the six foot six World War I pilot, who quit driving race cars back in 1914 and who now was preparing another entry for the Pike's Peak race. "Always wanted to win that race," Ted thought. "He's gone up that hill so many times he yodels when he snores now," and Ted laughed at his own joke. "But Walt and his type are what makes this sport continue. Always building race cars and trying to make them better. Just about had nervous prostration when I drove his car in that movie, thought I would crack it up for sure. I always felt he was kind of disappointed when I didn't."

> Hi Walt—he continued—This is a lousy piece of paper to write a letter on but I'm down at the beach and if I wait till I get back to the shop I might forget all about it or something, so here goes with just what there is at hand.
>
> Very glad to hear from you Walt, and it was a good idea of yours to check upon this appearance of mine in those western races. To be exact, I haven't made a definite decision. I have been told they are advertising my appearance, but I haven't heard from anybody and haven't made any commitments. This doesn't mean I am not coming out there, and it doesn't mean I'm thinking too much of coming either. To tell the truth, I'd like to rest very much.
>
> If I did come out there I would have to see my way clear that it would at least pay my expenses, and I've become accustomed to sleeping in a bed and not on the side of the road in a car. My boys bring the race car with the truck and they get all of their expenses paid, and they don't like to sleep on the side of the road either. Also, we are used to one thick steak a week—*all of us!*
>
> Frankly, I am a bit perturbed at promoters just taking for granted I'll appear and advertising to that effect, when they haven't made any arrangements. One thing for sure, I positively won't miss the 50 lap Trophy race at Williams Grove on October 24th.
>
> Glad to see Rogers win the Peak. Not that I have anything against Unser, but he's already won it many times. Guess it would burn some guys up to have a piece of lesser equipment beat them, but I think if a guy can beat the field with inferior equipment, he deserves just that much more credit. As long as the car meets all the rules, I think that is

ACTIVITY IN THE MINING TOWN

all that matters. If they don't want lesser equipment running, then the rules should be changed to exclude it.

I guess you've noted I'm going to be the National Champion again this year. The first time that anybody got it three years in a row. I'll probably end up Eastern Dirt Track Champ also. I had that last year, and I'm in the lead now.

I'm staying in the house trailer down at the beach right now, but tomorrow will leave for the Championship race at Du Quoin. Guess there isn't anything else to say, so,
Best of luck, always.—TED.

Du Quoin, Illinois, is located in the southeastern part of the state, not far from the Kentucky and Indiana lines. A town of about 7,500 people, the fairgrounds were about its only excuse for being on the map. There was some coal mining and a brisk saloon business, but that was about all. Save for the annual Fair the town goes about its business in a manner that tabs it as being depressing.

The fairgrounds is another matter. Built over strip mining territory, it probably has one of the finest race tracks in the country. A full mile track, with a curved steel guard rail inside and out and a wire mesh fence encompassing the entire grounds. Inside the track, a channel of water 30 feet deep to hold speedboat races and water carnivals. Landscaped to perfection, it served as a sharp contrast to the town.

Paul Johnson was pulling into Du Quoin. Paul, the AAA Observer at Indianapolis, had a job to do. Always reliable Ike Welch was the AAA official in charge of this race and he had called Paul for help, to serve as Pit Steward. Noting the distressing aspects of the town, Paul was not too keen for his assignment. This was funny too—for a person who had followed racing a lifetime, it was the first time he could recall he didn't relish the thoughts of a race.

His spirits rose, however, when he spied a familiar car parked at the hotel. "Ted's here," he said. "Well, guess it isn't so bad after all. Inside that hotel you can't see this out here. Let's get in and join the fun."

Inside, the fun was strange. Ted was there talking to Ken Fowler and Bill Shoof. "Interest is lagging 'cause anyone can do 90 to 100 on the highway," Ted was saying, and when his listeners tired, moved to another group. Ted was talking in a loud voice and fast. Paul stopped. That didn't sound like Ted Horn. He never made excuses for the sport; he was always boosting it. Ted never imposed into conversations and he certainly isn't drinking—sounds as if he had something on his mind. He's trying to talk himself out—something's eating him, that's for sure. Guess I'll register and forget seeing him.

Ted rose and dressed early. Hearing an exclamation from his wife, turned and asked, "What's the matter?" "I only brought two dresses," she answered, "and this one's soiled." "Wear the other one," Ted answered, "anything wrong with it?" "Only that it's green," came the quiet answer.

Ted was silent for a long time, and when he did answer it was in an offhand manner. "Go ahead and wear it. It doesn't matter that much."

At 10:30 the familiar Ted Horn team arrived at the race track. Ted slowly pulled to a parking place, then sought out Paul Johnson. "Paul," he said, after shaking hands, I have a favor to ask. Can I put my car with the family next to my pit. Gotta reason." Paul thought a minute. That's strange; he never wanted women and kids around before. "Sure, guess it's OK if you want to," was the permission. "Say, where's Jughead?"

"Might go on to California, so I left him in Paterson this time," Ted returned, as he walked rapidly down the track. "Huh," thought Paul, "Never did that before. Never saw a guy that depended so much on another. You'd think he'd take him to the coast, too." But Paul hadn't read Woestman's letter. He wasn't going to the coast.

Ted walked the track—then qualified. It seemed as if he was in a hurry to end these preliminaries. He spent much time at his car, always returning to supervise a bit of preparation to Beauty. One of these jobs consisted of a minor weld, and as Ike Welch secured the welder, noted how exacting Ted was over the method the work was being done. "Wish we had more like him," Ike remarked. "Does everything himself and leaves nothing to chance."

A group was forming on the main stretch to talk. In it were Harry Bennett, Sol Silbermann, Welch, Lee Oldfield and Eddie Pummell. The conversation, too, was distressing. "Don't look up into those stands," said one, "There's so few people it makes you want to go home." Another said, "Can you tell me the reason for this race? Ted has the Championship sewed up, it's late in the year, due to get bad weather, and no point to it at all." His question was unanswered. Ted appeared. Today, Ted was joining all groups and conversing. Silbermann spoke, Sol Silbermann, Chief Metallurgist AAA Contest Board, and President of Metallurgical Service Company in Indianapolis. Another of racing's great benefactors who since 1935 had installed his equipment yearly at the Indianapolis Speedway and gave freely of his time and knowledge, inspecting vital parts that were to be subjected to stress in the race.

"Hello Ted, we were just talking about magnufluxing Championship cars for this type of event. What do you think of it?"

Ted's answer came at once. "Great idea. I'm for it all the way; should be compulsory, same as Indy."

"What about your spindles, Ted," Silbermann added, "had them magnafluxed lately?"

"No I haven't," Ted answered, "Not since spring, but I have new ones ordered. In fact I expect them when I get back, but I figured these would last a race or two."

As Ted returned to his car, Welch remarked, "He uses the lightest spindles in the game, too," and as he noted Johnson coming towards him, looked at his watch. "Well, let's go, get this one over with. Come on Paul, we ride the pace car."

Welch and Johnson settled in the lead car, then pulled out. Glancing at the sky, Ike remarked, "Look, the sun is shining, but it still is cloudy and cold. Brrr! how are they coming back there, Paul?"

"Can't line up," was the answer. "You'd think those guys were trying this for the first time instead of being the best in the business. Darn it, don't they want to race?"

"Wouldn't blame them if they didn't," Ike answered.

"Three times around now. That's enough. Wave 'em in line Paul, we can't do this all day."

But still they refused to form. Two more laps—then, "This is it. VandeWater has the green out; hit the inside."

Paul watched as the field was off. Around the turn in a group and down the back stretch. Out of the far turn and speed picked up as they came down in front of the empty stands. Now in the bottom turn and out onto the stretch—then, DUST—although the track was hard and damp—MORE DUST AND A CAR IN THE AIR. It's white with a blue tail and it's coming down as a blue one also rises. Welch jumps in the pace car and they speed to the turn—then down the stretch, and stop.

He lay there, where Beauty had tossed him. Beauty, beautiful Beauty—Beauty turned Beast. Three feet from the outside rail he was lying on his back, with one arm outstretched and one leg doubled back. One boot was off, but there were no cuts or abrasions, and he wasn't breathing. On his chest were the words, "Ted Horn, National Champion, 1946-47."

And Paul whispered to himself, "He was a Champion, a great Champion."

And Fate closed a book and wrote: "FINIS."

CHAPTER X

Reminiscenses and Tributes

WEEKS later a group was sitting in the office of Sol Silbermann. An interview was taking place and facts were being searched. Silbermann placed his glasses on the desk and picked up a piece of metal. Looking steadily at it he began to speak, "The break in this spindle was what we call a transverse break. It didn't just happen. It was there all along, gradually reaching the point where it would give way. In fact there is no such thing as crystallization of metal as we use the term. Breaks start and enlarge," then he paused and thought before continuing his testimony. Suddenly he looked up. "Before we go any farther, I want to say right now, Ted Horn died as a martyr. He died so that all race cars be magnafluxed before racing on any AAA track."

Back in Anderson, Indiana, Paul Johnson was pacing the floor and holding a clipping in his hand. "It's wrong, it's wrong," he said to himself. "They say when they took his boot off his right foot a dime fell out. That's wrong; it was his left boot," and he felt a five cent piece in his pocket. "Found this darn thing at Du Quoin and meant to give it to Ted, but felt that was kid stuff. Wish I had, now," and Paul Johnson is a realist, not easily convinced of the supernatural. "Wonder if Rex Mays intends to drive. Loaded right up that day and wouldn't finish the race. He was right alongside Ted, too. Just wouldn't talk to anyone. Darn the luck."

In Pendleton a jeweler sat in a little room in the back of the store and looked at a newspaper. "He wouldn't want me to feel bad, but he told me . . . was going to start that fund with the Du Quoin race . . . the one for the kids. Said he had the Championship and from here on out it was for the kids," and he wept a little.

In Richmond, Virginia a man was standing by a window holding a newspaper in his hands. He was looking towards

Strawberry Hill and his mind kept repeating over and over, "He was the best friend I ever had—if it hadn't rained, if it hadn't rained." And in Warrenton, a business man put down his paper and said, "He was a modest and unassuming Champion, and I never knew a more unselfish man."

In a room at an Indianapolis hotel a newspaper reporter was asking the man in the sick bed for a statement. He repeated, "You can say for me, Ted Horn was the greatest day-in-day-out race driver I ever knew," and Cotton Henning closed his eyes. A friend, fearful of Cotton's condition, broke some cheering news. "The new Maserati is in New York, Cotton. Landed off the boat yesterday." "Yes," Cotton answered, "I know it. Ted knew it too, up there at Du Quoin, before it happened." And Cotton thought—the first Maserati and Cummings, the same day. The second Maserati and Ted—the same day.

And in Reading, Pennsylvania a man turned on his car radio, "Good evening, ladies and gentlemen, let's go to press," said Walter Winchell. "Du Quoin, Illinois, October 10th, Ted Horn, National Auto Racing Champion, was killed here today in a race," and the man turned the radio off and turned his car towards home. Then he sat down and wrote:

FAREWELL TED

The Speed World mourns the passing
Of the blonde and blue-eyed Ted.
The brightest star the sport has known
In many a year is dead.

His was a life of daring
As he rode to fortune and fame,
And added new color and glory
To the dangerous speedway game.

Yes, Ted is gone but in our hearts
We shall ever hold him dear;
And as the cars go speeding by
We'll always feel he's near.

Farewell—O gallant Champion,
We shall never forget your name.
In the sport you lived and died for—
You have earned eternal fame.

—Harold Mohn.

And Harold Mohn had never known Ted Horn except from the grandstands at Reading.

"LET THERE BE LIGHT."

The Lord is my Shepherd: I shall not want.

He maketh me to lie down in green pastures: He leadeth me beside the still waters.

He restoreth my soul: He leadeth me in the paths of righteousness for His Name's sake.

Yea, though I walk through the valley in the shadow of death, I will fear no evil: for thou art with me, Thy rod and Thy staff they comfort me.

Thou preparest a table before me in the presence of mine enemies: Thou anointest my head with oil, my cup runneth over.

Surely goodness and mercy shall follow me all the days of my life: and I will dwell in the house of the LORD forever.

Surely, goodness and mercy shall follow me all the days of my life: and I will dwell in the house of the LORD forever.

More than a thousand people, from all walks of life, attended the funeral at the Quinlan Funeral Home in Paterson. From Los Angeles, Washington, Philadelphia, Virginia, Ohio, Indiana, New York, presidents of corporations, race drivers, and children. Jug was there, and Dick, and Jim Lamb, Ike Welch, Roy Richwine, Tom Frost, Earl Twining. They were all there, and Walt Ader, Tommy Hinnershitz, Tommy Mattson, Joie Chitwood, Lee Wallard, Buster Warke and Jimmy Gibbons carefully and tenderly carried the casket. In front formed the honorory pall bearers; Wilbur Shaw, Frank Delroy, Harry Schleiman, E. H. Eaton, Johnny Moore, Gene Stonecipher, Ed Moss, Rocky Neerlemer, Captain Paul Schappert, Brick Melville, Paul Probst, Bert Ross, Vince Tulley, M. C. Pritzbur, Norris Freel, Frank Shershin, Charles Simoneck and Ken Walter, and they all looked at the floral piece that adorned the lid of the casket, a maroon floral blanket on which the numeral "1" was embossed in white—those were Baby's colors, and Baby had never let Ted down.

Ted left his mother and a brother in Los Angeles, his wife in Reading, and three daughters; Loretta, Theresa, and Gayeleen, who was born February 8, 1949, four months after her father was buried in Cedar Lawn Cemetery, Clifton, N. J.

Col. A. W. Herrington, Chairman of the Contest Board, said: "Ted was a friend, a gentleman and a great competitor, and a true sportsman in the highest and truest sense of the word. He lived the life of the Champion that he was."

James Lamb, Secretary of the Contest Board, announced that No. 1 would be blanketed for the coming season, in respect to the great Champion.

Eight weeks following Ted's funeral, patient, kindly and lovable Cotton Henning passed away of a heart condition. It was as if he was happy to go and see his great friend, Ted Horn. Pete De Paolo said, "It is my belief that Cotton's death was hastened with the loss of Ted; he idolized him." Into the capable hands of Lee Wallard went the wheel of the Maserati, the driver "who had made the grade."

Williams Grove management, through Roy Richwine, announced the No. 1 pit would be sealed for all time, with a suitable marker to tell future generations the reason. A movement was announced to organize a Ted Horn Foundation, to carry on the great work the great Champion had started, especially with the "youngsters." If only one of these projects materialize, Ted will feel highly honored, and humble.

In no manner has it been the thought of the author to establish the fact that Ted Horn was the greatest driver of all time. Were I to make that statement, the first objector, from wherever he is, would be Ted Horn. He was a great Champion, and a great man. Surely goodness and mercy followed him all the days of his life, and through life Ted was writing the last sentence of his biography,"*Best of Luck Always.*—Ted Horn."

Ted Horn, as a driver, represented everything that was necessary to make a National Driving Champion, and would serve as an ideal for any boy who desired to make a success in the racing profession. In my book, he ranks with the topmost drivers of all time. He was not only a great winner, but a gracious loser.

(Signed) SETH KLEIN,
Vice-President,
Marmon-Harrington Co.
(Official AAA Starter, Indianapolis Speedway)

Ted Horn, no matter for whom he was working or what product he was promoting, invariably pitched in to do the best kind of job he knew how. With complete devotion to his work and unmatched ability to produce wins at the track, he was always "up-front" for himself and those who counted upon him. In all the years of our business association to advertise Riverside tires, Montgomery Ward found Ted Horn a gentleman, a hard worker and a man of his word. Racing lost a valuable asset in his untimely passing—but he will always live on in the memory of those he worked with and called his friends.

(Signed) JOHN A. MARTIN,
Ass't Retail Sales Manager
Montgomery Ward & Company

Ted Horn won the first race I ever drove in at Riverside, California, Labor Day, 1931. Since that time we have raced against each other many times, both winning our share of races. From Ted's record for the past three seasons, I consider him the best of all the National Champions, at least since I started racing. He was a real Champion, and above all, a regular fellow.

(Signed) REX MAYS.

Ted Horn's unquestionable character, true sportsmanship and love for competition has caused him to remain in the heart of the racing world.

(Signed) LOUIS MEYER,
Vice-President,
Meyer & Drake Engineering Corp.

Ted Horn met every prerequisite of the ten qualifications of a true sportsman. First, he didn't boast. Second, he never quit. Third, he made no excuses. Fourth, he was a cheerful loser. Fifth, he was a quiet winner. Sixth, he always played fair. Seventh, he was willing to learn. Eighth, he had courage. Ninth, he played the game according to the rules and Tenth, he, above all, was honest. Ted was definitely an asset to the great sport of Auto Racing. We shall miss him.

Roy Richwine,
Williams Grove Speedway

In addition to Ted Horn being the undisputed Champion automobile driver of this era, he was unquestionably the most loved and respected driver of his time. These characteristics qualified him as the sport's outstanding goodwill ambassador. His passing was an irreparable loss to automobile racing.

(Signed) Wilbur Shaw,
President,
Indianapolis Motor Speedway

In the passing of Ted Horn it is my personal opinion we have lost a man whose character, ability, mannerisms, showmanship and temperament have done more for auto racing than that which has ever been exhibited on our speedways, and a compilation of these facts cannot fail to indicate a necessary observance of the need for development of these characteristics by future Champions and future drivers.

(Signed) I. W. (Ike) Welch,
Zone Supervisor,
American Automobile Assn.

Statistical Data

COMPLETE 1948 RECORD

Date	Track	Length	Type	Finish
Sun., Mar 21	Lakewood Spdwy., Atlanta, Ga.	1 Mi.	Sprints	1
Sun., Apr. 4	Reading, Pa. Fairgrounds	½ Mi.	Sprints	1
Sun., Apr. 11	Williams Grove Speedway	½ Mi.	Sprints	1
Sun., Apr. 18	Trenton, N.J. Fairgrounds	1 Mi.	Sprints	1
Sun., Apr. 25	Arlington Downs, Texas	100 Mi.	Nat. Ch.	1
Sun., May 2	Reading, Pa. Fairgrounds	½ Mi.	Sprints	1
Sun., May 9	Trenton, N.J. Fairgrounds	1 Mi.	Sprints	1
Sun., May 16	Salem, Indiana	½ Mi.	Sprints	1
Sat., May 22	Richmond, Va. Old Fairgrnds.	½ Mi.	Sprints	1
Sun., May 23	Williams Grove Speedway	½ Mi.	Sprints	1
Mon., May 31	Indianapolis Motor Spdwy.	500 Mi.	Sw'stakes	4
Sun., June 6	Wisconsin State Fairgrnds.	100 Mi.	Nat. Ch.	3
Sat., June 12	Mineola, N.Y. Fairgrounds	½ Mi.	Sprints	1
Sun., June 13	Dayton, Ohio Speedway	½ Mi.	Sprints	1
Sun., June 20	Langhorne, Pennsylvania	100 Mi.	Nat. Ch.	9
Sun., June 27	Williams Grove Speedway	½ Mi.	Sprints	1
Sun., July 11	Williams Grove Speedway	½ Mi.	Sprints	1
Sun., July 18	Charlotte, N. C.	½ Mi.	Sprints	1
Sun., July 25	Winchester, Ind. Spdwy.	½ Mi.	Sprints	1
Sat., July 31	Harrington, Del. Fairgrnds.	½ Mi.	Sprints	1
Sun., Aug. 8	Martinsville, Va. Spdwy.	½ Mi.	Sprints	1
Sun., Aug. 15	Wisconsin State Fair	100 Mi.	Nat. Ch.	3
Sat., Aug. 21	Springfield, Illinois	100 Mi.	Nat. Ch.	1
Sun., Aug. 22	Dayton, Ohio Speedway	½ Mi.	Sprints	1
Sun., Aug. 29	Wisconsin State Fair	200 Mi.	Nat. Ch.	3
Sat., Sept. 4	Du Quoin State Fairgrnds.	100 Mi.	Nat. Ch.	3
Mon., Sept. 6	Lakewood Spdwy., Atlanta, Ga.	100 Mi.	Nat. Ch.	0
Fri., Sept. 10	Hamburg, N.Y. (Night)	½ Mi.	Sprints	1
Sat., Sept. 11	Port Royal, Pennsylvania	½ Mi.	Sprints	1
Sun., Sept. 12	Williams Grove Speedway	½ Mi.	Sprints	2
Sun., Sept. 19	Springfield, Illinois	100 Mi.	Nat. Ch.	3
Fri., Sept. 24	Springfield, Massachusetts	½ Mi.	Sprints	1
Sat., Sept. 25	Springfield, Massachusetts	½ Mi.	Sprints	1
Sun., Oct. 3	Trenton, N.J. Fairgrnds.	1 Mi.	Sprints	1

STATISTICAL DATA

A.A.A. TRACK RECORDS
Held By
TED HORN
As of October 19, 1948

Date	Track	Distance	Time	MPH
Mar. 6, 1938	El Centro, California	1 lap	38.14	94.39
Mar. 20, 1938	Phoenix, Arizona	5 laps	2:47.8	67.00
Sept. 5, 1938	Altoona, Penna.	10 laps	7:19.96	92.05
Sept. 16, 1939	Hughesville, Penna.	1 lap	25.8	69.8
Sept. 16, 1939	Hughesville, Penna.	10 laps	4:36.2	65.2
Oct. 7, 1939	Danbury, Conn.	1 lap	26.9	66.9
Oct. 7, 1939	Danbury, Conn.	10 laps	4:37.5	64.9
Oct. 7, 1939	Danbury, Conn.	25 laps	11:44.5	63.87
Oct. 14, 1939	Raleigh, N. C.	1 lap	27.3	65.9
May 8, 1940	Union Raceway, N. J.	8 laps	3:47.2	63.4
Sept. 6, 1940	Rutland, Vermont	10 laps	4:48.2	62.5
Sept. 7, 1940	Dunkirk, N. Y.	1 lap	27.42	65.65
Sept. 7, 1940	Dunkirk, N. Y.	10 laps	4:42.22	63.78
Sept. 7, 1940	Dunkirk, N. Y.	30 laps	14:18.8	62.9
Sept. 21, 1940	Allentown, Penna.	30 laps	14:12.62	63.3
Sept. 28, 1940	Richmond, Va. (Old)	1 lap	24.44	73.65
Sept. 28, 1940	Richmond, Va. (Old)	30 laps	13:39.7	65.8
Oct. 26, 1940	Columbia, S. C.	1 lap	42.6	84.5
Oct. 26, 1940	Columbia, S. C.	5 laps	3:39	82.2
Oct. 26, 1940	Columbia, S. C.	15 laps	11:47.5	76.3
June 23, 1946	Greensboro, N. C.	25 laps	11:57.2	62.7
July 2, 1946	Atlanta, Ga. Lakewd. Sp.	50 mi.	36:22	82.5
July 20, 1946	Du Boise, Penna.	1 lap	27.81	64.7
July 20, 1946	Du Boise, Penna.	10 laps	10:18.12	58.2
Aug. 18, 1946	Skowhegan, Maine	1 lap	26.7	67.4
Aug. 18, 1946	Skowhegan, Maine	8 laps	3:37.0	66.4
Aug. 18, 1946	Skowhegan, Maine	20 laps	9:34.0	62.7
Oct. 12, 1946	Richmond, Va. (New)	8 laps	3:15.0	73.8
Oct. 12, 1946	Richmond, Va. (New)	20 laps	8:27.0	71.0
Oct. 19, 1946	Raleigh, N. C.	8 laps	4:03.2	59.2
Mar. 30, 1947	Atlanta, Ga. Lakewd. Sp.	8 laps	5:28.0	87.83
July 13, 1947	Bainbridge, Ohio	90 laps	1:03:00.0	85.7
Aug. 3, 1947	Dover, N. J.	30 laps	14:08.8	63.6
Aug. 23, 1947	Hamburg, N. Y.	1 lap	26.3	68.4
Aug. 29, 1947	Essex Jct., Vermont	1 lap	23.3	75.09
Aug. 29, 1947	Essex Jct., Vermont	20 laps	9:23.9	63.8
Aug. 31, 1947	Keller, Virginia	1 lap	28.24	63.7
Aug. 31, 1947	Keller, Virginia	8 laps	3:57.04	60.7
Aug. 31, 1947	Keller, Virginia	20 laps	10:59.11	54.6
Sept. 5, 1947	Rutland, Vermont	1 lap	25.9	69.4
Sept. 5, 1947	Rutland, Vermont	8 laps	3:36.9	66.3
Sept. 5, 1947	Rutland, Vermont	18 laps	8:14.4	65.3

STATISTICAL DATA

Date	Track	Distance	Time	MPH
Sept. 6, 1947	Port Royal, Penna.	1 lap	25.05	71.8
Sept. 6, 1947	Port Royal, Penna.	20 laps	9:02.19	66.3
Sept. 12, 1947	Uniontown, Penna.	25 laps	9:26.45	79.4
Sept. 13, 1947	Washington, Penna.	1 lap	25.66	70.1
Sept. 13, 1947	Washington, Penna.	8 laps	3:35.25	66.8
Sept. 19, 1947	Springfield, Mass.	8 laps	3:36.92	66.3
Sept. 19, 1947	Springfield, Mass.	20 laps	9:08.92	65.5
Sept. 20, 1947	Springfield, Mass.	1 lap	25.87	69.5
Sept. 21, 1947	Dover, N. J.	25 laps	12:27.2	60.2
Sept. 26, 1947	Uniontown, Penna.	8 laps	3:02.04	78.5
Sept. 26, 1947	Uniontown, Penna.	20 laps	7:32.89	79.4
Oct. 3, 1947	Harrington, Delaware	20 laps	9:41.31	61.9
Oct. 11, 1947	Richmond, Va. (New)	1 lap	23.79	75.6
Nov. 2, 1947	Arlington Downs, Tex.	95 laps	1:10:25.2	70.7
Nov. 9, 1947	Atlanta, Ga. Lakewd. Sp.	1 lap	38.8	92.7
Nov. 16, 1947	Jacksonville, Florida	1 lap	23.0	78.2
Nov. 16, 1947	Jacksonville, Florida	20 laps	8:43.53	68.7
Nov. 30, 1947	Macon, Georgia	1 lap	25.61	70.2
Nov. 30, 1947	Macon, Georgia	8 laps	3:34.0	67.2
Nov. 30, 1947	Macon, Georgia	20 laps	9:30.0	63.1
Mar. 21, 1948	Atlanta, Ga. Lakewd. Sp.	3 laps	2:06.23	85.55
Mar. 21, 1948	Atlanta, Ga. Lakewd. Sp.	20 mi.	13:37.06	89.3
Apr. 4, 1948	Reading, Penna.	25 laps	11:10.41	67.1
Apr. 17, 1948	Williams Grove, Penna.	1 lap	24.93	72.2
Apr. 17, 1948	Williams Grove, Penna.	10 laps	4:23.14	68.4
Apr. 17, 1948	Williams Grove, Penna.	30 laps	13:34.21	66.3
Apr. 18, 1948	Trenton, N. J.	20 laps	14:44.33	81.4
May 22, 1948	Richmond, Va. (Old)	25 laps	11:09.44	67.22
May 31, 1948	Indianapolis Motor Sp.	350 mi.	2:56:16.22	119.135
June 12, 1948	Mineola, N. Y.	20 laps	9:43.96	61.64
July 11, 1948	Williams Grove, Penna.	50 laps	23:02.12	65.117
July 18, 1948	Charlotte, N. C.	1 lap	25.2	71.42
July 18, 1948	Charlotte, N. C.	3 laps	1:20.1	67.41
July 25, 1948	Winchester, Indiana	1 lap	20.86	86.27
July 25, 1948	Winchester, Indiana	8 laps	2:51.6	83.91
July 25, 1948	Winchester, Indiana	20 laps	7:11.04	83.51
Aug. 8, 1948	Martinsville, Virginia	1 lap	26.21	68.87
Aug. 8, 1948	Martinsville, Virginia	3 laps	1:26.2	62.64
Aug. 8, 1948	Martinsville, Virginia	10 laps	4:44.8	63.2
Aug. 8, 1948	Martinsville, Virginia	25 laps	13:30.0	55.55
Aug. 22, 1948	Dayton, Ohio	8 laps	2:54.8	88.8
Aug. 22, 1948	Dayton, Ohio	20 laps	7:26.06	87.1
Sept. 10, 1948	Hamburg, N. Y.	3 laps	1:30.46	59.69
Sept. 10, 1948	Hamburg, N. Y.	25 laps	12:40.69	59.15
Sept. 24, 1948	Springfield, Mass.	15 laps	7:32.27	59.72
Oct. 3, 1948	Trenton, N. J.	1 lap	40.13	89.7
Oct. 3, 1948	Trenton, N. J.	3 laps	2:08.08	84.32

STATISTICAL DATA

POSITIONS WON BY TED HORN IN A.A.A. POINT STANDINGS

Year	Position	Circuit	Points
1931	83	Pacific Southwest	0.75
1932	20	Pacific Southwest	39.74
1933	2	Pacific Southwest (B)	220.76
1934	10	Pacific Southwest	87.43
	14	Eastern	318.00
	39	Midwestern	15.00
1935	20	Pacific Southwest	52.15
	23	Eastern	233.00
	23	Midwestern	70.00
1936	3	Pacific Southwest	12.85
	32	Eastern	36.00
	8	Midwestern	163.50
	3	NATIONAL CHAMPIONSHIP	825.00
1937	48	Eastern	32.00
	9	Central	206.00
	2	NATIONAL CHAMPIONSHIP	750.00
1938		Eastern	369.00
		Central	460.00
	4	NATIONAL CHAMPIONSHIP	660.00
1939	11	Eastern	270.00
	3	NATIONAL CHAMPIONSHIP	685.00
1940	3	Eastern	815.00
	4	NATIONAL CHAMPIONSHIP	625.00
1941	3	Central	152.00
1946	1	NATIONAL CHAMPIONSHIP	2448.00
1947	1	Eastern	940.00
	1	NATIONAL CHAMPIONSHIP	1920.00
1948	1	Eastern	765.00
	8	Midwestern	102.00
	1	NATIONAL CHAMPIONSHIP	1890.00

TED HORN'S COMPLETE INDIANAPOLIS RECORD

Year	Car	Qual. Speed	Race Speed	Finish
1934	Mick Special	...	...	..
1935	Ford V8	113.213	... (145 laps)	14
1936	Hartz-Miller	116.564	108.170	2
1937	Hartz-Miller	118.220	112.079	3
1938	Hartz-Miller	121.327	112.200	4
1939	Boyle-Miller	127.723	112.610	4
1940	Boyle-Miller	125.545	Flagged 199 laps	4
1941	Thorne-Sparks	124.297	113.824	3
1946	Boyle-Maserati	123.980	109.820	3
1947	Bennett-Maserati	126.564	114.799	3
1948	Bennett-Maserati	126.365	117.844	4

A.A.A. REGISTRATIONS

Year	Car Registration	Reg. No.	Driver Reg. No.	Date Issued
1931	Rajo Special	112	Temp.	3-31-31
1932	Horn Special	98	119	3-9-32
1933			63	3-5-33
1934			66	3-15-34
1935			57	5-26-35
1936	Miller Special	128	45	5-14-36
1937	Miller Special	119	3	3-20-37
1938	Riverside Special	2	2	1-31-38
1939	Riverside Special	150	4	2-27-39
	Riverside Tire Special	153		
1940	Riverside Tire Special	151	3	4-6-40
	Ted Horn Eng. Special	30		
1941	Riverside Tire Special	63	4	4-4-41
	Offenhauser Special	67		
1946	T.H.E. Special	54	55	4-23-46
	T.H.E. Special	53		
	T.H.E. Special	55		
1947	T.H.E. Special	101	1	3-20-47
	T.H.E. Special	201		
1948	T.H.E. Special	11	1	3-8-48
	T.H.E. Special	61		

TEMPORARY PERMITS

Number	Place	Date
130	Legion	3-31-31
33	Oakland	10-18-31
260	Legion	10-24-31
1034	Los Angeles	11-1-31
1832	Los Angeles	11-22-31
57	Legion	12-6-31
1123	Bakersfield	1-3-32
1543	El Centro	2-13-32

CREDITS

We desire to thank the following Speedway authorities for their help and cooperation in furnishing certain data and photos used in this book.

CLIFF BERGERE, Senior AAA Driver, Mileage leader Indianapolis Speedway. Champion Spark Plug Company. Toledo, Ohio.

AL BLOEMKER, Director of Public Relations, Publicity, Indianapolis Speedway. Indianapolis, Indiana.

GEORGE BURCH, President NARCO Inc. Pendleton, Indiana.

PETE DE PAOLO, Two time AAA Champion. Indianapolis winner 1925, Author. Los Angeles, California.

HARRY HARTZ, Former AAA Champion, Driver, Car Owner, Official. Studebaker Corp. South Bend, Indiana.

PAUL JOHNSON, AAA Observer, Steward. Anderson, Indiana.

CHARLES LYTLE, Hobby Photographer, Historian. Sharon, Pennsylvania.

ED. METZGER, Formerly Chief Mechanic, now team manager Cotton Henning Racing Stable. Indianapolis, Indiana.

TOM SMITH, Assistant Secretary, AAA Contest Board. Washington, D. C.

ART SPARKS, Art Sparks and Associates, Consulting Engineers. Pasadena, California.

I. W. (Ike) WELCH, Chief Observer Indianapolis Speedway and AAA Steward. Maywood, California.

W. WILBUR SHAW, President Indianapolis Motor Speedway Corporation.

The following contributed with specific incidents, data or research:

Lloyd Armstrong, Staff, Herald-Review. Decatur, Illinois.
Riley Brett, Team Mechanic, Indianapolis Speedway. Los Angeles, California.
Freddy Carpenter, AAA Eastern Driver. Albany, N. Y.
Rev. Chas. J. Child, Trinity Episcopal Church. Paterson, N. J.
W. P. Dodd, Photographer. Atlanta, Georgia.
E. M. Eaton, Vice-President's Office, Firestone Tire and Rubber Co. Akron, Ohio.
Bill Ferguson, Writer. Nashville, Tennessee.
Gordon E. Fish, Collector. Seattle, Washington.
Vern Fritch, Writer, Columnist. Detroit, Michigan.
Tom Frost, AAA Contest Board Member, Ford Dealer. Warrenton, Virginia.
Carl Green, President, Green Engineering. Paterson, N. J.
Mrs. Mary Horn. Los Angeles, California.
Mrs. Ted Horn. Reading, Pennsylvania.
Theresa Horn. Hawthorne, New Jersey.
John Hyland Sr., Vice-President, NARCO, Inc. Pendleton, Indiana.
Rajo Jack, Veteran Driver. Los Angeles, California.
Seth Klein, AAA Starter. Indianapolis, Indiana.
John Kozub, Photographer, Collector, Writer. Perth Amboy, New Jersey.
Harry Lewis, Designer, Automobile Body Builder. Los Angeles, California.
Dick McGeorge, Director Publicity, Champion Spark Plug Co. Toledo, Ohio.
Len Milde, Writer. Elyria, Ohio.
Jim Mitchell, Tennis Pro., Country Club of Virginia. Richmond, Virginia.

CREDITS

Harold F. Mohn, Author. Myerstown, Pennsylvania.
Don O'Reilly, Publisher, Speed Age Magazine. Hyattsville, Maryland.
Harold Overstreet, Writer. Syracuse, Indiana.
V. F. Schroeder, Montgomery Ward and Company. Chicago, Illinois.
Bob Shaffer, Sports Staff, Akron Beacon Journal. Akron, Ohio.
Sol Silbermann, President, Metallurgical Service Co. Inc. Indianapolis, Indiana.
Archie Smith, President Mill Products Company, Inc. Milwaukee, Wisconsin.
Roscoe Turner, Former President, United Racing Association. Bell, California.
Lou Vollmar, Bosch Products. Longmeadow, Massachusetts.
F. M. White, President Burd Piston Ring Company. Rockford, Illinois.
Ed Wintergust, Field Representative Gulf Oil Company. Indianapolis, Indiana.
Walt Woestman, Car Owner, Writer and Photographer. Altadena, California.
Bud Williams, Photographer. Union City, Indiana.

And special mention to Wm. J. Mickler of Tower Studios, official Indianapolis Speedway Photographer, for his splendid cooperation.

RUSS CATLIN.

VELOCEPRESS MANUALS – AUTOMOBILE BY MAKE

ALFA ROMEO GIULIA WORKSHOP MANUAL 1300 TO 2000cc 1962-1975
ALFA ROMEO GIULIA TECH MANUAL CARBURETED CARS FROM 1962
ALFA ROMEO GIULIA TECH MANUAL FUEL INJECTED CARS FROM 1969
ALFA ROMEO GIULIETTA & GIULIA 750 & 101 SERIES 1955-1965 WSM
AUSTIN-HEALEY SPRITE & MG MIDGET WORKSHOP MANUAL 1958-1971
BMW 600 LIMOUSINE FACTORY WORKSHOP MANUAL
BMW 600 LIMOUSINE OWNERS HAND BOOK & SERVICE MANUAL
BMW 2000 & 2002 1966-1976 WORKSHOP MANUAL
CORVAIR 1960-1969 WORKSHOP MANUAL
CORVETTE V8 1955-1962 WORKSHOP MANUAL
FERRARI HANDBOOK ROAD & RACE CARS (SERVICE/SPECS) 1948-1958
FERRARI 250GT SERVICE & MAINTENANCE by JIM RIFF 1956-1965
FERRARI 250GT & 250GTE FACTORY PARTS AND REPAIR MANUALS
FIAT 500 FACTORY WORKSHOP MANUAL 1957-1973
FIAT 600, 600D & MULTIPLA FACTORY WORKSHOP MANUAL 1955-1969
JAGUAR E-TYPE 3.8 & 4.2 SERIES 1 & 2 WORKSHOP MANUAL
JAGUAR MK 7, 8, 9 & XK120, 140, 150 WORKSHOP MANUAL 1948-1961
METROPOLITAN FACTORY WORKSHOP MANUAL
MGA & MGB OWNERS HANDBOOK & WORKSHOP MANUAL
MG MIDGET TC, TD, TF & TF1500 WORKSHOP MANUAL
PORSCHE 356 1948-1965 WORKSHOP MANUAL
PORSCHE 911 2.0, 2.2, 2.4 LITRE 1964-1973 WORKSHOP MANUAL
PORSCHE 911 2.7, 3.0, 3.2 LITRE 1973-1989 WORKSHOP MANUAL
PORSCHE 912 WORKSHOP MANUAL
PORSCHE 914/4 & 914/6 1.7, 1.8, 2.0 LITRE 1970-1976 WSM
TRIUMPH TR2, TR3, TR4 1953-1965 WORKSHOP MANUAL
VOLKSWAGEN TRANSPORTER, TRUCKS & WAGONS 1950-1979 WSM
VOLVO 1944-1968 ALL MODELS WORKSHOP MANUAL

VELOCEPRESS TECHNICAL BOOKS - AUTOMOBILE

HOW TO BUILD A FIBERGLASS CAR
HOW TO BUILD A RACING CAR
HOW TO RESTORE THE MODEL 'A' FORD
MASERATI OWNER'S HANDBOOK
PERFORMANCE TUNING THE SUNBEAM TIGER
SOUPING THE VOLKSWAGEN
SOLEX CARBURETORS (EMPHASIS ON UK & EU AUTOMOBILES)
SU CARBURETORS (EMPHASIS ON UK AUTOMOBILES)
WEBER CARBURETORS (EMPHASIS ON ALFA & FIAT)

VELOCEPRESS BOOKS & GUIDES - AUTOMOBILE

COMPLETE CATALOG OF JAPANESE MOTOR VEHICLES
FERRARI 308 SERIES BUYER'S AND OWNER'S GUIDE
FERRARI BROCHURES AND SALES LITERATURE 1968-1989
FERRARI SERIAL NUMBERS PART I - ODD NUMBERS TO 21399
FERRARI SERIAL NUMBERS PART II - EVEN NUMBERS TO 1050
HENRY'S FABULOUS MODEL "A" FORD
MASERATI BROCHURES AND SALES LITERATURE

VELOCEPRESS BOOKS – AUTO RACING

CARRERA PANAMERICANA - MEXICAN ROAD RACE (BOOK OF)
DIALED IN - THE JAN OPPERMAN STORY
VEDA ORR'S NEW REVISED HOT ROD PICTORIAL

www.VelocePress.com

www.ingramcontent.com/pod-product-compliance
Lightning Source LLC
Chambersburg PA
CBHW080731230426
43665CB00020B/2697